AF869180

INVITATION · TO

"C"

INVITATION · TO

"C"

Lawrence McNitt

PETROCELLI BOOKS
Princeton, New Jersey

Copyright © 1987 Petrocelli Books, Inc.
All rights reserved
Printed in the USA
First Printing

Library of Congress Cataloging-in-Publication Data

McNitt, Lawrence L.
Invitation to "C"

Includes Index

1. C (Computer program Language) I. Title
QA76.73. C15M37 1986 005.13'3
86–22597

ISBN 0–89433–280–5

Contents

PREFACE ix

PART I INTRODUCTION TO C

1 INTRODUCTION 3
1.1 Why C? 3
1.2 Developing and Running the Program 8
1.3 Printing Messages 11
1.4 Arithmetic 16
1.5 For Loops 19
1.6 Test at Beginning of Loop 21
1.7 Test at End of Loop 23
1.8 Programming Process 25

2 PRIMITIVE PROGRAMS 29
2.1 Program Organization 29
2.2 Variables and Type Declarations 34
2.3 Arithmetic Expressions 39
2.4 Relational Expressions 46
2.5 Bit Operations 51
2.6 Primitive Input and Output 60
2.7 Comments 67

3 ELEMENTS OF PROGRAM FLOW 75
3.1 FOR 75

3.2 WHILE 88
3.3 DO . . . WHILE 96
3.4 IF 101
3.5 IF . . . ELSE 108

4 ARRAYS 121
4.1 Numeric arrays 121
4.2 String Arrays 129
4.3 Multidimensional Arrays 134
4.4 Internal Representation of Arrays 139

5 FUNCTIONS 143
5.1 Standard Functions 143
5.2 Function Definitions 151
5.3 Arguments 155
5.4 Array Arguments 162
5.5 Scope 168
5.6 Recursion 172

6 PROGRAM FLOW REVISITED 177
6.1 Switch 177
6.2 Break 179
6.3 Continue 184
6.4 Go to 186

7 POINTERS 191
7.1 Pointers and Addresses 191
7.2 Pointers and Functions 196
7.3 Pointers and Arrays 201
7.4 Pointer Arrays 210

8 ADDITIONAL FEATURES 213
8.1 Structures 213
8.2 Unions 221
8.3 Fields 222
8.4 Miscellaneous 226
8.5 Disk Files 230

PART II APPLICATIONS

9 MATHEMATICS 239
9.1 Series and Sequences 239
9.2 Numerical Calculus 254
9.3 Matrix Operations 270
9.4 Simultaneous Linear Equations 282

10 DATA ANALYSIS 289
10.1 Summary Measures 289
10.2 Sorting 302
10.3 Linear Curve Fitting 310
10.4 Nonlinear Curve Fitting 325

11 INFORMATION REPRESENTATION 341
11.1 ASCII Codes 341
11.2 Strings 345
11.3 Binary Integers 348
11.4 Floating Point 357
11.5 Hex Dumps of Files 361
11.6 Hex Memory Dumps 367

12 PERFORMANCE 375
12.1 Subscripts or Pointers 375
12.2 Formatted or Unformatted I/O 385
12.3 Local or Global Variables 389
12.4 Increment or Add 394

APPENDICES
A Reserved Words 403
B Format Codes 405
C Special Symbols 407
D Operators 409
E Standard Functions 411

INDEX 413

Preface

C is a general-purpose language used widely in systems programming to create operating systems, compilers, and system utilities. It has a rich set of operators and includes the modern flow of control and data structures. Source programs are more concise and compact than Pascal and similar languages.

C was designed for and developed concurrently with Bell Laboratory's UNIX operating system, but is available for other systems including CP/M and MS-DOS for microcomputers. The UNIX operating system, compilers, and many application programs are written in C. Many microcomputer system software houses are adopting C as their primary programming language.

The data types more closely match the data representations of modern computers than other higher-level languages. The primitive operations defined for the language are closer to the operations available with the machine language instruction set. Programs written in C are efficient because they reflect the capabilities of modern computers. There is little incentive to use assembly language.

C's main emphasis has been systems programming, but it is also a practical applications programming tool for those systems needing optimum execution-time performance.

Part I introduces the C language, giving simple examples illustrating its features. Part II applies it to several application areas. This book can serve as a text for a short course in C or for a full course in applications programming. The numerous examples and applications make the book ideal for self-study or as a supplementary text for computer science courses.

C language usage has grown steadily since the early 1970s. It came into its own as a standalone language with the microcomputers of the 1980s. Serious students of computing will enjoy the exciting world of C in polishing their programming skills.

PART I

Introduction to C

1

Introduction

This book explores the C language and its applications. It features many example programs, starting with simple ones illustrating features of the language. Part II contains applications chapters demonstrating the C language for a variety of problems.

This introductory chapter sets the stage for C language programming. It introduces those features which set it apart from other higher-level languages.

1.1 Why C?

C is a general-purpose programming language developed in 1972 by Dennis Ritchie of Bell Labs. Its economy of expression, modern flow of control, and extended set of operators makes C a powerful tool for both systems and applications programming.

SYSTEMS AND APPLICATIONS PROGRAMMING

Although developed as a systems programming language for Bell Lab's UNIX operating system, C is also useful for applications programming. It provides memory addressing facilities that are like machine language. Thoughtful use of these features results in programs with highly efficient run-time performance.

Although C was developed concurrently with UNIX, it is not tied to that system. C compilers exist for other operating systems, including the IBM System/370 and microcomputers running the CP/M and MS-DOS operating systems. The implementation of C on microcomputers has greatly extended its potential market.

Several microcomputer software houses have adopted C as their primary development language because it offers machine independent portability among diverse computer families while retaining much of the run-time efficiency of a machine language. Portability and run-time efficiency account for C's success.

PORTABILITY

There are many diverse families of computers and more are on the drawing boards. Each family has its own machine language instruction set and methods of addressing memory. They even differ in their internal number representations. Programs written in machine language for one family do not easily convert to another family.

Higher-level languages such as FORTRAN, COBOL, Pascal, and C are machine independent. They are not tied to specific machine language statements and their programs are easier to transport to another family. C is not inherently more portable than other higher-level languages.

EFFICIENCY AND MACHINE LANGUAGE

C offers greater run-time efficiency than other higher-level languages. It provides an extended set of primitive operators which improve its efficiency.

Many computer families use single-address instructions with one or more accumulators. They operate much like calculators. To add two numbers, the processing steps are

1. Enter the first number.
2. Add the second number.
3. Record the sum.

The machine language instruction set includes instructions for loading the accumulator, adding a value to it, and storing the updated contents. The symbolic machine language, also called assembly language, for the operation

$$X = Y + Z$$

for a simple computer follows:

```
LOAD Y
ADD Z
STORE X
```

Several major factors limit the portability of symbolic machine languages. The computer families differ in their instruction sets. Common instructions—such as load, add and store—have no agreement on names or codes. Each family differs in its number of accumulators and how to use them. There are differences in addressing modes and how to specify them among the computer families.

HIGHER-LEVEL LANGUAGES LOSE RUN-TIME EFFICIENCY

Higher-level languages provide machine independent specification of operations. The following statements represent the simple problem in several languages:

X = Y + Z	FORTRAN
X := Y + Z;	Pascal
X = Y + Z;	PL/1
LET X = Y + Z	BASIC
X = Y + Z;	C

Higher-level languages use compilers or interpreters to translate the source program into machine language. Compilers translate the entire program from beginning to end prior to execution. Most FORTRAN, Pascal, PL/1 and C translators are compilers. Interpreters translate and execute each statement in an interleaved fashion.

BASIC is slow because most BASIC translators are interpreters rather than compilers. Programs with slow execution time have loops requiring many iterations. Interpreters retranslate the source statements each time through the loop. Interpreted programs run 20 to 100 times slower than compiled programs because compiled programs do not require retranslation of source statements each time through a loop.

Most C language translators are compilers with the advantage of faster execution times, an advantage available to all compiled higher-level languages.

REASONS FOR C EFFICIENCY

It is difficult to make a compiler for a machine independent higher-level language which also effectively uses the machine language instruction set. Sophisticated optimizing compilers improve the run-time performance of compiled programs but are expensive and add to the compilation time. Some computer vendors provide two compilers; the debugging compiler for program development and the optimizing compiler for production of final object programs.

Wise use of C's extended operators reduces the need for optimizing compilers. The extended operators describe specialized operations which are difficult to identify without a complex optimizing compiler.

Consider the task of incrementing a memory location by the value 1. The higher-level statement

```
X = X + 1
```

describes the operation in a form used by many higher-level languages. A nonoptimizing compiler might produce the following sequence of machine language statements:

```
LOAD X
ADD =1
STORE X
```

The assembler program that translates symbolic machine language to absolute machine language uses the symbol =1 to specify the location of the numeric constant.

Many machine language instruction sets include instructions to increment (add 1) and decrement (subtract 1) a memory location without using the accumulator. For such systems the single instruction

```
INCR X
```

would add the value 1 to the contents of X. An optimizing compiler will convert the instruction

```
X = X + 1
```

to the single increment instruction.

The C language includes the operator symbols + + for increment and − − for decrement. The statement

```
X++
```

adds (increments) to X, and

```
X--
```

decrements X. A C compiler uses the more efficient increment and decrement instructions.

There are other extended operators like the + + and − − operators. These give the compiler information that allows it to do a ciently as those of other higher-level languages. Using the extended operators will provide better run-time performance.

The extended operators constitute one of C's major contributions to programming language. They improve execution speed by streamlining memory accesses and tell the compiler more about the intended task. It can then generate efficient machine language code.

The extended operators have an obvious limitation. Programmers who are unfamiliar with C find these programs more difficult to read. The nonC programmer will not know what the statement

```
X++
```

means, but a FORTRAN programmer can pick up a Pascal program and read it with a fair understanding. This is not true for other programmers who pick up a C program using the extended operators.

BITS AND BYTES

Another feature of C which has endeared it to the systems programmer is the definition of primitive operations defined for bit strings. A bit is a binary digit having the two values 0 and 1. Common operations, described later, include and, or, exlusive or, complementation, shift, and rotate. C builds these bit operations into the language. Other languages define subroutines to handle bit strings, but their performance suffers because of the overhead inherent in the subroutine mechanism.

REGISTER REFERENCE

Some implementations of C allow explicit reference to accumulators and other internal registers of the machine. The variable name AX may refer to the accumulator. The command

```
AX = Z
```

would move the contents of the memory location into the accumulator.

Careful use of register references can speed execution on the intended computer family. Transporting the program to another family will result in programs that work, but will not achieve improved efficiency because the machine-specific register references no longer apply. Most of the other extended operations give the intended efficiency improvements regardless of the computer family involved.

1.2 Developing and Running the Program

There are several mechanical steps needed to enter a program into a system, to compile it, and to run the compiled object program. Entering a program into the system requires a program editor. The C compiler compiles the program to obtain an object program. Some systems require a separate link step if the output of the C controller is in intermediate form, not yet ready for execution.

PROGRAM EDITOR

Entering a program into the system and editing it requires a program editor. Each system has its own—sometimes primitive—text editor which can be used to create and maintain the C source program. The choice of editor is personal.

Some word processing systems include a nondocument mode which leaves out their special document formatting control characters. Beware of word processors that do not have this feature.

The two major classes of editors are line editors and screen editors. A line editor uses implied line numbers to reference lines for the editing operations of deletion, insertion, and modification. Line editors are for printing terminals which have no video display.

Screen editors require terminals with video display output and cursor movement capability. The cursor movement keys allow two-dimensional movement to any point within the text. Screen editors are much easier to use than line editors.

Program editors are available from several sources. The operating system may include an editor such as TEXT, ED, EDLIN, or SEE. Commercial C systems may include a program editor. User groups have several public domain editors for specific computer systems. Some specialized editors are available commercially which perform a syntax check of each line of the program as it is entered.

Programmers who work with several languages often select a favorite program editor and use it for editing all source programs. This bypasses the need to remember editing commands for several editors.

COMPILE THE PROGRAM

A compiler is a program that translates the source program into an object program. Many systems give the name CC to the C compiler. The command

CC PROG1

will compile the source program PROG1.C to generate an object program, PROG1.O or PROG1.OBJ. Many operating systems include a name and an extension to identify files.

The extension C designates a C source file. Extensions for object programs and the name CC for the C compiler are not standard.

LINK THE PROGRAM

Some systems require a separate link step to prepare the program for execution. The name "bind" is also used for this step. For such systems the command

LINK PROG1

or

BIND PROG1

will accept the intermediate file created by the C compiler and generate an executable program with an appropriate extension for use by the operating system.

RUN THE PROGRAM

Executing the program requires typing the name of the program. The command

PROG1

executes the final program prepared by the previous steps.

DIFFERENCES AMONG SYSTEMS

This is the time to read the language reference manual for your implementation of C. It will give the commands needed to compile and run your programs. The most common sequence is

```
CC PROG1
PROG1
```

or

```
CC PROG1
LINK PROG1
PROG1
```

Exercises

1. Select a program editor. Learn how to add new lines to the end of the text, delete existing lines, insert new lines, and make corrections to existing lines. Name the C source files in a manner appropriate to your system. Most systems require the extension .C to identify C source programs.

2. From your C language reference manual determine the commands needed to compile, link (if necessary), and execute your programs.

1.3 Printing Messages

Sections 1.3 and 1.4 introduce the C language by comparing similar programs written in C, Pascal, and BASIC. C is rarely taught as the first language. BASIC is the most common first language, is widely taught in high schools, and comes "free" with most microcomputers. Pascal is gaining popularity as the first college-level programming language.

C PROGRAM TO PRINT TWO LINES

The first C program prints a short exerpt from "She was a Phantom of Delight" from William Wadsworth. The two lines

> And now I see with eye serene,
> The very pulse of the machine.

are taken out of context, but they reflect the exciting anticipation of a programmer embarking on a new computer adventure.

The C program printing the two lines follows:

```
main()
{ printf("And now I see with eye serene,\n");
} printf("The very pulse of the machine.\n");
```

The key word "main" followed by the parentheses is required. The parentheses are required even though parameters are not specified. The braces—{ and }—define blocks of the program as the BEGIN/END words of Pascal. The printf function is the standard formatted print procedure which corresponds to the PRINT and PRINT USING of BASIC or the WRITE and WRITELN of Pascal. The purpose of the \n symbol is to advance to the beginning of the next output line.

PASCAL PROGRAM TO PRINT TWO LINES

The structure of C is closer to Pascal than it is to the BASIC translators provided on microcomputers. The Pascal program that prints the same two lines follows:

```
PROGRAM SIMPLE1;
BEGIN
   WRITELN  ('And now I see with eye serene,');
   WRITELN  ('The very pulse of the machine.')
END.
```

The output is similar to that of the C program.

C programs are more compact than corresponding Pascal programs; they use braces rather than the words BEGIN and END. C requires a semicolon at the end of each statement within a block; Pascal adds a null statement if the last statement of a BEGIN/END block has a terminating semicolon. C has no terminating punctuation mark; Pascal requires the terminating period.

BASIC PROGRAM TO PRINT TWO LINES

The following BASIC program prints the same two lines:

```
10 PRINT "And now I see with eye serene,"
20 PRINT "The very pulse of the machine."
30 END
```

The output is the same as before.

BASIC requires fewer programming preliminaries than either C or Pascal, but suffers from more primitive control structures and subroutines. Its simplicity is both its strength and its weakness. BASIC is easy to learn but is quickly outgrown by the serious programmer.

C PROGRAM ONE-LINER

The line

I came, I saw, I conquered.

is attributed to Julius Ceasar. The following C program uses one statement to print the entire statement:

```
main()
   {  printf("I came, I saw, I conquered.\n");
   }
```

The braces must bracket the program statement. They can be on the same line:

```
main()
   { printf("I came, I saw, I conquered,\n"); }
```

There is nothing to prohibit placing the entire program on one line. The following program does this:

```
main()  {  printf("I came, I saw, I conquered.\n"); }
```

Packing too much detail into one line reduces program readability.

PASCAL PROGRAM ONE-LINER

The following Pascal program is similar to the first of the three C programs:

```
PROGRAM simple2;
BEGIN
   WRITELN ('I came, I saw, I conquered.')
END.
```

The output is the same as before.

Pascal also allows packing details on one line, but the resulting programs are not as readable. Both the Pascal program and the first of the C programs indented the lines containing the inner part of the program block. Although this indentation is optional, it improves readability and is common practice.

BASIC PROGRAM ONE-LINER

The following BASIC program also prints the saying using one output statement:

```
10 PRINT "I came, I saw, I conquered."
20 END
```

Again BASIC gets straight to the point without preliminaries.

C MULTIPLE-LINE PROGRAM

C, Pascal, and BASIC allow continued output to a print line. The line

I came, I saw, I conquered.

consists of three phrases. The following C program uses one statement for each phrase:

```
main()
  {
       printf("I came,");
       printf(" I saw,");
       printf(" I conquered.\n");
  }
```

The first two printf statements do not give the code \n—called newline—telling the output device to advance to the beginning of the next output line. The three statements produce output in the following form:

```
I came, I saw, I conquered.
```

PASCAL MULTILINE PROGRAM

The following Pascal program also prints each phrase separately:

```
PROGRAM simple3;
BEGIN
   WRITE ('I came,');
   WRITE (' I saw,');
   WRITELN (' I conquered.')
END.
```

Again, the output is placed on one line. The Pascal WRITELN procedure terminates the current line and advances to the beginning of the next line. The WRITE procedure does not terminate the current output line.

BASIC MULTILINE PROGRAM

The following BASIC program also uses a separate output statement for each phrase:

```
10 PRINT "I came,";
20 PRINT " I saw,";
30 PRINT " I conquered."
40 END
```

The dangling semicolon at the end of lines 10 and 20 means that more is to follow on the same line. The absence of punctuation at the end of line 30 signifies the end of the output.

EXERCISES

1. Type in and run the C programs of this section using your computer and the C language.

2. Write a program to print the following lines from "The Raven" by Edgar Allan Poe:

"Once upon a midnight dreary
    while I pondered weak and weary,
Over many a quaint and curious
    volume of forgotten lore,"

3. Write a program that prints your name and address as you would write it on an envelope.

1.4 Arithmetic

Most computer programs do arithmetic with numbers. Integers are the simplest numbers and are the least susceptible to computer idiosyncrasies. The example of this section computes the area and circumference (length of perimeter) of a rectangle.

For a rectangle having length *L* and width *W*, the formula

$$A = L * W$$

gives the area, and

$$C = 2 * (L + W)$$

gives the circumference. The symbol $*$ represents multiplication and is consistently used for this purpose by most programming languages.

C PROGRAM

The following C program assigns the value 40 as the length, the value 30 as the width, computes the area and circumference, and prints the results:

```
main()
{
    int length, width, area, circum;
    length = 40;
    width = 30;
    area = length * width;
    circum = 2 * (length + width);
      printf("length                %d\n", length);
      printf("width                 %d\n", width);
      printf("area                  %d\n", area);
      printf("circumference         %d\n", circum);
}
```

The variables length, width, area, and circum are all integers and are declared such by the statement beginning with the keyword int. The printf procedures include the symbol %d which specifies the printing location of an integer value. This program consists of one variable declaration statement, four assignment and calculation statements, and four output statements.

The program output follows:

```
length            40
width             30
area              1200
circumference     140
```

PASCAL PROGRAM

The similar Pascal program follows:

```
PROGRAM simple4;
VAR
  length,
  width,
  area,
  circum
    : INTEGER;
BEGIN
  length := 40;
```

```
  width := 30;
  area := length * width;
  circum := 2 * (length + width);
  WRITELN ('Length                    ', length);
  WRITELN ('Width                     ', width);
  WRITELN ('Area                      ', area);
  WRITELN ('Circumference             ', circum)
END.
```

Pascal and C programs have similar structures, but C is less rigid than Pascal. This is both a curse and a blessing. The more relaxed nature of C makes it more flexible for experienced programmers, but it also gives inexperienced programmers enough rope to hang themselves.

BASIC PROGRAM

The following BASIC program also computes the area and circumference of a rectangle having length 40 and width 30:

```
10 LET L  = 40
20 LET W = 30
30 LET A  = L * W
40 LET C  = 2 * (L + W)
50 PRINT "LENGTH",L
60 PRINT "WIDTH",W
70 PRINT "AREA",A
80 PRINT "CIRCUMFERENCE",C
90 END
```

BASIC does not distinguish between integer and real (fractional) numbers; this makes it easier to learn. The price paid is slower execution speed of programs requiring extensive calculation with integers. Real arithmetic is much slower than integer arithmetic for microcomputers.

Exercises

1. Implement the program of this section on your system.

2. Write a program that computes the area and circumference of a circle of radius 5.

3. Write a program that computes the surface area and volume of a box 4 feet long by 2 feet wide by 6 inches deep.

1.5 For Loops

BASIC, Pascal, and C have FOR loops. The FOR statement includes an initialization part, an increment or decrement part, and a termination part. Typical FOR statements for the three languages are

BASIC:	FOR I = 1 TO N
Pascal:	for i := 1 to n do
C:	for (i = 1; i <= n; i = i + 1)

The example programs of this section compute and print a table of squares for the integers 1, 2, . . . , 5 using the FOR loop control statement. This is the output:

```
1    1
2    4
3    9
4    16
5    25
```

C PROGRAM

The C program generating the table of squares follows:

```
main()
{
    int i, n, s;
    n = 5;
    for (i = 1; i <= n; i++)
       {
           s = i * i;
           printf("%d     %d\n", i, s);
       }
}
```

Notice the i+ + part of the FOR statement. This command increments the value of i by 1 each time through the loop. This does the same thing as the command i = i + 1 but may execute more efficiently if the computer has an appropriate increment machine language instruction.

The command s = i * i squares each value of i by multiplying it by itself. The printf procedure has two %d parameters; one for the contents of i, the other for the contents of s.

The FOR command controls only the following statement. The braces combine the s = i * i and printf statements into one block to be controlled by the FOR statement. This is similar to Pascal's use of the BEGIN/END delimiters defining compound statements.

PASCAL

The following Pascal program performs a similar function:

```
PROGRAM simple5;
VAR
  i, n, s : INTEGER;
BEGIN
  N := 5;
  FOR I := 1 TO N DO
     BEGIN
         S := I * I;
         WRITELN (I, '     ', S)
     END
END.
```

This program also generates a table of squares for the values 1, 2, . . . , 5.

BASIC

The following BASIC program also generates a table of squares:

```
10 LET N = 5
20 FOR I = 1 TO N
30     LET S = I * I
```

```
40      PRINT I,S
50 NEXT I
60 END
```

Exercises

1. Enter and run the program of this section.

2. Write a program to generate the sum of the first five integers.

3. Write a program to generate the product of the first five integers.

1.6 Test at Beginning of Loop

There are two general-purpose looping constructs available in many languages; one performs its test at the beginning of the loop and the other at the end. The test at the beginning of the loop is more common. Most languages use the keyword WHILE to identify the general loop with the test at the beginning.

The programs of this section perform the same task as those of Section 1.5. They use a WHILE construct with the test at the beginning of the loop. They generate a table of squares with an output as follows:

```
1   1
2   4
3   9
4   16
5   25
```

C PROGRAM

The following program uses the general looping construct with the test at the beginning of the loop:

```
main()
{
    int i, n, s;
```

```
    n = 5;
    i  = 0;
    while (i < n)
       {
          i++;
          s = i * i;
          printf("%d      %d\n", i, s);
       }
}
```

The key word "while" is immediately followed by the test in parentheses. Looping continues while the condition is true. When the condition fails, control continues with the rest of the program and the program terminates. The braces enclose the body of the loop.

PASCAL PROGRAM

The following Pascal program accomplishes the same task:

```
PROGRAM simple6;
VAR
  i, n, s : INTEGER;
BEGIN
  n := 5;
  i  := 0;
  WHILE (i < n) DO
    BEGIN
      i := i + 1;
      s := i * 1;
      WRITELN (i, '      ', s)
    END
END.
```

Pascal and C are similar in their implementation of the WHILE construct. C uses braces, while Pascal uses the key words BEGIN and END to define the scope of the loop.

BASIC PROGRAM

Many BASIC systems do not include the general looping constructs. The following BASIC program illustrates a form of the WHILE statement available for some systems:

```
10 LET N = 5
20 LET I = 0
30 WHILE I < N
40      LET I = I + 1
50      LET S = I * I
60      PRINT I, S
70 WEND
80 END
```

This differs from Pascal and C in using the key word WEND to define the end of the loop.

Exercises

1. Enter and run the program of this section.

2. Write a program to calculate the sum of the first five integers.

3. Write a program to calculate the product of the first five integers.

1.7 Test at End of Loop

The second general-purpose looping construct performs the test at the end of the loop. Many languages use the keywords REPEAT and UNTIL for this mechanism. C uses DO . . . WHILE, a variant of the WHILE loop.

The REPEAT/UNTIL form continues looping until the test is satisfied. If the test is false, looping continues; if it is true, looping stops. This is the opposite of the WHILE loop which loops if the condition is true and stops when it fails.

The DO . . . WHILE of C keeps the same relational comparison as the WHILE loop. The loop continues if the test is satisfied and stops when the test fails. The test is performed at the end of the loop.

The programs of this section perform the same task as for sections 1.5 and 1.6. They generate a table of squares for the values 1, 2, . . . , 5. The output is:

```
1    1
2    4
```

```
3    9
4    16
5    25
```

C PROGRAM

The following C program uses the DO . . . WHILE mechanism:

```
main()
{
    int i, n, s;
    n = 5;
    i  = 0;
    do
      {
        i++;
        s = i * i;
        printf("%d      %d\n", i, s);
      }
    while (i < n);
}
```

The test is at the end of the loop. Looping continues while the test is true and stops when the test fails. The key words do and while define the scope of the loop. The command i++ increments the contents of i.

PASCAL

The corresponding Pascal program follows:

```
PROGRAM simple7;
VAR
  i, n, s : INTEGER;
BEGIN
  n := 5;
  i  := 0;
  REPEAT
    i := i + 1;
    s := i * i;
    WRITELN (i, '      ', s)
  UNTIL (i >= n)
END.
```

The test is done at the end of the loop. The REPEAT/UNTIL construct continues looping when the test fails and stops when the test fails.

BASIC PROGRAM

The REPEAT/UNTIL construct is not common, but the following illustrates a program for those systems that have this looping mechanism:

```
10 LET N = 5
20 LET I  = 0
30 REPEAT
40       LET I  = I + 1
50       LET S = I * I
60       PRINT I,S
70 UNTIL I >= N
80 END
```

The test is at the end of the loop and looping continues while the test is false.

Exercises

1. Enter and run the program of this section.

2. Write a program to calculate the sum of the first five integers.

3. Write a program to calculate the product of the first five integers.

1.8 Programming Process

The programming process consists of several steps:

1. define the problem
2. develop the algorithm
3. code the program
4. test the program
5. debug the program

6. document the program
7. place the program in production
8. maintain the program.

Beginning programmers tend to focus on step 3. As problems and their programs become larger and more complex, an inordinate amount of time is spent on steps 4 and 5. To prevent wasting time on these steps, additional attention must be given to steps 1 and 2. Documentation is necessary if the program is to serve the needs of people other than the original programmer. Many companies are finding that they spend more effort maintaining the program over its average 6 to 12-year life than they did creating it initially. This, in a nutshell, describes the programming process.

WHAT CONSTITUTES A GOOD PROGRAM?

Software consists of the computer programs that make the computer work. These include systems programs comprising the operating systems, its language translators, and utilities. They also include applications programs devoted to user tasks. Program quality is important whether it is a systems program or an applications program.

What is a good program? Why is one program better than another? Is there such a thing as a bad program? Is it possible to label programs good, better, and best? Is it possible to label programmers? Is a good programmer one who writes good programs?

The following is a list of desirable qualities for computer programs:

1. work correctly
2. clear, readable, easy to understand
3. fast execution speed
4. compact (small amount of memory)
5. easy for beginners to learn
6. efficient for experienced operators

7. quickly programmed
8. portable; easy to convert to other computers.

Some of these qualities are mutually conflicting. Optimizing the program's execution speed may increase its memory requirements and limit its portability. Finishing a program as quickly as possible does not leave time for optimizing other qualities. A program that is easy for a beginner to learn is often annoying to the experienced operator.

The program must work correctly; that is why it is first on the list. Software engineering is the study of the science and methods of computer programming. It has elevated the second quality to the same level as the first; every program should be clear, readable, and easy to understand. The programmer chooses other qualities to fit the problem. The program should be appropriate to its task and to the people who will be using it.

C AND READABILITY

Experienced programmers who have had no prior contact with Pascal may pick up Pascal programs and read them with comprehension. This is not always possible with C programs. Many of the extended operators defined in C are not discernible to the programmer who has had no prior contact with the language. Programmers who want to make effective use of C need to learn the new operators.

The question is not whether C programs are readable to programmers who have never had prior experience with C, but whether the programs are readable by experienced C programmers. Readability has much to do with how the program uses the standards established by the organization.

As programmers work together on projects for their organization, they will develop standard names, methods and programming styles. C is not as readable as Pascal. This is inherent in the nature of the language and results from its concern for run-time performance. Readability depends more on the development of and adherence to local standards.

2

Primitive Programs

This chapter adds flesh and blood to the basic C programs introduced in the previous chapter. It gives a more complete explanation of program organization, use of variables, arithmetic operations, and input/output. It discusses readability issues including indentation, blank lines, and comments.

2.1 Program Organization

A C program, consisting of one or more building blocks called functions, is a function invoked from the operating system by typing its name. Every function has a pair of parentheses following it, and any arguments are designated by variables or expressions contained within the parentheses.

DECLARATIONS

The variable declarations follow the name of the function and its arguments. The primary purposes are to declare integer, real, and other variable types, and to identify and dimension vectors and matrices.

MAIN FUNCTION

The root, or main, part of the program is identified with the name main() which usually contains no arguments. This tells the compiler where program execution begins. It also determines the root of a hierarchical program which contains a main program, which calls subroutines, which in turn call lower-level subroutines.

BRACES

The braces { and } define the body of a function. The symbol { denotes the beginning of the function body. The body contains one or more program statements used to perform a specific task. The symbol } marks the end of the function body. The opening and closing brace come in pairs, and are delimiters for the body of the function.

FUNCTION LIBRARY

The C language does not contain built-in commands for input and output; these are provided through a library of C functions. The printf function used in Chapter 1 is an example of such a library function. These functions reside in a standard library and are available. If the program references a function not defined within the program, it will search the standard library. If the function is not defined within the standard library or another named library, the compiler or linker will give an error message.

SEMICOLONS

A semicolon marks the end of each C program statement. This differs subtly from Pascal which uses semicolons to separate program statements. The rule for C is easier to apply.

LOWERCASE CONVENTION

Most older languages like FORTRAN and COBOL are written in uppercase only. The reason had more to do with the restrictions of keypunch machines and punched cards than with readability. Most modern languages including Pascal and C have roots reaching back to ALGOL rather than to FORTRAN and COBOL. Although ALGOL's roots reach back to the time of early FORTRAN and COBOL implementations, it was more commonly implemented on computers employing punched paper tape which allowed both lower and uppercase.

ALGOL and its descendants make predominant use of lowercase letters. The primary reason is the inconvenience of holding down a shift to obtain an uppercase letter or of using the shift-lock key to toggle between lowercase and uppercase. Uppercase letters offer improved readability, but require extra typing effort.

Pascal is not case sensitive. The variable names APPLE, apple, Apple, and aPpLe all refer to the same memory location. C is case sensitive. The variables designate three different variables. The same is true of function names.

Library function names are lowercase and the reserved key words such as int and main() must be lowercase. User-defined names may be either uppercase or lowercase. Most C programmers use lowercase for variable names, reserving uppercase for defined constants and symbolic names.

EXAMPLE PROGRAM WITHOUT BLANK LINES

The following program calculates the area and circumference of a rectangle having a length of 40 feet and a width of 30 feet:

```
main()
  {
      int length, width, area, circum;
      length = 40;
      width = 30;
      area = length * width;
      circum = 2 * (length + width);
      printf("Length                  %d\n",length);
      printf("Width                   %d\n",width);
      printf("Area                    %d\n",area);
      printf("Circumference           %d\n",circum);
  }
```

The output follows:

```
Length          40
Width           30
Area            1200
Circumference   140
```

The area is 1,200 square units and the circumference is 140 units.

The function name main() with no arguments designates the main, or root, portion of the program. The declaration statement beginning with the key word int declares that the four variables are to contain integer numbers.

The braces enclose the body of the main program which contains the declaration statement and the executable program statements. The first two executable statements assign the values 40 and 30 to the variables length and width, respectively. The next two executable statements compute the area and circumference. The final four statements print the results.

The four output statements call the standard library function printf to format the output. The output goes to the standard output device. This is the video screen for interactive systems having video output. It is the printer for batch systems which require that the job be submitted in batch mode.

BLANK LINES FOR READABILITY

The following program adds blank lines to separate parts of the program:

```
main()
  {
       int length, width, area, circum;

       length = 40;
       width = 30;
       area = length * width;
       circum = 2 * (length + width);

       printf("Length          %d\n",length);
       printf("Width           %d\n",width);
```

```
        printf("Area              %d\n",area);
        printf("Circumference     %d\n",circum);
  }
```

The blank lines improve readability by calling attention to the natural divisions in the program.

PROGRAM STYLE

Program style includes indenting subordinate parts of a program and adding appropriate blank lines. The purpose is to aid readability, thus improving the maintainability of the program. If a major portion of a program's lifetime programming cost is in the area of maintenance, anything that can be done to improve maintainability is worth consideration.

ALTERNATE CONVENTION FOR UPPERCASE

An organization may adapt the conventions for internal use. Some use uppercase letters for all user-supplied variable and function names, reserving lowercase for system supplied names including standard library functions. The following program uses uppercase variable names:

```
main()
  {
        int LENGTH, WIDTH, AREA, CIRCUM;
        LENGTH = 40;
        WIDTH = 30;
        AREA = LENGTH * WIDTH;
        CIRCUM = 2 * (LENGTH + WIDTH);

        printf("Length            %d\n",LENGTH);
        printf("Width             %d\n",WIDTH);
        printf("Area              %d\n",AREA);
        printf("Circumference     %d\n",CIRCUM);
  }
```

Exercises

1. Write a program to compute the area and circumference of a circle.

2. Write a program that computes the volume and surface area of a box that is 12 feet long, 3 feet wide, and 2 feet deep.

3. Write a program that computes the pound weight of water in a tank that is 6 feet long, 4 feet wide, and 2 feet deep.

4. Write a program to compute the surface area and volume of a cylindrical tank that is 6 feet long by 4 feet in diameter.

5. Write a program that computes the surface area and volume of a sphere that is 6 feet in diameter.

2.2 Variables and Type Declarations

A variable is a quantity that may assume any one of a set of values. The variable name references the quantity. If the quantity changes, the variable name references the new quantity. The programmer must state the name of the variable and its type. Variables must be declared before they are used.

VARIABLE NAMES

Variable names consist of letters, digits, and the underscore character _. The first character must be a letter. The name cannot contain spaces and may be of any length, but only the first eight characters are treated as significant. The names coat_size_small and coat_size_large appear to be distinct names, but they use the same first eight characters. The compiler assumes that they are the same variable. It is poor practice to exceed the eight-character limit.

KEY WORDS

Most languages have a set of reserved words which cannot be used as user-supplied names. C is no exception. It is wise to check the list of reserved words for your implementation of C as there may be differences from one compiler to another. The following list is typical:

auto	do	for	return	switch
break	double	goto	sizeof	typedef
case	else	if	short	union
char	entry	int	static	unsigned
continue	extern	long	struct	while
default	float	register		

Do not use one of the reserved words as a variable name.

It is also good practice to avoid common function names for variable names. While it is true that the compiler knows that main() is a function name and main is a variable name, it confuses the programmer who reads the program.

DATA TYPES

The most common data types and their standard sizes in bits are summarized below:

Type	*Bits*	*Description*
char	8	External characters, ASCII or EBCDIC
short	16	Short integer
long	32	Long integer
int	—	32 for mainframes, 16 for minis and micros
float	32	Short floating point (real)
double	64	Double precision floating point

Not all C compilers for microcomputers implement long, float, and double number representations. Systems programming does not often use floating point, but applications programming does.

The "int" type specification uses the standard internal integer representation defined for the computer's machine language. Programs written for large IBM and other mainframe computers may need their int declarations changed to long declarations.

The terms long, short, and unsigned are adjectives for the type int. The combination long int, short int, or unsigned int is assumed even though the object int is usually omitted. The declaration

```
long a, b, c, d;
```

is equivalent to the declaration

```
long int a, b, c, d;
```

which includes the object of the adjective long.

FORMAT CODES FOR PRINTF FUNCTION

The following summarizes the format % codes for the printf function:

Code	*Number type*
%d	Decimal integer
%o	Octal (base 8) integer
%x	Hexadecimal (base 16) integer
%u	Unsigned decimal
%f	Decimal format for float or double
%e	Scientific notation format for float or double
%g	Decimal or scientific notation, whichever is shorter
%c	Single character
%s	Character string

An optional number immediately following the symbol % specifies a field size. The code %5d specifies an integer field of 5 positions. The number will be right-justified within that field. The code %5.2f specifies a floating decimal format with two places to the right of the decimal point. The letter l may be used as a length modifier specifying that the data item is a long rather than a short int.

A minus sign before the field size specification results in left justification within the field. The code %-5d left justifies the number within the 5-digit field.

SPECIAL CHARACTERS

Character constants are written in the form 'A' or 'a' within single quotes. Even the space can be written this way:

```
ch = ' ';
```

The C language provides a set of escape sequences with the backslash character \ followed by a character. The common escape characters follow:

Description

Newline (carriage return and line feed)
Carriage return only
Form feed (eject page)
Single quote
Horizontal tab
Backspace
Backslash
Null character

The most common escape character is the newline symbol \n.

DATA TYPES AND FORMATS

The following program defines several data types and uses the printf codes for output:

```
main()
  {
       char a;
       int b;
       long c;
       float d;
       double e;

       a = 'd';
       b = 125;
       c = 49250312;
       d = 1274.25;
       e = 2.718281828459;

       printf("a    %c\n",a);
       printf("b    %5d\n",b);
       printf("c    %10ld\n",c);
       printf("d    %8.2f\n",d);
       printf("e    %16.10e\n",e);
  }
```

The printed output follows:

```
a   d
b      125
c      49250312
d    1274.25
e      2.7182818284E0
```

The code for printing the long integer is %10ld. The letter 1 signifies a long integer data type. The variable types and the code specifications match.

FACTORIAL TABLE

The factorial function n! gives the value 1 for $n = 0$ and the product of the first n integers for n greater than or equal to 1. The following program computes the values for n! for $n = 1, 2, \ldots, 5$:

```
main()
  {
     int n, i, p;

     n = 5;
     p = 1;
     for (i = 1; i <= n; i++)
       {
          p = p * i;
          printf("%3d       %6d\n", i, p);
       }
  }
```

The output follows:

```
1     1
2     2
3     6
4    24
5   120
```

The values are right-justified in the usual way for numbers. The values for i are right-justified in a field of size 3 and the values for p are right-justified in a field of size 6.

SYNTAX ERRORS

The compiler will catch syntax errors from incorrect use of the language. Error messages will not always identify the underlying problem. While learning a new language, it is good to explore the error handling capabilities of the system by introducing intentional errors. This can be done by using inconsistent spellings of variable names or by misspelling system names. Failure to include proper braces or parentheses is a rich source of syntax errors.

Exercises

1. Write a program to compute the sum of the squares of the first five integers.

2. Write a program to compute the gross pay in dollars and cents for a person earning $8.65 per hour for 47.5 hours.

3. Write a program using the float data type to compute the area and circumference of a rectangle having length 12.25 and width 6.75. Limit the output to two places to the right of the decimal point.

4. Write a program using the long int type to compute the factorial table for n! for $n = 1, 2, \ldots, 10$.

5. Modify the program of exercise 4 to compute n! for $n = 1, 2, \ldots, 30$. Does an error message result? If so, why? Is 30! too large to be represented by a 32-bit integer? What is the largest signed integer that a 32-bit integer can represent?

2.3 Arithmetic Expressions

C includes the four common operations add, subtract, multiply, and divide as well as several dozen more. The following lists the standard arithmetic operators:

Operator	*Description*
+	Add
−	Subtract
*	Multiply
/	Divide
%	Modulo (remainder after integer division)

These are binary operators because they combine two input values to obtain one result.

EXAMPLES

The statement

```
z = x + y
```

adds the values contained in *x* and *y* and places the sum in *z*. The expression

```
z = x * y
```

places the product of *x* and *y* into the variable *z*.

More than one operation can be performed on one line. The expression

```
a = 3 * b + c / 2
```

follows the usual precedence ordering, with multiplications and divisions performed before additions and subtractions.

PARENTHESES

Parentheses override the natural precedence ordering. The expression

```
3 * (b + c) / 2
```

in the statement

```
a = 3 * (b + c) / 2
```

performs the addition first because the parentheses override the normal order of operations.

NEGATION

The unary minus operator negates the value of the variable or constant on the right. A unary operator has only one argument. The statement

```
a = -b
```

places the negative of *b* into the variable *a*.

VARIABLE TYPE AND ARITHMETIC

Integer and floating point are distinct types of numbers. Each has its own machine language instruction codes. There will be one set of machine language instructions for integer addition, subtraction, multiplication, and division. There will be another set of instructions for floating point numbers.

Most computer programming languages, including C, permit mixing the integer and floating point within a single expression. Integer values are converted to floating point for the evaluation of mixed-mode expressions. It is not wise to make excessive use of such expressions because of this.

If the variable *a* is integer and the variable *b* is floating point, the statement

```
a = b
```

converts from floating point to integer during the data movement. The statement

```
b = a
```

converts from integer to floating point.

INTEGER DIVISION AND MODULO OPERATION

The addition or subtraction of two integers gives an integer result. One integer will not always divide evenly into another integer. Integer division gives the integer quotient and ignores the remainder.

Assume that the variables *a, b,* and *c* are integers. The statement

```
a = b / c
```

places the integer quotient in *a*. The modulo operator % gives the remainder. The expression a = b % c

places the remainder of the integer division in *a*.

PROGRAM ILLUSTRATING INTEGER DIVISION

The following program illustrates the integer division and modulo operations:

```
main()
  {
      int dividend, divisor, quotient, remainder;
      dividend   = 20;
      divisor    = 3;
      quotient   = dividend \ divisor;
      remainder  = dividend % divisor;

      printf("Dividend              %5d\n", dividend);
      printf("Divisor               %5d\n", divisor);
      printf("Quotient              %5d\n", quotient);
      printf("Remainder             %5d\n", remainder);
  }
```

The output follows:

```
Dividend     20
Divisor       3
Quotient      6
Remainder     2
```

Dividing the integer 3 into the integer 20 gives the quotient 6 with remainder 2.

PROGRAM COMPUTING GROSS AND NET PAY

The following program computes gross pay as hours worked times pay rate, taxes as 14 percent of the difference between gross pay and $50.00, and net pay as gross pay less taxes.

```
main()
  {
      float rate, hours, gross, tax, net;
```

```
    rate  = 6.75;
    hours = 38.6;
    gross = rate * hours;
    tax   = .14 * (gross - 50.0);
    net   = gross - tax;

    printf("Hours worked          %7.1f\n", hours);
    printf("Pay rate              %7.2f\n", rate);
    printf("Gross pay             %7.2f\n", gross);
    printf("Taxes                 %7.2f\n", tax);
    printf("Net pay               %7.2f\n", net);
}
```

All variables are real (floating point) and monetary output is in dollars and cents.

The output follows:

```
Hours worked     38.6
Pay rate         6.75
Gross pay      260.55
Taxes           29.48
Net pay        231.07
```

INCREMENT AND DECREMENT

The following summarizes the operators for incrementing or decrementing a variable:

Operator	*Description*
++a	Preincrement a, a = a + 1
a++	Postincrement a, a = a + 1
--a	Predecrement a, a = a - 1
a--	Postdecrement a, a = a - 1

The preincrement and predecrement operations take place before the variable is used. The postincrement and postdecrement operations occur after the variable is used.

In many expressions there is no effective difference between the pre and post operations, but there is a difference for some expressions.

There is another class of operators performing a function similar to that of the increment and decrement operators. The following lists these operators:

Operator	*Description*
a += b	Sum, a = a + b
a −= b	Difference, a = a − b
a *= b	Product, a = a * b

OBJECT PROGRAM EFFICIENCY

The purpose of these extended operators is to give the compiler information about the task rather than to make the programmer's task easier. Many machine language instruction sets include increment and decrement instructions.

The operators +=, −=, and *= combine the assignment and arithmetic operations into a composite operator. Compilers can effectively use information about these operations when applied to subscripted variables (vectors and matrices).

PROGRAM USING EXTENDED OPERATORS

The following program uses the pre and postincrement and decrement operators on both integer and real variables:

```
main()
  {
      int i, n, preincr, postincr, predecr;
      float fpreincr, fi, fsum, fprod;

      preincr   = 10;
      postincr  = 10;
      predecr   = 10;
      fpreincr  = 10.0;
      fsum      = 0.0;
      fprod     = 1.0;
      n         = 5;
      fi        = 0.0;

      for (i = 1; i <= n; i++)
```

```
        {
            ++preincr;
            postincr++;
            --predecr;
            ++fpreincr;
            fi ++;
            fsum += fi;
            fprod *= fi;

            printf("%5d  %5d  %5d", preincr, postincr, predecr);
            printf("  %5.0f  %5.0f  %5.0f\n", fpreincr, fsum, fprod);
        }
}
```

The output follows:

```
11    11    9    11     1      1
12    12    8    12     3      2
13    13    7    13     6      6
14    14    6    14    10     24
15    15    5    15    15    120
```

This program illustrates the use of the extended operators for both integer and real variables. There is no effective difference between pre and post operations.

DIFFERENCE BETWEEN PRE AND POST OPERATIONS

The following program performs the preincrement and postincrement operations as part of the printf statement:

```
main()
  {
     int preincr, postincr, i, n;

     n = 5;
     preincr  = 10;
     postincr = 10;
     for (i = 1; i <= n; i++)
       {
          printf("%5d  %5d\n", ++preincr, postincr++);
       }
  }
```

This time there is a difference between preincrementing and postincrementing as the following output shows:

```
11    10
12    11
13    12
14    13
15    14
```

The preincrement operator performs the incrementing *before* using the contents of the variable. The postincrement operator performs the incrementing *after* the contents of the variable is used. The incrementing takes place in both cases. Both variables were initialized to the value 10 before execution of the FOR loop.

Exercises

1. Write a program using the += operator to calculate the sum of the first 5 integers.

2. Write a program using the *= operator and floating point variables to calculate n! as the product of the first *n* integers. Test using an *n* of 30.

3. Use the increment and decrement operators in the process of calculating the values for the expression

$$(10 - x)/(10 + x)$$

for the values $x = 0, 1, 2, \ldots, 10$.

4. Use the increment operator in the process of calculating the area and circumference of each of a series of boxes having sides of length 1, 2, . . . , 5.

5. Compute the velocity in feet per second and distance traveled in feet for an object accelerating at the rate of 32.2 feet per second for 5 seconds.

2.4 Relational Expressions

Relational operators compare two values and return a result of 0 if the comparison is false and 1 if the comparison is true. The standard relational operators follow:

Operator	*Description*
$>$	Greater than
$>=$	Greater than or equal
$<$	Less than
$<=$	Less than or equal
$==$	Equal
$!=$	Not equal

The expression

$$3 < 4$$

returns the value 1 representing the result true since the value 3 is less than the value 4 and the relation is true. The expression

$$3 >= 4$$

returns the result 0 since the relation is false.

The C language permits assigning the results of a relational comparison to variables. The statement

$$a = b < c$$

assigns the result 1 or 0 to the variable *a* depending on whether or not *b* is less than *c*.

The result of a relational comparison can be used as part of a larger arithmetic expression. The statement

$$a = (b < c) * d$$

multiplies the value of *d* by the result of the relational comparison. The value of $(b < c)$ can assume only the value 0 or the value 1. The result will be to assign the value of *d* to the variable *a* if the relation is true, and the value 0 if the relation is false.

LOGICAL OPERATORS

The common logical operations include AND, OR, and NOT. The following summarizes the common logical operators:

Operator	*Description*
&&	AND, true if both are true

: :	OR, true if at least one is true
!	NOT, true to false or false to true

The NOT operator has only one operand which is to the right. The other two are binary operators which require two operands, one on each side of the operator symbol. (period).

Logical operators operate on the results of relational comparisons. The expression

```
(a < b) && (b < c)
```

results in the value 1 (true) if both relational comparisons are true. If either comparison is false, the result will be 0 (false).

The expression

```
(a < b) :: (b < c)
```

results in the value 1 (true) if either or both of the comparisons is true. The result is 0 (false) only if both of the comparisons are false.

The expression

```
!(a < b)
```

compares the values contained in *a* and *b*. The subexpression

```
(a < b)
```

returns the value 1 if *a* is less than *b* and the value 0 otherwise. The negation (NOT) operator switches the result 1 (true) to 0 (false) or the result 0 (false) to 1 (true).

PROGRAM ILLUSTRATING RELATIONS AND LOGIC

The following program illustrates several relational comparisons and logical operations and their computed results:

```
main()
  {
      int a, b, c, d;
```

```
        a = 3;
        b = 4;
        c = 12;

        d = a < b;
        printf("a < b      %d\n", d);
        d = a >= b;
        printf("a>=b    %d\n", d);
        d = c == a * b;
        printf("Line 3     %d\n", d);
        d = (a < b) && (b < c);
        printf("Line 4     %d\n", d);
        d = (a >= b) :: (c >= b);
        printf("Line 5     %d\n", d);
        d = a != b;
        printf("Line 6     %d\n", d);
        d = !((a < b) && (b < c));
        printf("Line 7     %d\n", d);
}
```

The output follows:

```
a < b      1
a >= b     0
Line 3     1
Line 4     1
Line 5     1
Line 6     1
Line 7     0
```

The results are 1 for true and 0 for false.

OVERTIME PAY

Many companies pay hourly employees by the week and give time-and-a-half for overtime exceeding 40 hours. The bonus is an extra 50 percent for each hour over 40 hours. Let h be the hours worked and r be the hourly pay rate. The expression

$$r * h$$

gives the regular pay for all hours including overtime, and

$$.5 * r * (h - 40)$$

gives the extra 50 percent bonus.

The comparison

$$(h > 40)$$

returns the value 1 if overtime is involved and the value 0 if there is none. The combined expression

$$(h > 40) * .5 * r * (h - 40)$$

returns the 50 percent overtime bonus if overtime is involved or the value 0 if there is none.

The following program uses this approach to calculate the gross pay including time-and-a-half for overtime.

```
main()
  {
      float rate, hours, overtime, regular, gross;

      rate     = 8.25;
      hours    = 51.8;

      overtime = (hours > 40.0) * 0.5 * rate * (hours - 40.0);
      regular  = rate * hours;
      gross    = overtime + regular;
      printf("Hours worked     %7.1f\n", hours);
      printf("Pay rate         %7.2f\n", rate);
      printf("\n");
      printf("Regular pay      %7.2f\n", regular);
      printf("Overtime pay     %7.2f\n", overtime);
      printf("\n");
      printf("Total pay        %7.2f\n", gross);
  }
```

The output follows:

```
Hours worked       51.8
Pay rate           8.25

Regular pay      427.35
Overtime pay      48.67

Total pay        476.02
```

The IF statements of Chapter 3 provide a method that is easier to understand. Some situations need results of logical operations similar to those given in the overtime pay program.

Exercises

1. Write a program that makes the following comparisons and prints the logical results 1 and 0:

a. 5 < 6
b. 5 >= 6
c. 5 == 5
d. 5 != 5
e. 5 > 5

2. Write a program that performs the following logical operations and prints the results:

a. (5 < 6) && (12 > 12)
b. (5 < 6) :: (12 > 12)
c. !(5 < 6)
d. !(12 > 12)
e. (5 < 6) && ((12 > 12) :: (3 * 4 = 12))

3. Use the overtime program to calculate the pay for an employee working 35.6 hours at an hourly pay rate of $6.95.

4. Use the overtime program to calculate the pay for an employee working 47.5 hours at an hourly pay rate of $9.25.

2.5 Bit Operations

C includes a set of bit operations which are useful for the systems programmer. The following summarizes these operations:

Operation	*Description*
&	Bitwise AND
:	Bitwise inclusive OR

∧	Bitwise exclusive OR
~	One's complement
<<	Left shift
>>	Right shift

They are almost universally available in the machine language instruction set. A good C compiler can translate these operations directly into the appropriate machine language instructions.

BINARY NUMBERS

A bit is a binary digit. It can assume only one of the two values 0 and 1. The following table lists the first few binary numbers and compares them with their corresponding decimal numbers:

Binary	*Decimal*
0	0
1	1
10	2
11	3
100	4
101	5
110	6
111	7
1000	8
1001	9
1010	10
1011	11
1100	12

HEXADECIMAL AND OCTAL

Hexadecimal (base 16) and octal (base 8) numbers provide a convenient coding scheme for large binary numbers. The following table compares the corresponding binary, octal, and hexadecimal numbers:

Binary	*Octal*	*Hexadecimal*
0	0	0

1	1	1
10	2	2
11	3	3
100	4	4
101	5	5
110	6	6
111	7	7
1000	10	8
1001	11	9
1010	12	A
1011	13	B
1100	14	C
1101	15	D
1110	16	E
1111	17	F
10000	20	10
10001	21	11

CONVERTING FROM BINARY TO CODED FORM

Converting from binary to octal or octal to binary is easy. Each octal digit corresponds to three binary bits. The bits are arranged in groups of three from the right. Consider converting the binary number

1101111001

to octal. Commas in the number

1,101,111,001

form the bits into groups of three. Convert each group into the corresponding octal digit using the table above, and this octal number results:

1571

Converting from binary to hexadecimal requires grouping the bits into groups of four from the right. The binary number

1101111001

becomes

11,0111,1001

when placed in the proper groups of four. Converting each group into the corresponding hexadecimal digit gives

379

as the corresponding hexadecimal number.

CONVERTING CODED NUMBERS TO BINARY

Converting from octal to binary also involves groups of three bits. Each octal digit converts to its three-bit counterpart. The octal number

2537

converts to the binary number

010,101,011,111

which becomes

10101011111

without the commas and with zero suppression.

The hexadecimal number

E38A

converts to the binary number

1110,0011,1000,1010

with commas marking the groups of four bits, and

1110001110001010

without the commas.

HEXADECIMAL IS MOST COMMON

Rarely is binary information displayed in bit form. It is usually displayed in octal or hexadecimal coded form. Most modern computers use hexadecimal codes. Each 8-bit byte (character) contains two 4-bit hexadecimal digits some call nibbles. Each 16-bit integer contains 4 hexadecimal digits. Each 32-bit floating point value corresponds to 8 hexadecimal digits.

NEGATIVE NUMBERS

Most computers use a scheme for which the leftmost bit designates the sign of the number. The leftmost bit is 0 for positive numbers and 1 for negative numbers. The three major schemes for representing negative numbers are signed magnitude, one's complement, and two's complement.

The following table compares the three schemes for a hypothetical computer allowing signed 8-bit numbers:

Decimal	*Signed magnitude*	*One's complement*	*Two's complement*
−5	10000101	11111010	11111011
−4	10000100	11111011	11111100
−3	10000011	11111100	11111101
−2	10000010	11111101	11111110
−1	10000001	11111110	11111111
−0	10000000	11111111	
0	00000000	00000000	00000000
1	00000001	00000001	00000001
2	00000010	00000010	00000010
3	00000011	00000011	00000011
4	00000100	00000100	00000100
5	00000101	00000101	00000101

The three schemes are identical for positive numbers. Their differences become apparent only for negative numbers. Two's complement notation is the only one of the three which does not have the negative zero anomoly. This is the primary reason why it has become the most popular.

COMPLEMENTATION

A number is complemented by forming its one's complement. This is a bit-by-bit complement of the original number. The binary number

001001010111

has

110110101000

as its complement. One's complement negative numbers are bit-by-bit complements of the corresponding positive numbers.

Two's complement numbers are formed in two steps. First, form the one's complement number, then add the value 1 to the one's complement. This applies to converting negative numbers to positive or vice versa.

Signed magnitude numbers require changes to the leftmost bit only. The other bits remain unchanged whether the number is positive or negative.

PROGRAM GENERATING HEXADECIMAL CODES

The following program uses the postincrement and postdecrement operators to generate corresponding negative and positive integers and displays the results using hexadecimal codes:

```
main()
  {
      int n, i, incr, decr;

      incr  = 0;
      decr  = 0;
      n     = 6;

      for (i = 0; i <= n; i++)
          printf("%4x    %4x\n", decr--, incr++);
  }
```

The printed output follows:

```
   0    0
FFFF    1
FFFE    2
FFFD    3
FFFC    4
FFFB    5
FFFA    6
```

The format code %4x specifies output in hexadecimal within a field of four columns. Notice that the negative numbers are in two's complement notation. The hexadecimal number

```
FFFF
```

corresponds to the binary number

```
1111111111111111
```

which is the two's complement of the binary number

```
0000000000000001.
```

BITWISE LOGICAL OPERATORS

Consider the binary numbers 1010 and 1100. The AND operator combines the two numbers bitwise, giving a 1 if both operands contain a 1 in that location and a 0 otherwise. The "and" of 1010 and 1100 is 1000. The following portrays the operation:

```
1010
 &
1100
----
1000
```

The inclusive OR operation returns a 1 if at least one of the two operands contains a 1 in the corresponding bit positions. The following shows the inclusive OR operation:

```
1010
 :
1100
----
1110
```

The exclusive OR operation returns a 1 if only one of the operands contains a 1 in the required bit position. The following illustrates the exclusive OR operation:

```
 1010
  ^
 1100
----
 0110
```

SHIFT OPERATIONS

The C operators << and >> shift left and shift right, respectively. The variable containing the binary number is the lefthand operand. The righthand operand gives the number of bit positions for the shift. The expression

```
a << 3
```

shifts the contents of a left three bits. The expression

```
a >> 1
```

shifts the contents of a right one bit.

Each hexadecimal digit corresponds to a group of four bits. The expression

```
a << 4
```

shifts the contents of a left one 4-bit hexadecimal digit. Each byte corresponds to a group of eight bits. The expression

```
a >> 8
```

shifts the contents of a right one byte.

PROGRAM ILLUSTRATING LOGICAL OPERATIONS

The following program demonstrates the common logical operations

```
main()
  {
       unsigned int a, b, c;
```

```
        a = OXF5A3;
        b = OX94E6;

        printf("First operand         %4x\n", a);
        printf("Second operand        %4x\n", b);
        c = a & b;
        printf("Logical and           %4x\n", c);
        c = a : b;
        printf("Logical or            %4x\n", c);
        c = a /\ b;
        printf("Exclusive or          %4x\n", c);
        c = ~b;
        printf("Complement of b       %4x\n", c);
        c = b << 4;
        printf("Shift b left 4        %4x\n", c);
        c = b >> 4;
        printf("Shift b right 4       %4x\n", c);
}
```

The output follows:

```
First operand        F5A3
Second operand       94E6
Logical and          94A2
Logical or           F5E7
Exclusive or         6145
Complement of b      6B19
Shift b left 4       4E60
Shift b right 4       94E
```

The variables are unsigned integers so that the shift operations will work properly. A right shift of a signed integer results in the sign bit propagating in from the left. A right shift of an unsigned integer does not propagate the sign bit.

Exercises

1. Write a program comparing the decimal and hexadecimal representations of the numbers $-12, -11, \ldots, 12$.

2. Write a program showing the hexadecimal representation of the floating point numbers $-12.0, -11.0, -10.0, \ldots, 12.0$.

3. Write a program that first places the hexadecimal number 7F05 into a variable, then extracts the four hexadecimal digits and places in the rightmost four bits of four other variables.

4. Write a program that takes the rightmost four bits of each of four variables and packs them into one 16-bit unsigned integer.

2.6 Primitive Input and Output

Input and output facilities are not built into C language commands. They are added to the language as functions in a standard library. Some systems require the statement

```
#include <stdio.h>
```

near the beginning of the source file; others automatically search the standard library.

FILE COPY PROGRAM

The purpose of the following program is to make a copy of a file:

```
main()
  {
     int c;

     while ((c = getchar()) != EOF)
        putchar (c);
  }
```

Some systems require the explicit definition of the name EOF using a statement of the form

```
# define EOF -1
```

before the main() statement of the source file. Some systems use 0 rather than −1.

UNIX-based systems process this program in a predictable manner. Standard input comes from the keyboard and standard output goes to the video display. Redirection of standard I/O gives flexibility to the program.

Give a program the name "copy" and run it without using the redirection feature. If the input line is

```
Now is the time
```

some systems will echo each character, giving an output line of the following appearance:

```
NNooww iiss tthhee ttiimmee
```

Other systems use an input buffering scheme that will give output having the following appearance.

```
Now is the time
Now is the time
```

In both cases the typed character appears on the screen and the putchar function returns it to the screen.

The copy program checks each incoming character for an end of file symbol designated EOF in the program. Determine the method for generating the EOF character for your computer system and terminal.

REDIRECTION

UNIX provides redirection of standard input and output. Standard input can be redirected to come from a file instead of the keyboard. Standard output can be redirected to the printer or to a file instead of the video screen.

Giving the name of the program by itself as in the command

```
copy
```

results in standard input coming from the keyboard and standard output going to the screen. The command

```
copy >filename
```

redirects the standard output to a file. The > symbol designates output redirection. This allows direct entry from the keyboard to a file.

The command

copy <filename

redirects standard input from a file. The symbol < defines redirection of standard input. The copy program lists the file to the video screen.

The command

copy <filename1 >filename2

copies the file to another location and assigns a different name, providing backup copy.

If the name printer specifies a printing device, the command

copy <filename >printer

lists the file on the printer. Some systems use the redirection parameter >* to send the standard output to the printer. The command

copy <filename >*

uses this convention.

The Microsoft MS-DOS and PC-DOS operating systems include the redirection of standard input and output using the UNIX convention. This is a powerful feature that adds to the usefulness of programs written in C or any other language.

FORMATTED INPUT

The scanf function operates like the printf function. It uses many of the same symbols of the form %d, %f, etc. This is a primary way of obtaining values from the standard input device, including the keyboard.

The scanf requires a different type of variable reference. Functions accept data from the calling routine through the argument list. In computer science terminology, the parameters are actual values. The function accepts actual values but cannot return actual values to the calling routine.

A second type of argument gives the numerical address of the variable rather than its value. The function can place results in the required address. If *x* is the name of a variable, then &x is its address.

The function scanf requires the addresses of the variables to receive the results of the input scan. The function call is of the form

```
scanf("%d %f", &a, &b);
```

which reads an integer value for the variable *a* and a floating point value for the variable *b*. The symbols &a and &b give scanf the required addresses for the variables *a* and *b*.

A summary of the control characters follows:

Symbol	*Description*
%d	Decimal integer
%f	Floating point number
%c	Character
%s	Character string
%o	Octal integer
%x	Hexadecimal integer
*	Skip field (%*d, %*f, etc.)

Blanks, tabs, and newlines (\n) are called whitespace and are ignored by scanf during input.

UNLABELED INPUT

The following program computes the area and circumference of a rectangle, obtaining the length and width from standard input:

```
main()
  {
      int length, width, area, circum;
```

```
        scanf("%d %d", &length, &width);
        area   = length * width);
        circum = 2 * (length + width);

        printf("Area                %7d\n", area);
        printf("Circumference       %7d\n", circum);
    }
```

This program does not give a prompt message. The user provides the data in the proper order or redirects standard input to a data file containing the values. If the file FILE1 contains the data

```
40  30
```

and the program name is PROG1, the command

```
PROG1 <FILE1
```

results in the following standard output sent to the video screen:

```
Area                1200
Circumference        140
```

PROMPT MESSAGES FOR INTERACTIVE DATA ENTRY

Interactive data entry from the keyboard works best when the program provides prompt messages. The following program includes a prompt message:

```
main()
  {
      int length, width, area, circum;

      printf("Length and width ? ");
      scanf("%d %d", & length, &width);
      area   = length * width;
      circum = 2 * (length + width);

      printf("\n");
```

```
        printf("Area             %7d\n", area);
        printf("Circumference    %7d\n", circum);
  }
```

The keyboard is the default standard input device. Using the keyboard for interactive data entry results in the following interaction and output sent to the video screen:

```
Length and width ? 40 30
Area              1200
Circumference      140
```

REQUEST EACH VALUE SEPARATELY

Requesting more than one value on one line of keyboard input is not usually recommended. The following program requests the length and width separately:

```
main()
  {
        float length, width, area, circum;

        printf("Length ? ");
        scanf("%f", &length);
        printf("Width  ? ");
        scanf("%f", &width);

        area   = length * width;
        circum = 2.0 * (length + width);

        printf("\n");
        printf("Area             %7.2f\n", area);
        printf("Circumference    %7.2f\n", circum);
  }
```

The following interaction results:

```
Length ? 27.5
Width  ? 15.3

Area             420.75
Circumference     85.60
```

This program uses floating point variables rather than integer variables.

FILE-ORIENTED PROGRAMS

The following program is a file-oriented program rather than a program assuming keyboard entry and video or printer output:

```
main()
  {
      float length, width, area, circum;

      scanf("%f", &length);
      scanf("%f", &width);

      area   = length * width;
      circum = 2.0 * (length + width);

      printf("%7.2f\n", length);
      printf("%7.2f\n", width);
      printf("%7.2f\n", area);
      printf("%7.2f\n", circum);
  }
```

This program includes no explanatory messages.

If the program name is PROG4 and the input file FILE2 contains

```
27.5
15.3
```

then the command

```
PROG1 <FILE2 >FILE3
```

sends the following values to FILE3:

```
 27.50
 15.30
420.75
 85.60
```

Exercises

1. Write an interactive program to compute the area and circumference of a circle.

2. Write an interactive program to compute the gross pay for a person working 37.5 hours at an hourly rate of $6.75.

3. Write an interactive program requesting acceleration in feet per second and time in seconds, and which computes the velocity in miles per hour and distance in feet at the time specified.

4. If your system allows standard input/output redirection, write a program similar to that of exercise 2. The hours worked and pay rate are accepted from an input file. The hours worked, pay rate, and gross pay are sent to an output file.

2.7 Comments

Programming style, including comments within the program, are important tools for program readability. Aesthetics have no bearing on the execution of the program, but the appearance is important for those reading the source program listing. There are many ways to write a given program. The example programs of this chapter contrast many program styles for the simple problem of calculating the area and circumference of a rectangle.

JUMBLED MESS

The following program jams everything together in a disorganized mess:

```
main(){int length,width,area,circum;length=40;width=30;
area=length*width;circum=2*(length+width);
printf("Length    %d\n",length);printf("Width              %d\n",width);
printf("Area      %d\n",area);printf("Circumference   %d\n",circum);}
```

The output follows

```
Length          40
Width           30
```

```
Area            1200
Circumference   140
```

The program works, but the source program listing is hard to read. Many programmers using the BASIC language adopt this style in their efforts to improve execution speed and limit the memory requirements of the source program. There is no reason to make source programs unreadable when using compiled programs.

ONE STATEMENT PER LINE

The following program places one program statement only per line:

```
main()
  { int length, width, area, circum;
     length  = 40;
     width   = 30;
     area    = length * width;
     circum = 2 * (length + width);
     printf("Length              %d\n", length);
     printf("Width               %d\n", width);
     printf("\n");
     printf("Area                %d\n", area);
     printf("Circumference       %d\n", circum);}
```

The output is the same as before, but program readability is greatly improved. Some C programs pack multiple statements of the same class on one line as in

```
length = 30; width = 40;
```

which is acceptable.

INDENTING SUBORDINATE PARTS

The following program indents subordinate parts of the program

```
main()
  {
        int length, width, area, circum;
        length  =  40;
        width   =  30;
        area    =  length * width;
        circum  =  2 * (length + width);
        printf("Length             %5d\n", length);
        printf("Width              %5d\n", width);
        printf("Area               %5d\n", area);
        printf("Circumference      %5d\n", circum);
  }
```

The output follows:

```
Length              40
Width               30
Area              1200
Circumference      140
```

Paragraphing, another name for identing, contributes to readability. Most C programmers indent their programs. There are slight differences in style. Some place the braces in the same column as the outer lines and indent only the inner lines; others use the style given.

The program also uses the format code %5d to control the numerical output. The resulting values are right-justified in the 5-digit field, which is normal practice for integers. Floating point values in a column are normally aligned around their decimal points, if possible.

BLANK LINES

Blank lines in the program listing form white space separating parts of the program. The same technique is useful for separating parts of the output. The newline character \n in a statement of the form

```
printf("\n");
```

prints a blank line. Most program editors permit the insertion of blank lines into the source program.

The following program includes blank lines for white space:

```
main()
  {
      int length, width, area, circum;

      length  =  40;
      width   =  30;

      area    =  length * width;
      circum  =  2 * (length + width);

      printf("Length              %5d\n", length);
      printf("Width               %5d\n", width);
      printf("\n");
      printf("Area                %5d\n", area);
      printf("Circumference       %5d\n", circum);
  }
```

The output follows:

```
Length            40
Width             30
Area            1200
Circumference    140
```

The output includes a blank line separating the problem parameters, length and width, from the results, area and circumference.

COMMENTS

Adding comments to the source program can improve readability. Small programs may not need many comments. Large programs should be commented. One or more lines of comments should be at the beginning of the program, giving its purpose. Other comments may describe how to use the program, give information about the variables, and give the purpose of each section of the program. Comments in C begin with the symbol /* and end with the symbol */.

The best comments describe *what* the program does rather than *how*. The program statements themselves describe how. Most C programmers do not comment each variable name, but rather choose meaningful names. The following program comments each variable name to show the manner of such commenting:

```
main()      /* Program
                 SZ173
               Purpose
                 Compute the area and circumference
                 of a rectangle using assignment
                 statements to specify parameters.
               Programmer
                 Larry McNitt
               Date
                 1/8/85
               System
                 IBM PC
            */
  {

    /* Variable declarations for main */
    int length,       /* Length of rectangle */
        width,        /* Width of rectangle */
        area,         /* Area of rectangle */
        circum;       /* circumference of rectangle */

    /* Problem parameters */
    length = 40;
    width  = 30;

    /* Process parameters */
    area   = length * width;
    circum = 2 * (length + width);

    /* Output both parameters and results */
    printf("Length                  %5d\n", length);
    printf("Width                   %5d\n", width);
```

```
    printf("\n");
    printf("Area              %5d\n", area);
    printf("Circumference     %5d\n", circum);
  }
```

The output is the same as for the previous program. Organizations set commenting practices as standards for their programmers. If programs are commented in a consistent manner, they will be easier to read and less costly to maintain.

COMMENTING OUTPUT

Output should be commented for the same reason that the program listing should be commented. It is good practice to include some initial identifying messages if the program is to run interactively from the terminal. These messages may include the name of the program and a one to three-line description of its purpose.

A final message indicating normal termination of the program is also good practice. This reassures the user and also identifies the end of multiple-page printed output.

The following program includes additional identifying messages for the output:

```
main()     /* Program
                SZ173
              Purpose
                Compute the area and circumference
                of a rectangle using assignment
                statements to specify parameters.
              Programmer
                Larry McNitt
              Date
                1/8/85
              System
                IBM PC
           */
  {
      /* Initial message */
      printf("/n");
```

```
    printf("Program SZ173\n");
    printf("\n");
    printf("Compute the area\n");
    printf("and circumference\n");
    printf("for a rectangle.\n");

    /* Variable declarations for main */
    int length,     /* Length of rectangle */
        width,      /* Width of rectangle */
        area,       /* Area of rectangle */
        circum;     /* circumference of rectangle */

    /* Problem parameters */
    length = 40;
    width  = 30;

    /* Process parameters */
    area   = length * width;
    circum = 2 * (length + width);

    /* Output both parameters and results */
    printf("\n");
    printf("Length           %5d\n", length);
    printf("Width            %5d\n", width);
    printf("\n");
    printf("Area             %5d\n", area);
    printf("Circumference    %5d\n", circum);

    /* Final message */
    printf("\n");
    printf("End of program SZ173\n");
}
```

The output follows:

```
Program SZ173

Compute the area
and circumference
for a rectangle.

Length          40
Width           30
```

```
Area              1200
Circumference      140

End of program SZ173
```

Exercises

1. Write a commented program to compute the area of a circle.

2. Write a commented program to compute the gross pay of an employee, including time-and-a-half for overtime.

3. Write a commented program to compute n! (factorial) for a specified value of *n*.

4. Write a commented program that computes velocity in feet per second, velocity in miles per hour, and distance in feet of an object accelerating at a specified rate in feet per second for a specified time in seconds.

5. Write a commented program that computes the surface area and volume of a sphere of specified diameter.

3

Elements of Program Flow

Many activities are repetitive. Accumulating the sum of a set of values requires repeated addition. Computing a compound interest table requires repetitious calculating and printing for each line of the table. Searching for the first occurrence of a value requires repeating the test.

A program loop consists of a sequence of one or more statements to be executed repeatedly. All programming languages contain control statements to alter the normal sequential flow of execution within the program. C provides three general looping control structures: FOR, WHILE, and DO . . . WHILE.

A Boolean (logical) variable has two possible values: 1 (true) and 0 (false). A Boolean expression containing relational operators also gives the same two values. Boolean expressions provide a mechanism for the conditional execution of a portion of the program. This gives the program its decision-making capability. IF statements and IF . . . ELSE statements give flexibility to the program.

3.1 FOR

The FOR loop of C provides looping control by using a control variable and an automatic updating feature. The required information for the looping process includes the name of the control variable, its initial value, its final value, the way it is updated, and the statement representing the body of the loop.

The control variable can be any type, including floating point, although it will usually be integer. C is quite flexible in its choice of loop control variables, but FORTRAN and Pascal do not permit floating point (real) loop control variables.

EXAMPLE FOR STATEMENTS

The FOR loop control statement contains three parts and has the form

```
for (ei; e2; e3)
```

with three expressions controlling initialization, test for end of loop, and updating in that order.

The statement

```
for (i = 1; i <= n; i = i + 1)
```

represents the most common type which performs the body of the loop *n* times. The variable *i* is the loop control variable and assumes the values 1, 2, . . . , *n*. The statement

```
for (i = 1; i <= n; i++)
```

accomplishes the same thing using the increment operator for the loop control variable.

The similar statement

```
for (i = n; i >= n; i--)
```

performs the loop *n* times, counting from *n* to 1 in descending order.

The FOR statement in C is more flexible than it is for other languages. The expressions may be omitted entirely, although the semicolons must still be present. The statement

```
for (;;)
```

specifies an infinite loop. C provides a BREAK command to break out of the middle of a loop.

The statement

```
for (; x > e;)
```

includes only the test for end of loop. This is similar to the WHILE statement.

BODY OF THE LOOP

The body of the loop must contain a single statement. That statement may be a compound statement contained within braces. The statement

```
for (i = 1; i <= 5; i++)
        printf("%d\n", i);
```

repeats the print statement five times. A semicolon terminates the printf statement which is controlled by the FOR mechanism.

The statement

```
for (i = 1; i <= n; i++)
  {
    s = i * i;
    printf("%d      %d\n", i, s);
  }
```

repeats the compound statement *n* times. No semicolon follows the right brace.

LET ME COUNT THE WAYS

One of Elizabeth Barret Browning's famous verses begins:

> How do I love thee? Let me count the ways.
> I love thee to the depth and breadth and height
> My soul can reach, when feeling out of sight.

The following C program makes up in output volume what it lacks in linguistic elegance and taste:

```
main()
  {
      int number, count;

      printf("How do I love thee?\n");
      printf("Let me count the ways.\n");

      number = 5;
      for (count = 1; count <= number; count++)
        printf("%d\n", count);
  }
```

The output follows:

```
How do I love thee?
Let me count the ways.
1
2
3
4
5
```

If this program does not count high enough to suit the occasion, a simple change to the final value for the control variable will increase the count.

TABLE GENERATION

Charles Babbage, in the early 1800s, conceived the idea of an automatic machine he called the analytical engine, which could both calculate and print mathematical tables for navigation and other purposes. His vision was unattainable until the first working computers of the 1940s. What was one of their main applications? Calculating and printing mathematical tables.

The following program generates a table giving the velocity in feet/sec and distance in feet for an object accelerating at 8 feet/sec/sec:

```
main()      /* Velocity and distance table */
  {
        int a,      /*Acceleration in feet/sec/sec */
            t,      /* Time in seconds */
            f,      /* Final time */
            v,      /* Velocity in feet/sec */
            d;      /* Distance in feet */

        printf("Time      Velocity      Distance\n");
        a = 8;
        f = 5;

        for (t = 1; t <= f; t++)
          {
                v = a * t;
                d = a * t * / 2;
                printf("%5d      %5d       %5d\n", t, v, d);
          }
  }
```

The output follows:

```
Time     Velocity     Distance
   1         8            4
   2        16           16
   3        24           36
   4        32           64
   5        40          100
```

This program illustrates one of the main uses of braces—to form a compound statement for the body of a loop.

FLOATING POINT VARIABLES

The following program generates a similar table, but uses floating point variables for acceleration, velocity, and distance:

```
main()
  {
        int   time, final;
        float accel, velocity, distance;
```

```
    printf("Time      Velocity      Distance\n");
    accel = 8.0;
    final  = 5;

    for (time = 1; time <= final; time++)
      {
         velocity  = accel * time;
         distance = 0.5 * accel * time * time;
         printf("%4d      %9.2f      %10.2f\n",
           time, velocity, distance);
      }
}
```

The output follows:

```
Time      Velocity      Distance
   1          8.00           4.00
   2         16.00          16.00
   3         34.00          36.00
   4         32.00          64.00
   5         40.00         100.00
```

This program contains a mixed-mode expression. The variable time is integer while acceleration, velocity, and distance are floating point.

FLOATING POINT LOOP CONTROL VARIABLE

The following program adds a floating point loop control variable:

```
main()
  {
    float time, final, accel, velocity, distance;

    printf("Time      Velocity      Distance\n");
    accel = 8.0;
    final  = 5;

    for (time = 1; time <= final; time++)
      {
         velocity  = accel * time;
```

```
            distance = 0.5 * accel * time * time;
            printf("%6.1f      %9.2f      %10.2f\n",
               time, velocity, distance);
         }
}
```

The output is the same as for the previous program.

SQUARE ROOT TABLE

The following program uses the FOR loop to generate the values 1.0, 1.1, . . . :

```
#include      <math.h>

main()       /* Square root table */
  {
     double value, first, last, step, root;

     first  = 1.0;
     last   = 2.0;
     step = 0.1;
     printf("Value      Square root\n");

     for (value = first; value <= last; value += step)
        {
           root = sqrt(value);
           printf("%7.2f      %16.11f\n", value, root);
        }
}
```

The output follows:

```
Value        Square root
   1.00          1.00000000000
   1.10          1.04880884817
   1.20          1.09544511501
   1.30          1.14017542509
   1.40          1.18321595661
   1.50          1.22474487139
   1.60          1.26491106406
   1.70          1.30384048104
```

```
1.80        1.34164078649
1.90        1.37840487520
```

This program looks like it should generate the square root table for the values 1.0, 1.1, . . . , 2.0, but it stops one value short. The reason is the finite precision of the floating point numbers. Floating point representation of integer values is not a problem. Fractional numbers must be approximated.

The binary representation of .1 is a repeating binary fraction, and must be rounded with cumulative errors. The generated value for 2.0 is slightly greater than 2.0, causing the test for end of loop to fail when we expect it to execute one last time. Use care with floating point loop control variables.

Most systems require the #include statement

```
#include <math.h>
```

when accessing the standard math functions including the square root. Math functions do their calculations on double precision and return double precision results. When using single precision floating point, the C compiler generates the instructions needed to convert between standard 32-bit floating point and double precision 64-bit floating point.

STANDARD MATH FUNCTIONS

C compilers differ in their choice of standard math functions. The following are usually available:

Name	*Description*
abs()	Absolute value of an integer
acos()	Arccosine
asin()	Arcsine
atan()	Arctangent
cos()	Cosine
exp()	Exponential
fabs()	Absolute value of a floating point number
frand()	Random number within interval 0-1

log()	Natural logarithm
pow(a,b)	*a* raised to power *b*
rand()	Random integer
srand()	Set seed for random number generator
sin()	Sine
sqrt()	Square root
tan()	Tangent

NONSTANDARD INITIALIZATION AND UPDATE

All three expressions are usually present with the FOR loop control mechanism. The following program generates the square root table, but does the initializing and updating outside the FOR loop mechanism:

```
#include <math.h>

main()      /* Square root table */

  {
      double value, first, last, step, root;

      first  = 1.0;
      last   = 2.0;
      step   = 0.1;
      printf("Value      Square root\n");

      value = first;
      for (; value <= last;)
          {
              root = sqrt(value);
              printf("%7.2f      %16.11f\n", value, root);
              value + = step;
          }
  }
```

The output is the same as before. Although rare, this form is possible. The statement

```
value + = step;
```

performs the same operation as

```
value = value + step;
```

but is more easily optimized by the compiler.

CHARACTER CONTROL VARIABLE

The following program illustrates the FOR loop control construct with a character loop control variable:

```
main()
  {
      int code;
      char c;

      for(c = 'A'; c <= 'E'; c++)
        {
          code = c;
          printf("%c     %3d\n", c, code);
        }
}
```

The output follows:

```
A    65
B    66
C    67
D    68
E    69
```

This program lists the uppercase letters A, B, . . . , E with their corresponding code numbers. Each printable symbol has an 8-bit code. IBM mainframe computers use a coding scheme called EBCDIC (Extended Binary Coded Decimal Interchange Code). Most other computers use another scheme called ASCII (American Standard Code for Information Interchange). The ASCII code for the symbol A is the decimal number 65.

C permits character-typed variables in arithmetic expressions. The character code is used as if it were a number, which it is to the computer. C is quite permissive in allowing the programmer to mix types.

CHARACTER CONTROL VARIABLE WITH DECREMENT

The following program decrements the character control variable in the FOR construct:

```
main()
  {
       int code;
       char c;

       for(c = 'E'; c >= 'A'; c--)
         {
            code = c;
            printf("%c      %3d\n, c, code);
         }
}
```

The output follows:

```
E   69
D   68
C   67
B   66
A   65
```

GENERATING CHARACTER VALUES

Each character has a corresponding code number. It is possible to use the number corresponding to the character. It is also possible to use the character defined by the number. An 8-bit byte can represent 256 possible symbols.

The first 31 ASCII symbols relate to communication and printer control and are nonprintable symbols. The next 97 symbols vary only slightly among computers that use the ASCII scheme. The final 128 symbols are highly nonstandard. The original ASCII code defines only seven bits; the eighth is a parity bit for checking the accuracy of transmission.

The following program generates and prints the symbols corresponding to ASCII codes 33, 34, . . . , 126:

```
main()      /* List printing symbols*/
 {
       int code;
```

```
    char c;
    for (code = 33; code <= 64; code++)
      {
        c = code;
        printf("%c", c);
      }
    printf("\n");

    for (code = 65; code <= 96; code++)
      {
        c = code;
        printf("%c", c);
      }
    printf("\n");

    for (code = 97; code <= 126; code++)
      {
        c = code;
        printf("%c", c);
      }
    printf("\n");
}
```

The output follows:

```
!"#$%&'()*+,-./0123456789:;<=>?@
ABCDEFGHIJKLMNOPQRSTUVWXYZ[\]^_'
abcdefghijklmnopqrstuvwxyz{:}~
```

INTERACTIVE DATA ENTRY

One use of the FOR loop construct is as a counter controlling the number of times through the loop. This is used in repeated data entry and for repetitive calculations. The following program calculates the sum of a set of values using interactive data entry:

```
main()      /* Compute sum */
  {
    int number, count;
    float value, sum;
```

```
    printf("\nCompute the sum of\n");
    printf("a set of values.\n");

    printf("\nNumber of values ? ");
    scanf("%d", &number);
    printf("\nValue\n");

    sum = 0.0;
    for (count = 1; count <= number; count++)
      {
        printf("No. %2d ? ", count);
        scanf("%f", &value);
        sum += value;
      }

    printf("\nSum      %10.2f", sum);
}
```

A sample test run follows:

```
Compute the sum of
a set of values.

Number of values ? 3

Value
No. 1 ? 12.7
No. 2 ? 19.1
No. 3 ? 15.6
Sum            47.40
```

Exercises

1. Write a program that will print a table listing all the letters from A to Z with their corresponding code numbers.

2. Write a program that will print all the letters A through Z on the same line.

3. A Fibonacci sequence begins with the numbers 1 and 1 and forms each successive number as the sum of the previous two numbers. The first few values of the sequence are

1, 1, 2, 3, 5, 8. Write a program that generates the first 15 terms of the sequence.

4. Write a program to compute the average of the following test scores:

83 70 91 84 85.

Use interactive data entry.

3.2 WHILE

The three loop control structures are FOR, WHILE, and DO . . . WHILE. The FOR loop specifies the initial value, test for end of loop, and loop control variable modification. It is useful as a loop counter and as a method of generating data values for use within the loop.

The WHILE and DO . . . WHILE loops are generalized looping structures. Both employ a test using a variable or expression. It is the responsibility of the programmer to initialize and update the variables used in the loop control test.

The WHILE statement performs its test at the beginning of the loop. If the test fails the first time, the loop will not execute. The DO . . . WHILE loop performs its test at the end of the loop. The loop statements will execute at least once. In both cases the loop is executed when the test is true and terminates when the test fails.

RELATIONAL OPERATORS

The relational operators are:

Operator	*Description*
<	Less than
<=	Less than or equal
>	Greater than
>=	Greater than or equal
==	Equal
!=	Not equal

Example relational expressions are

```
count <= 25
```

which is 1 (true) if the value of count is less than 25 and 0 (false) otherwise,

```
amount != -999.0
```

which is true if the value of amount does not equal −999.0, and

```
(count / 2) < (size - diff)
```

if the expression on the left is greater than that on the right.

COMPOUND LOGICAL EXPRESSIONS

Compound Boolean (logical) expressions are formed from simple expressions using combinations of AND and OR operators. The compound expression

```
(count < number) && (amount > 0)
```

uses the AND logical connective &&. The result of the compound expression is true if count is less than number and amount is greater than 0.

The compound expression

```
(big > verybig) :: (amount < 0)
```

is true if big is greater than verybig or amount is less than 0; otherwise, the expression is false.

A compound expression formed with the OR operator is true if at least one of the logical subexpressions is true. The compound expression is false only if both subexpressions are false. A compound expression formed with the AND operator is true only if both subexpressions are true. It is false if at least one of the subexpressions is false.

NEGATION

The NOT operator symbol ! negates the righthand operand. It converts the value 1 (true) to 0 (false) and vice versa. The expression

```
!(amount < big)
```

is true if amount is not less than big. The expression

```
(amount >= big)
```

has the same result and is easier to read.

If the result is a logical variable, the expression

```
!result
```

negates it. The C language contains many functions that return logical results. The function iscntrl() returns the value 1 if the argument is a control character and a 0 otherwise. The expression

```
!iscntrl(c)
```

returns the value 1 (true) if c does not contain a control character.

WHILE SYNTAX

The WHILE statement form

```
while (exp)
 {
      s1;
      s2;
  }
```

is most common.

If the loop body contains only one statement, the form

```
while (exp)
   s1;
```

is used, although some prefer the one-line form

```
while (exp) s1;
```

if there is enough space on the line.

SQUARE ROOT TABLE

The following program uses the WHILE loop construct to generate a table of square roots:

```
#include <math.h>

main()      /* Square root table */
  {
      float value, root;

      value = 1.0;
      while (value <= 1.5)
        {
            root = sqrt(value);
            printf("%7.2f     %14.10f\n", value, root);
            value += 0.1;
        }
  }
```

The output follows:

```
1.00    1.0000000000
1.10    1.0488088131
1.20    1.0954451561
1.30    1.1401754618
1.40    1.1832159758
```

The program includes the math.h library for the sqrt function computing square roots. The floating point requires rounding fractional numbers. The result of the rounding operation causes the final test to fail for the loop, giving the square root of 1.5. Not all computer systems and C languages fail this test.

Some languages use a small deviation—called fuzz—

for comparison tests involving floating point numbers. If the values are nearly equal, the ==, <=, and >= will return the result 1 (true) and the test != will return the result 0 (false).

TEST USING FUZZ

The following program includes a small "fudge factor" (fuzz) so that the square root table continues to the expected point:

```
#include <math.h>

main()      /* Square root table */
  {
      float value, root;

      value = 1.0;
      while (value <= 1.5001)
        {
          root = sqrt(value);
          printf("%7.2f      %14.10f\n", value, root);
          value += 0.1;
        }
  }
```

The output follows:

```
1.00      1.0000000000
1.10      1.0488088131
1.20      1.0954451561
1.30      1.1401754618
1.40      1.1832159758
1.50      1.2247449160.
```

FOR LOOP REVISITED

The following program uses the FOR construct—

```
for (; exp;)
```

—which is similar to the WHILE construct:

```
#include <math.h>

main()      /* Square root table */
  {
      float value, root;

      value = 1.0;
      for (;value <= 1.5001;)
        {
           root = sqrt(value);
           printf("%7.2f      %14.10f\n", value, root);
           value += 0.1;
        }
  }
```

The output is the same as before.

COMPUTE FACTORIAL

For integer values of *n* greater than 0, the expression n! has a value equal to the product of the first *n* integers. The value for 0! is defined to be 1. The value for 1! is 1. The value for 5! is $1 \times 2 \times 3 \times 4 \times 5 = 120$.

The following program uses the FOR loop to generate the integers needed to calculate the factorial:

```
main()      /* Factorial */
  {
      int count, number;
      long product;

      number = 10;
      product = 1;

      for (count = 1; count <= number; count++)
        product *= count;

      printf("Number      %10d\n", number);
      printf("Factorial   %101d\n", product);
  }
```

The output follows:

```
Number           10
Factorial   3628800
```

The value of n! grows very large for large values of *n*. Defining the variable containing the product as a long integer permits numbers up to 31 bits. This is the equivalent of nine decimal places. Even long integers cannot represent values much larger than 11!. Most floating point representations cannot represent numbers greater than 70!.

PROGRAM USING WHILE LOOP

The following program uses the WHILE loop for calculating the factorial:

```
main()     /* Factorial */
  {
      int count, number;
      long product;

      number = 10;
      product =  1;

      count = 1;
      while (count <= number)
        {
          product *= count;
          ++count;
        }

      printf("Number      %10d\n", number);
      printf("Factorial   %101d\n", product);
  }
```

The output is the same as that of the previous program. Explicit statements must be added to initialize the value of count and to increment it each time through the loop.

USING TRAILER VALUE TO TERMINATE DATA ENTRY

A common method of terminting data entry is to use a special trailer value and to test for that value every time through the loop. The WHILE statement requires that the variables used by the test have meaningful values before entering the loop. This is necessary because the WHILE construct tests at the beginning of the loop.

The following program reads a set of floating point values and computes their sum using the special value −999.0 as a trailer value designating the end of the data:

```
main()       /* Trailer value  -999 */
  {
      float value, sum, trailer;

      trailer = -999.0
      sum = 0.0;

      scanf("%f", &value);
      while (value != trailer)
        {
           sum += value;
           scanf("%f", &value);
        }
      printf("Sum       %10.2f\n", sum);
  }
```

If the file FILE1 contains the values

```
2.4
3.8
1.2
-999.0
```

and the program is SUM, the command

```
SUM <FILE1
```

reads the data from the data file and displays the result

```
Sum          7.40
```

on the video screen.

It is also possible to enter the values from the keyboard, but the program gives no prompt messages. The following session illustrates obtaining the values from the keyboard:

```
SUM
2.4
3.8
1.2
-999.0
Sum         7.40
```

Exercises

1. Write a program using the WHILE construct to compute the sum of the first 15 integers.

2. Write a program using the WHILE construct and floating point variables to compute the sum of the squares of the first 15 integers.

3. Write a program using the WHILE construct to generate a square root table for the values 10.0, 10.2, . . . , 14.0.

4. Write a program using floating point variables to compute the value of 30!.

5. Write a program to compute the average of the test scores

88 73 77 81 92

using a WHILE loop and the special trailer value of −1.0.

3.3 DO . . . WHILE

The DO . . . WHILE looping construct performs its test at the end of the loop and always executes the body of the loop at least once. The body of the WHILE loop will not execute at all if the beginning-of-the-loop test fails the first test. The DO . . . WHILE construct is an exit-controlled loop, the least commonly used looping method.

The DO . . . WHILE loop is of the form

```
do
    statement
while (expression);
```

in which the statement is a single statement or a compound statement enclosed in braces.

SQUARE ROOT TABLE

The following program uses the DO . . . WHILE construct to control looping as it generates a square root table:

```
#include      <math.h>

main()      /* Square root table */
  {
       float value, root;

       value = 1.0;
       do
         {
              root = sqrt(value);
              printf("%7.2f      %10.6f\n", value, root);
              value + = 0.1;
         }
       while (value <= 1.50001);
  }
```

The output follows:

```
1.00        1.000000
1.10        1.048809
1.20        1.095445
1.30        1.140175
1.40        1.183216
1.50        1.224745
```

The only difference between this program and the similar program in Section 3.2 is the location of the test at the end of the loop. The upper limit of 1.50001 allows for round-off error accumulated from the repeated additions of the value 0.1. Most computers cannot represent the decimal fraction .1 exactly in internal binary form.

INFINITE LOOPS

It is easy to write WHILE and DO . . . WHILE loops that never terminate. These infinite loops result in runaway programs that fill the screen with output if the loop contains an output statement. If the infinite loop does not contain an input or output statement, the computer will apparently be doing nothing, but it will be feverishly repeating the loop until you stop it.

Every system has its "panic button." This may consist of a break key on the keyboard. Some systems require pressing the control key and break key simultaneously. Still other systems use the control/c combination consisting of holding the control key down and typing the letter c. Determine how your system stops an executing program.

The WHILE and DO . . . WHILE constructs require that the programmer take responsibility for initializing and updating the necessary variable or variables used in the test. If the loop never reaches the stopping point, the loop will be infinite.

PROGRAM WITH INFINITE LOOP

The following program is identical to the previous except that the statement

```
value += 0.1;
```

has been removed:

```
#include     <math.h>

main()      /* Square root table */
  {
     float value, root;

     value = 1.0;
     do
       {
          root = sqrt(value);
          printf("%7.2f      %10.6f\n", value, root);
       }
     while (value <= 1.50001);
  }
```

The updating does not take place; the test will never fail. The stopping condition will never be reached; the computer will get into an infinite loop. Each time through the loop the computer will send the line

```
1.0        1.000000
```

to the video display. The only recourse is to hit the panic button to stop the runaway program.

STOPPING DATA ENTRY WITH TRAILER VALUE

The following program calculates the sum of a set of floating point values using the trailer value −999.0 to signal the end of the data entry:

```
main()      /* Form sum of a set of values*/
  {
       float value, sum, trailer;

       trailer = -999.0;
       sum   = 0.0;
       scanf("%f", &value);

       do
         {
             sum += value;
             scanf("%f", &value);
         }
       while (value  != trailer);

       printf("Sum      %7.2f\n", sum);
  }
```

If the file FILE1 contains the values

```
19.6
27.5
15.2
-999.0
```

and the program name is SUM, the command

```
SUM <FILE1
```

uses input redirection to redirect standard input to the file FILE1. The output follows:

```
Sum        62.30
```

The program includes an initial scanf command to establish the initial value for the input variable. The variable sum is cleared to 0.0 before beginning the process loop. Each time through the loop the program adds the current value to sum, reads the next value, and makes its end of loop test. The scanf comes at the end of the loop so that the input value can be tested, thus keeping the program from adding the trailer value −999.0 to the sum.

Exercises

1. Write a program using the DO . . . WHILE loop to compute the sum of the first 15 integers.

2. Write a program using the DO . . . WHILE loop to compute the sum of the squares of the values 10.0, 10.2, . . . , 14.0.

3. Write a program using the DO . . . WHILE loop to generate a square root table for the values 100, 110, 120, . . . , 300.

4. Write a program using the DO . . . WHILE loop and a trailer value of −1.0 to compute the average of the test scores

88 73 77 91 92.

5. Write a program to compute the sum of the terms

$$x^n/n!$$

for the value $x = 2$ and $n = 0, 1, 2, \ldots$ until the value of the last term is less than .000001.

3.4 If

The simplest conditional statement is

```
if (condition)
  statement;
```

or

```
if (condition)
  statement;
else
  statement;
```

Similar statements abound in life. "If it is raining when I leave the house, I will take an umbrella." The statement, "it is raining when I leave the house" will be either true or false. If it is true, the action statement, "I will taken an umbrealla," goes into effect.

Within a bank's computer programs is a conditional statement to the effect, "IF customer checking account balance is less than zero, THEN send 'account overdrawn' notice to customer." Within a payroll program is a statement similar to, "IF hours worked is greater than 40, THEN compute overtime pay at time-and-a-half."

FLOW OF CONTROL

The normal flow of control in a program is from beginning to end; some call it from top to bottom because the beginning of the program is toward the top of the screen. Looping constructs override this natural order, but the body of the loop is still executed sequentially from the first to the last statement. After finishing the looping process, the program continues in sequential fashion with the statements immediately following the loop.

The IF statement provides a short single-statement conditional execution. It slips an additional statement into the sequence of statements if the condition is true. By using braces to form compound statements, the extra statement can be a complex portion of the C program containing loops and other IF statements.

OVERTIME PAY

An organization pays time-and-a-half for overtime beyond 40 hours per week. Gross pay is the hourly pay rate times the number of hours worked. Overtime hours earn an additional 50 percent.

The following program uses a simple IF statement to add the overtime factor:

```
main()      /* Calculate gross pay */
  {
      float rate, hours, gross;

      rate  = 9.25;
      hours = 47.5;

      gross = rate * hours;
      if (hours > 40.0)
        gross = gross + 0.5 * rate * (hours - 40.0);

      printf("Pay rate           %8.2f\n", rate);
      printf("Hours worked       %8.1f\n", hours);
      printf("Gross pay          %8.2f\n", gross);
  }
```

The output follows:

```
Pay rate            9.25
Hours worked        47.5
Gross pay         474.06
```

IF . . . ELSE

The following program uses the IF . . . ELSE construct to calculate gross pay with overtime:

```
main()      /* Calculate gross pay */
  {
      float rate, hours, gross;
```

```
      rate   = 9.25;
      hours = 47.5;

      if (hours > 40.0)
        gross = 40.0 * rate + 1.5 * rate * (hours - 40);
      else
        gross = hours * rate;

      printf("Pay rate           %8.2f\n", rate);
      printf("Hours worked       %8.2f\n", hours);
      printf("Gross pay          %8.2f\n", gross);
  }
```

The output follows:

```
Pay rate          9.25
Hours worked     47.50
Gross pay       474.06
```

MAXIMUM VALUE

Another application of the simple IF statement is searching for the maximum among a set of values. The statement

```
if (value > maximum)
  maximum = value;
```

updates the value of the variable "maximum" to reflect the new value if it is larger.

The variable "maximum" can be initialized to an extremely small value or to the first data value. A trailer value of −999.0 within the data values signals the end of data entry. Use of a trailer value suggests using the WHILE or DO . . . WHILE looping constructs.

The following program uses the DO . . . WHILE looping statements and reads the first data item before starting the looping section of the program:

```
main()     /* Maximum value */
  {
      float value, maximum;
```

```
    scanf("%f", &value);
    maximum = value;

    do
      {
          if (value > maximum)
            maximum = value;
          scantf("%f", &value);
      }
    while (value > -999.0);

    printf("Maximum value     %9.2f\n", maximum);
}
```

Let the data file FILE1 contain the values:

```
25.95
17.95
31.49
-999.0
```

Using <FILE1 to redirect system input results in the following output:

```
Maximum value          31.49
```

SALES COMMISSION

A business pays its sales force on a commission basis of 5 percent of the first $10,000, 8 percent of the second $10,000, and 10 percent of the sales above $20,000. Determine the commissions for each of the following amounts: $12,700.00, $8,275.73, and $32,500.00. Place the sales amounts in a file and use the value −1.0 to signal end of data.

The following program outputs the sales amount and corresponding commission for each sales amount:

```
main()     /* Sales commission */
  {
    float
      amount,     /*Amount of sales */
```

```
        comm,         /* Sales commission */
        amount;       /*5% for first $10,000 */
                      /* 8% for second $10,000 */
                      /* 10% for sales above $20,000 */

    scanf("%f", &amount);
    while (amount > -1.0)
      {
         if (amount <= 1000.0)
           comm = 0.05 * amount;
         if ((amount > 10000.00) && (amount <= 20000.0))
           comm = 500.0 + 0.08 * (amount - 10000.0);
         if (amount > 20000.0)
           comm = 1300.0 + 0.10 * (amount - 20000.0);
         printf("%9.2f     %7.2f\n", amount, comm);
         scanf("%f", &amount);
      }
}
```

If the data is contained in file FILE2 and the program name is COM1, the command

```
COM1 <FILE2
```

runs the program using FILE2 as standard input. The output follows:

```
12700.00       716.00
 8275.73       413.79
32500.00      2550.00
```

FREQUENCY COUNT FOR THE LETTER E

The standard library contains a function getchar() which fetches one character at a time from the standard input file. It will continue fetching characters until the end of the file. This is a primitive input function and it is up to the programmer to check for end of file.

The function getchar() returns an ASCII code interpreted as a positive integer between 0-255 when placed in a 16-bit or 32-bit integer. When it encounters the end of file, getchar() returns the value −1. This is why the result of getchar() is usually placed in an integer variable rather than a variable of type char.

The following program reads a text file and counts the number of occurrences of the letter e, both lowercase and uppercase:

```
#define     EOF     -1

main()      /* Frequency count */
  {
     int count, letter;

     count = 0;
     letter = getchar();

     while (letter != EOF)
       {
          if ((letter == 'E') :: (letter == 'e'))
             ++count;
          letter = getchar();
       }

     printf("Frequency     %d\n", count);
  }
```

The statement

```
#define     EOF     -1
```

defines the symbol EOF to be the value returned by getchar() if it encounters an end of file. The program fetches one character at a time and compares it with both "e" and "E" as it counts the frequency.

The file FILE3

```
Now is the time
for all good men
to come to the aid
of their party.
```

contains the text to be processed. The output

```
Frequency      6
```

results from using the program to count the frequency of the letters e and E.

PLACING getchar() IN THE WHILE TEST

If letter is an integer containing the latest character read from the file, then the logical expression

```
(letter != EOF)
```

returns the value true if the contents of letter does not indicate the end of the file.

The expression

```
(letter = getchar())
```

assigns the result of the getchar() function to the variable letter and makes that value available for use in a larger expression. The expression

```
((letter = getchar()) != EOF)
```

places the next character in the integer letter and compares it with the code returned if an end of file is encountered.

The expression

```
while ((letter = getchar()) != EOF)
```

means "while the next character is the end of file symbol." The following program uses this statement to accomplish reading the next character and testing for end of file:

```
#define     EOF     -1

main()     /* Frequency count */
  {
      int count, letter;
```

```
        count = 0;
        while ((letter = getchar()) != EOF)
          }
             if ((letter = = 'E' :: (letter = = 'e'))
               + +count;
          }

        printf("Frequency      %d\n", count);
  }
```

The output is the same as before.

Exercises

1. Write an interactive program with prompt messages requesting pay rate and hours worked for several employees and computing gross pay including time-and-a-half for overtime.

2. Write a program that computes the minimum of a set of data read from a file using input redirection.

3. Write a program that fetches text from a file forming the frequency count for each of the vowels a, e, i, o, and u.

4. Write a program that reads exam scores from a file redirected as the standard input device, computes the average score, and assigns a letter grade based on the following boundaries:

90-100%	A
80-89.9	B
70-79.9	C
60-69.9	D
0-59.9	F

3.5 IF . . . ELSE

The IF . . . ELSE conditional statement is of the form

```
if (expression)
  statement;
else
  statement;
```

and chooses one of the two statements on the basis of the logical expression. If the condition is true, the computer executes the first statement; if not, it executes the second.

ALTERNATION

Alternation refers to the process of choosing one of two possible courses of action. Either or both of the alternate statements can consist of compound statements within braces.

COMPUTE REGULAR AND OVERTIME PAY

A company pays time-and-a-half for overtime beyond 40 hours per week. Regular pay (up to 40 hours) and overtime pay are computed separately. Gross pay is the sum of regular pay and overtime pay.

The following program uses one IF . . . ELSE to calculate regular pay and another IF . . . ELSE statement to calculate overtime pay:

```
main()      /* Payroll */
  {
      float
        rate,                   /* Hourly pay rate */
        hours,                  /* Hours worked */
        regular,                /* Regular pay */
        overtime,               /* Overtime pay */
        gross;                  /* Gross pay */

      rate  = 9.24;
      hours = 47.5;

      if (hours <= 40.0)
        regular = rate * hours;
      else
        regular = rate * 40.0;

      if (hours <= 40.0);
        overtime = 0.0;
      else
        overtime = 1.5 * rate * (hours - 40.0);
```

```
    gross = regular + overtime;

    printf("Hours worked     %9.1f\n", hours);
    printf("Pay rate         %9.2f\n", rate);
    printf("Regular pay      %9.2f\n", regular);
    printf("Overtime pay     %9.2f\n", overtime);
    printf("Gross pay        %9.2f\n", gross);
}
```

The output follows:

```
Hours worked      47.5
Pay rate          9.24
Regular pay     369.60
Overtime pay    103.95
Gross pay       473.55
```

IF . . . ELSE WITH COMPOUND STATEMENTS

Both the regular and overtime pay calculations test the overtime condition. The program is easier to understand if the test is made only once as the following program demonstrates:

```
main()      /* Payroll */
  {
     float
        rate,              /* Hourly pay rate */
        hours,             /* Hours worked */
        regular,           /* Regular pay */
        overtime,          /* Overtime pay */
        gross;             /* Gross pay */

     rate  = 9.24;
     hours = 47.5;

     if (hours <= 40.0)
        {
           regular  = rate * hours;
           overtime = 0;
        }
```

```
    else
      {
        regular  = rate * 40.0;
        overtime = 1.5 * rate * (hours - 40.0);
      }

    gross = regular + overtime;

    printf("Hours worked       %9.1f\n", hours);
    printf("Pay rate           %9.2f\n", rate);
    printf("Regular pay        %9.2f\n", regular);
    printf("Overtime pay       %9.2f\n", overtime);
    printf("Gross pay          %9.2f\n", gross);
}
```

The output is the same as for the previous program.

EMPLOYEE FILE

The program easily extends to calculate the pay for a set of employees whose data is contained in a file. Let the file FILE4 contain the hours worked and hourly pay rate for four employees. The last record contains −1 as the hours worked and −1 as the pay rate to designate the end of the file. The data follows:

```
 47.5   9.24
 36.9   6.75
 26.4   8.75
 56.2   7.85
-1.0   -1.0
```

The following program calcualtes the regular pay, overtime pay and gross pay for each employee and places these figures and input parameters into the standard output file:

```
main()      /* Payroll with payroll */
  {
     float
        rate,               /* Hourly pay rate */
        hours,              /* Hours worked */
```

```
        regular,            /* Regular pay */
        overtime,           /* Overtime pay */
        grosspay;           /* Gross pay */

    scanf("%f %f", &hours, &rate);
    while (hours > -1)
      {

         if (hours <= 40.0)
            {
               regular   = rate * hours;
               overtime = 0.0;
            }
         else
            {
               regular   = rate * 40.0;
               overtime = 1.5 * rate * (hours - 40.0);
            }
         grosspay = regular + overtime;
         printf("%5.1f %7.2f %9.2f ", hours, rate, regular);
         printf("%9.2f %9.2f\n", overtime, grosspay);
         scanf("%f %f", &hours, &rate);
      }
}
```

The output of this program redirecting file FILE4 as standard input follows:

```
47.5    9.24    369.60    103.95    473.55
36.9    6.75    249.08      0.00    249.08
26.4    8.75    231.00      0.00    231.00
56.2    7.85    314.00    190.76    504.76
```

This program can accept data from the keyboard or from a data file. It may send the output to the video screen, printer, or to another data file.

NESTED IF . . . ELSE STATEMENTS

A distributor features two classes of products having quantity discount breaks for each class. The per-unit discount is

20 percent for 10 or more class A products. The discount is 5 percent for 100 or more class B products.

The following program computes the total purchase cost for an order given the product class, regular per-unit price, and order quantity:

```
main()      /* Quantity discount */
  {
      char
        class;         /* Classification */
      int
        number,        /* Number of records */
        count,         /* Counter for loop */
        quantity;      /* Quantity purchased */
      float
        price,         /* Per-unit price */
        amount;        /* Total amount with discount */

      scanf("%d", &number);
      for (count = 1; count <= number; count++)
        {
          scanf("%c %f %d", &class, &price, &quantity);

          if (class == 'A')
            if (quantity < 10)
              amount = price * quantity;
            else
              amount = 0.8 * price * quantity;
          else
            if (quantity < 100)
              amount = price * quantity;
            else
              amount = 0.95 * price * quantity;

          printf("%c %7.2f %5d", class, price, quantity);
          printf(" %9.2f\n", amount);
        }
  }
```

The program reads three values for each record. Let file FILE5 contain the following:

```
5
A 3.95 25
B 0.14 5
C 0.69 144
A 12.95 4
A 8.79 1
```

Each record contains the class code, the regular per-unit price, and the quantity.

The output corresponding to the data file follows:

```
A     3.95    25    79.00
B      .14     5      .70
B      .69   144    94.39
A    12.95     4    51.80
A     8.79     1     8.79
```

The output adds the total purchase amount to the input parameters.

QUANTITY DISCOUNTS USING BOOLEAN EXPRESSIONS

Boolean expressions provide an alternate method to nested IF statements. The following program uses Boolean expressions to test for product class and quantity for the quantity discount problem:

```
main()      /* Quantity discount */
  {
       char
         class;          /* Classification */
       int
         number,         /* Number of records */
         count,          /* Counter for loop */
         quantity;       /* Quantity purchased */
       float
         price,          /* Per-unit price */
         amount;         /* Total amount with discount */

       scanf("%d", &number);
       for (count = 1; count <= number; count++)
```

```
    {
       scanf("%c %f %d", &class, &price, &quantity);

       if ((class == 'A') && (quantity < 10))
         amount = price * quantity;
       if ((class == 'A') && (quantity >= 10))
         amount = 0.8 * quantity;

       if ((class == 'B') && (quantity < 100))
         amount = price * quantity;
       if ((class == 'B') && (quantity >= 100))
         amount = 0.95 * price * quantity;

       printf("%c %7.2f %5d", class, price, quantity);
       printf(" %9.2f\n", amount);
    }
}
```

The output is the same as for the previous program.

SERIES OF QUANTITY DISCOUNT BREAKS

A series of nested IF . . . ELSE statements of the type

```
if (condition)
  statement;
else if (condition)
  statement;
else if (condition)
  statement;
else
  statement;
```

is very useful. The nested IF comparisons continue only until the first true condition. Control passes to the statement following the last else statement immediately after executing the statement following the first true condition.

A manufacturer offers progressively higher discounts for a series of order quantities. The regular per-unit price is $19.95. For orders of 20 to 49 units the per-unit price is

$17.95; for 50 to 199 units it is $16.95; for orders of 200 or more, it is $15.95.

The nested IF statements for determining the price follows:

```
if (qualtity < 20)
  price = 19.95;
else if (quantity < 50)
  price = 17.95;
else if (quantity < 200)
  price = 16.95;
else
  price = 15.95;
```

It is also possible to use a series of IF statements using Boolean expressions of the form:

```
if (quantity < 20)
  price = 19.95;
if ((quantity >=20) && (quantity < 50))
  price = 17.95;
if ((quantity >= 50) && (quantity < 200))
  price = 16.95;
if (quantity >= 200)
  price = 15.95;
```

This form isn't as easy to read as the corresponding nested IF . . . ELSE statements.

For some situations, the use of Boolean expressions is the easiest to understand. Other situations are clearer with nested IF statements.

The following program uses the nested IF . . . ELSE statements for calculating the per-unit price and purchase amount including the quantity discount:

```
main()     /* Quantity discount price */
  {
     int
       quantity;     /* Quantity purchased */
     float
       price,        /* Per-unit price */
       amount;       /* Total purchase amount */
```

```
    scanf("%d", &quantity);
    while (quantity > 0)
      {

         if (quantity < 20)
           price = 19.95;
         else if (quantity < 50)
           price = 17.95;
         else if (quantity < 200)
           price = 16.95;
         else
           price = 15.95;

         amount = price * quantity;

         printf("%5d %7.2f", quantity, price);
         printf(" %9.2f\n", amount);

         scanf("%d", &quantity);
      }
  }
```

A quantity of 0 terminates the program. Let the file FILE6 contain the following quantities:

```
5
25
50
7
225
144
0
```

The output produced for the quantities in FILE 6 follows:

```
    5   19.95     99.75
   25   17.95    448.75
   50   16.95    847.50
    7   19.95    139.65
  225   15.95   3588.75
  144   16.95   2440.80
```

IF STATEMENT PROBLEMS

Several problems arise using IF statements that are deeply nested. A misplaced semicolon may cause a program to perform differently from that intended. Some deeply nested IF . . . ELSE statements are ambiguous to those reading the program although the compiler handles them in a consistent manner. Many ambiguities are removed by noting that C always associates an ELSE with the immediately preceding open IF statement. If that is not intended, then careful use of braces can force the compiler to associate the ELSE with the appropriate IF statement.

The ELSE portion of the IF . . . ELSE statement can be omitted entirely, but it is difficult to read nested IF . . . ELSE constructs within which some ELSE clauses are missing. Use care when writing, testing, and debugging nested IF . . . ELSE statements.

Exercises

1. Write a checkbook balancing program that reads transactions from the standard input file. Each transaction includes a transaction code: D for deposit, C for check, and S to terminate data entry. The value of the transaction will be positive. Deposits are added to the balance and checks are subtracted. The first value of the file contains the beginning account balance. Compute the service charge and ending balance and print them with appropriate labels. There is no service charge if the balance never falls below $200.00. The service charge is $.10 per check if the balance ever falls below $200.00.

2. Write a program that reads text data from the standard input file and counts the frequency for each vowel. Use a nested IF . . . ELSE statement.

3. Write a program that reads a set of four exam scores for each of five students, computes the average score for each student, and assigns a letter grade as follows:

90.00-99.99	A
80.09-89.99	B

70.00-79.99	C
60.00-69.99	D
00.00-59.99	F

Use a nested IF . . . ELSE construct to assign the letter grade.

4

Arrays

C provides arrays for containing vectors, matrices, and lists of values. The values may be integers, floating point numbers, characters, or Boolean values. A subscript references an individual value within the array. A simple list has one dimension only; more complex arrays have multiple dimensions.

4.1 Numeric Arrays

In mathematics, the vector X contains an ordered set of values $x_1, x_2, \ldots, x_n$. The value x_3 is the third element of the vector. The numbers to the lower right are subscripts. The symbol x_i designates the *i*th element of the vector.

In computer science, a vector is a one-dimensional array. A cell is an element of the array. Arrays are not limited to numerical values, but may be any variable type. The maximum size of the array is defined as the variable is declared.

The declaration

```
int apples[100];
```

defines the variable apples as an array of up to 100 integers. The declaration

```
float grapes[20];
```

defines the variable grapes to be an array of up to 20 floating point numbers. The declaration

```
char letter, linebuf[80];
```

declares the character variable letter and the character array 80 containing up to 80 characters.

SUBSCIPTS

Array subscripts are enclosed in brackets in the same manner as in the array declaration. The statement

```
value = a[i];
```

places the *i*th value of the array "a" in the variable "value". The statement

```
if (data[index] > max)
  max = data[index];
```

references the array "data" using the subscript "index".

C uses the subscript zero to reference the first element of an array. The computer associates the array name with the beginning memory location of the array. The subscripts are adjusted for the variable type size in bytes and added to the base memory address to give the address of the desired element.

The first element has a subscript of 0 and is the base address. The second element has a subscript of 1 which is added to the base address after adjusting for the element size.

Some programmers ignore the location referenced by the subscript zero even though that element wastes some storage space. Assembly language programmers are familiar with zero origin indexing and use it with C in the same manner they would when using machine language.

SUM OF THE ELEMENTS OF A VECTOR

The following program uses assignment statements to place values in the array and references those elements to calculate the sum:

```
main()     /* Sum elements of an array */
  {
      int
        value[3],       /* Vector of values */
        sum;            /* Sum of the values */

      value[0] = 19;
      value[1] = 12;
      value[2] = 15;
      value[3] = 14;

      sum = value[0] + value[1] + value[2] + value[3];

      printf("Sum     %d\n", sum);
  }
```

The output follows:

```
Sum     60
```

FOR LOOP GENERATES SUBSCRIPTS

A common use of the FOR loop is to generate subscripts for processing an array. The following program uses this approach to sum the array elements:

```
main()     /* Sum elements of an array */
  {
      int
        value[3],       /* Vector of values */
        index,          /* Index for array */
        sum;            /* Sum of the values */

      value[0] = 19;
      value[1] = 12;
      value[2] = 15;
      value[3] = 14;

      sum = 0;
      for (index = 0; index <= 3; index++)
        sum = sum + value[index];
```

```
    printf("Sum     %d\n", sum);
}
```

The output is the same as before. This approach is much more flexible and works for very large arrays.

INITIALIZE ARRAY VALUES

C provides the facility of initializing variable values at the time they are declared. The declaration

```
int k = 12;
```

defines the integer variable and initializes it to the value 12 at compile time. A separate assignment statement is unnecessary.

STATIC AND AUTOMATIC VARIABLES

An automatic variable is defined only during the current execution of a function and its subsidiary functions. When the function is finished, the variable disappears. If the function is reexecuted, a new instance of the variable is created.

A static variable is one that keeps its definition from one call of a function to the following call. Most variables are automatic; occasionally, static variables are needed. C permits the initialization of arrays only if they are static. The declaration

```
static float vector[20] = {21.8, 27.3, 15.6};
```

declares the variable vector to be a static floating point vector with up to 20 values and initializes the first three elements.

The array size can be inferred from the initialization list. The declaration

```
static int numbers[] = {12, 11, 19, 14, 15};
```

initializes the vector and dimensions it appropriately.

ARRAY INITIALIZATION

The following program initializes the array at the time of declaration:

```
main()      /* Sum elements of an array */
 {
    int
      index,      /* Index for array */
      sum;        /* Sum of the values */

    static int
      value[] = {19, 12, 15, 14};

    sum = 0;
    for (index = 0; index <= 3; index++)
      sum = sum + vaue[index];

    printf("Sum     %d\n", sum);
 }
```

The output is the same as before.

FOR LOOP FOR DATA ENTRY

The FOR loop can generate the needed subscripts for data entry as well as summing the elements of the vector. The following program obtains the values from the standard input device:

```
main()      /* Sum elements of an array */
 {
    int
      value[100],     /* Vector of values */
      index,          /* Index for array */
      sum;            /* Sum of the values */

    for (index = 0; index <= 3; index++)
      scanf("%d", &value[index]);
```

```
    sum = 0;
    for (index = 0; index <= 3; index++)
      sum = sum + value[index];

    printf("Sum      %d\n", sum);
  }
```

If this program runs using data entry from the keyboard, the interaction is as follows:

```
19
12
15
14
Sum    60
```

The input data can be redirected to a data file.

DATA FILE WITH NUMBER PREDEFINED

The average of a set of values is the sum divided by the number of values. One way to control the data entry is to include the number of values as the first element. The program reads that value and uses a FOR loop to control the entry.

The following program uses this approach:

```
main()      /* Average value */
  {
    float
      value[100],     /* Data vector */
      sum,            /* Sum of values */
      average;        /* Average value */
    int
      number,         /* Number of values */
      index;          /* Subscript for data vector */

    /* Get data */
    scanf("%d", &number);
    for (index = 1; index <= number; index++)
      scanf("%f", &value[index]);
```

```
    /* Compute average */
    sum = 0;
    for (index = 1; index <= number; index++)
      sum += value[index];
    average = sum / number;

    /* Output */
    printf("Number of values      %9d\n", number);
    printf("Average value         %9.2f\n", average);
}
```

Let the file FILE1 contain the following items:

```
4
27.5
15.6
19.1
14.2
```

The following output results from using the program to process the data file FILE1 using the command

```
AVG1 <FILE1
```

to redirect standard input to FILE1:

```
Number of values          4
Average value         19.10
```

FILE WITH TRAILER VALUE

A second approach to control input from a file is to use a trailer value and to test for that value for each item read from the file. The data file FILE2 contains the value −1.0 as its trailer value. The contents of the file follows:

```
27.5
15.6
19.1
14.2
-1.0
```

The following program computes the average of a set of values contained in a file checking for the value −1.0 signaling end of data entry:

```
main()      /* Average value */
  {
      float
      value[100],        /* Data vector */
      sum,               /* Sum of values */
      item,              /* New item */
      average;           /* Average value */
      int
        number,          /* Number of values */
        index;      Subscriptfordatavector */

      /* Get data */
      index = 0;
      scanf("%f", &item);
      while (item != -1)
        {
            + +index;
            value[index] = item;
            scanf("%f", &item);
        }
      number = index;

      /* Compute average */
      sum = 0;
      for (index = 1; index <= number; index+ +)
        sum + = value[index];
      average = sum / number;

      /* Output */
      printf("Number of values       %9d\n", number);
      printf("Average value          %9.2f\n", average);
  }
```

The output from using the program to process the data file FILE2 follows:

```
Number of values          4
Average value         19.10
```

Exercises

1. Write a program to read a set of integer values into an array. Compute their average, minimum and maximum values.

2. Write a program that will read a set of integer values into an array maintaining the array in ascending order. Inserting the *i*th value into its proper position may require moving some values to make room. Display the sorted list when finished.

3. Write a program to read a set of values into an array. Compute the sum and sum of squares of the values.

4. Write a program to read a set of values into an array. Count the number of values falling between −10.0 and 10.0.

4.2 String Arrays

Arrays are not limited to numerical values. They may contain data of any defined type, including characters. A character string is an array of characters. C defines a special type of variable length character string for which the null character '\0' serves as an end-of-string symbol.

PROGRAM USING ASSIGNMENT STATEMENTS

One method of assigning values to a character array is to use assignment statements to assign the value of individual characters. The following program uses this approach:

```
main()      /* Character array with assignment statements */
 {
     char
        line[4];     /* Array containing message */
     int
        i,           /* Index */
        n = 4;       /* Number of elements */

     line[0] = 'H';
     line[1] = 'e';
     line[2] = 'l';
     line[3] = 'l';
     line[4] = 'o';
```

```
      for (i = 0; i <= n; i++)
         printf("%c", line[i]);
      printf("\n");
   }
```

The output follows:

```
Hello
```

The assignment statements place the message one character at a time into the array. The printf statements display the message one character at a time.

INITIALIZING THE CHARACTER ARRAY

It is easier to initialize the message values within the declaration portion of the program. The following program uses this method:

```
main()      /* Character array with assignment statements */
   {
      static char
         line[] = {'H', 'e', 'l', 'l', 'o'};
      int
         i,            /* Index */
         n = 4;        /* Number of elements */

      for (i = 0; i <= n; i++)
         printf("%c", line[i]);
      printf("\n");
   }
```

The output is the same as before. The one initialization statement replaces the five assignment statements.

INITIALIZING CHARACTER ARRAY WITH SPECIAL STRING

Most implementations of the C language include a special string format using a null character, defined by '\0', to define the end of the string. These strings have already been used within printf and scanf functions. The string

"Hello"

includes the five characters and is terminated with the null character '\0'.

Double quotes enclose strings, single quotes enclose characters. The symbol 'E' designates the letter E while "E" designates a character string consisting of the letter E followed by the null character. The string "" is the null string consisting of only the null character '\0'.

The following program initializes the character array to the string "Hello":

```
main()      /* Character array with assignment statements */
  {
     static char
       line[] = {"Hello"};
     int
       i = 0;      /* Index */

     while (line[i] != '\0')
       {
          printf("%c", line[i]);
          ++i;
       }
     printf("\n");
}
```

The output is the same as before. This initialization is easier because each symbol does not need to be enclosed in single quotes. The result is not exactly the same as for the previous program because of the addition of the null character '\0' to the array designating the end of the string.

STRING OUTPUT

Now that the character array contains a string in the proper C format, the printf function can print the entire string by using the s format code. The following program demonstrates this:

```
main()      /* Character array with assignment statements */
  {
        static char
          line[] = {"Hello"};
        int
          i = 0;      /* Index */

        printf("%s\n", line);
  }
```

The output is still the same as for the previous programs. It consists of the following line:

```
Hello
```

DECIMAL AND HEXADECIMAL CODES

The printf %c, %d, and %x codes are surprisingly flexible. They represent character, decimal integer, and hexadecimal output respectively. Although %d and %x are normally used with integers, they may also be used with character data types.

C does not allow direct assignment of strings to character arrays of the form

```
line = "Are you sure?";
```

but most implementations include a string copy function, called strcpy, which accomplishes the same task.

The statement

```
strcpy(target, source);
```

moves the string contained in the source to the target character array. The statement

```
strcpy(line, "Are you sure?");
```

assigns the string "Are you sure?" to the character array.

The following program assigns the message to a character array, prints the message on one line, then prints each character and gives its decimal code and corresponding hexadecimal code:

```
main()      /* Character array with assignment statements */
  {
      char
        line[80];      /* Character array */
      int
        i = 0;         /* Index */
      strcpy(line, "Are you ready?");

      printf("%s\n", line);

      while (line[i] != '\0')
        {
          printf("%c     %4d     %2x\n",
            line[i], line[i], line[i]);
          ++i;
        }
  }
```

The output follows:

```
Are you ready?
A     65    41
r    114    72
e    101    65
      32    20
y    121    79
o    111    6F
u    117    75
      32    20
r    114    72
e    101    65
a     97    61
d    100    64
y    121    79
?     63    3F
```

Exercises

1. Write a program that places a short message into a character array and computes the frequency of each of the five vowels. Count the uppercase and lowercase forms as the same letter.

2. Write a program that computes the average exam grade for each of several students whose grades are contained in a file. Place the letters 'A', 'B', 'C', 'D', and 'F' in a character array. Calculate the subscript for the letter grade using the following schedule:

90-99.99%	A
80-89.99	B
70-79.99	C
60-69.99	D
0-59.99	F

3. Write a program that places a string into a character array and outputs the string, placing each word on a separate line. For example, the string "How are you doing?" will appear as:

```
How
are
you
doing?
```

4.3 Multidimensional Arrays

A two-dimensional array is an array of arrays. All elements of the array are of the same type. Consider the table of values

12	11	19
14	17	15

which contains two rows and three columns.

The declaration

```
int table[w2]s[w3]s;
```

allocates space for a two-dimensional table having two rows and three columns. C reads this as an array of arrays in which there are two arrays, each having three elements.

INITIALIZATION OF TABLE

The declaration

```
static int table[2][3] = {{12, 11, 19}, {14, 17, 15}};
```

initializes the array and its values. The following program initializes a two-dimensional table and prints its values in readable form:

```
main()      /* Initialize int matrix */
  {
      static int
        table[2][3] = {{12, 11, 19}, {14, 17, 15}};
      int
        nrows = 2,
        ncols = 3,
        i,
        j;

      for (i = 0; i < nrows; i++)
        {
          for (j = 0; j < ncols; j++)
            printf("%5d ", table[i][j]);
          printf("\n");
        }
  }
```

The output follows:

```
12   11   19
14   17   15
```

COMPUTE ROW SUMS AND COLUMN SUMS

Both column and row subscripts start with the value zero. C uses zero-origin indexing for subscripts. The declaration statement gives the number of rows and the number of columns. The highest number subscript for a dimension is one less than the size of the dimension.

C uses the form x[i][j] to designate subscripts; most

languages use the form x(i,j) or x[i,j] to reference the element in row i and column j of x. C is also very free in using pointers and address calculations to reference arrays.

The following program adds commands to form the row and column sums of the values in the table:

```
main()      /* Form row and column sums */
  {
      static int
        table[2][3] = {{12, 11, 19}, {14, 17, 15}};
      int
        nrows = 2,
        ncols = 3,
        i,
        j,
        sum;

      /* List table */
      printf("Table of values\n");
      for (i = 0; i < nrows; i++)
        }
           for (j = 0; j < ncols; j++)
             printf("%5d ", table[i][j]);
           printf("\n");
        }
      /* Row sums */
      printf("\nRow     Sum\n");
      for (i = 0; i < nrows; i++)
        {
            sum = 0:
            for (j = 0; j < ncols; j++)
              sum += table[i][j];
            printf("%3d %5d\n", i, sum);
        }
      /* Column sums */
      printf("\nCol        Sum\n");
      for (j = 0: j < ncols; j++)
        {
            sum = 0;
            for (i = 0; i < nrows; i++)
              sum += table[i][j];
```

```
            printf("%3d %5d\n", j, sum);
        }
}
```

The output follows:

```
Table of values
      12    11    19
      14    17    15

Row     Sum
  0      42
  1      46

Col     Sum
  0      26
  1      28
  2      34
```

DATA ENTRY FROM A FILE

Initializing the vaues of an array at the time it is declared is not practical for a program that is to be reused with other sets of data. Obtain data from the keyboard or use redirection to obtain it from a data file. Let the file FILE14 contain the data for the table in the following form:

```
2 3
12
11
19
14
17
15
```

The first line contains the dimensions, and the data values follow.

The following program forms the row and column sums for a table of values obtained from the standard input device:

```
main()      /* Form row and column sums */
  {
      int
        table[20][30],
        nrows,
        ncols,
        i,
        j,
        sum;

      /* Get data */
      scanf("%d %d", &nrows, &ncols);
      for (i = 0; i < nrows; i++)
        for (j = 0; j < ncols; j++)
            scanf("%d", &table[i][j]);

      /* List table */
      printf("Table of values\n");
      for (i = 0; i < nrows; i++)
        {
            for (j = 0; j < ncols; j++)
              printf("%5d ", table[i][j]);
            printf("\n");
        }

      /* Row sums */
      printf("\nRow      Sum\n");
      for (i = 0; i < nrows; i++)
        {
            sum = 0:
            for (j = 0; j < ncols; j++)
              sum += table[i][j];
            printf("%3d %5d\n", i, sum);
        }
      /* Column sums */
      printf("\nCol       Sum\n");
      for (j = 0: j < ncols; j++)
        {
            sum = 0;
            for (i = 0; i < nrows; i++)
              sum += table[i][j];
```

```
            printf("%3d %5d\n", j, sum);
        }
}
```

The output is similar to that of the previous program:

CHARACTER ARRAYS

C allows two-dimensional character and number arrays. Store and access individual characters like individual numbers in a table. The handling of character strings in two-dimensional arrays is more complex.

Exercises

1. Write a program that will read a set of exam scores into a table. Let the rows represent students and the columns represent exams. Compute the average grade for each student and the average grade for each exam.

2. Write a program that reads a table of values into a two-dimensional array. Compute the minimum and maximum values for each row and the minimum and maximum values for each column.

4.4 Internal Representation of Arrays

Most programming languages, including C, store two-dimensional arrays row by row. The array x is stored as x[0][0], x[0][1], . . . for the first row. The element x[1][0] immediately follows the last element of the first row.

The statement

```
float x[20][40];
```

declares the floating point variable x with up to 20 rows and 40 columns. The C reference x is the base address for element x[0][0].

The reference x[2][4] is the element in the third row and fifth column. The first two rows contain 80 elements. Row one is in locations x+0, . . . , x+39. Row two is in locations x+40, . . . , x+79. The element x[2][4] is in location x+80+4 = x+84. The reference x[84] refers to the same element.

The location of x[i][j] is

x + i*c + j

for an array having c columns. The reference x[i*c + j] gives the same location as x[i][j]. C programmers can reference a two-dimensional array in its natural form or as its one-dimensional equivalent.

CHARACTER ARRAYS

The following program illustrates the definition of a two-dimensional character array and references the array as if it had one dimension:

```
#define    N LINES    4
#define    LENGTH     80

main()     /* Array of strings */
  {
      char
        message[NLINES][LENGTH];
      int
        number = NLINES,
        i;

      strcpy(message, "Now is the time");
      strcpy(message[80], "for all good men");
      strcpy(message[160], "to come to the aid");
      strcpy(message[240], "of their party.");

      for (i = 0; i < number; i++)
        printf("%s\n", message[i*LENGTH]);
  }
```

The names NLINES and LENGTH are given the meaning 4 and 80 respectively. There are four lines, each having a maximum length of 80 characters. A message is to be stored in each line in C string format with the null symbol '\n' indicating the end of the string.

The first line begins at location message[0][0] which is also message[0]. The second line begins at location message[1][0] which is also message[80]. Each line has a beginning location specified by both two- and one-dimensional references. The function strcpy places the messages in their appropriate locations. The printf function displays them using the %s code for strings.

The output follows:

```
Now is the time
for all good men
to come to the aid
of their party.
```

Exercises

1. Write a program that declares a five-row by five-column integer array and uses FOR loops to fill the array with zeros.

2. Write a program that declares a five-row by five-column integer array and uses FOR loops to fill the array with zeros and ones. All values should be zero except the main diagonal elements for which the row and column subscripts are equal.

3. Write a program that reads character strings from the keyboard using the scanf function and places them in a two-dimensional array row by row. Count the total number of words.

4. Write a program that reads character strings from the keyboard using the scanf function and places them in a two-dimensional array row by row. Count the frequency of each vowel, combining uppercase and lowercase for each letter.

5

Functions

C functions bring order and discipline to large programs. Divide large programs into modules, each to perform a needed task. Subdivide large tasks into smaller units, defining each as a module. In C, these modules are named functions and organize the program into manageable chunks.

Functions bring order out of chaos. Organize large programs into hierarchical trees. The main program calls functions, which call lower-level functions, until the lowest-level functions accomplish the processing steps.

The organization chart of a program looks like a company organization chart consisting of the president, vice presidents reporting to the president, department heads reporting to the vice presidents, and so on.

Loose coupling is the property which makes functions within a large program independent of each other. Limit communication between functions to argument lists. Cohesion is an important factor. An internally cohesive function does only one task; combining two or more unrelated tasks in one function is poor practice.

This chapter discusses functions and their uses. Functions include predefined functions from the standard library and user-defined functions. The relative merits of global and local variables will be discussed, and types of function variable references will be compared.

5.1 Standard Functions

C includes numerous predefined functions in its standard libraries. Systems differ in their choice of standard functions and in their names. Determine the standard functions available for your system. There are many standard functions to consider; the following groups them according to function.

The form of the C function is like the function

$$y = f(x)$$

in mathematics. The variable x is the argument to the function. The result of the function is $f(x)$; it may be assigned to a variable or used in a larger expression. The expression

$$z = f(x) * g(y)$$

computes the product of the results $f(x)$ and $g(y)$, placing the result in z.

STANDARD MATH FUNCTIONS

Most standard math functions assume double precision arguments and double precision results. Exceptions include functions requiring integer arguments or results. Many systems include the following standard math functions:

Name	*Description*
abs(x)	Absolute value, integer = abs(integer)
fabs(x)	Absolute value, double = fabs(double)
acos(x)	Arccosine, result in radians
asin(x)	Arcsine, result in radians
atan(x)	Arctangent, result in radians
cos(x)	Cosine, argument in radians
sin(x)	Sine, argument in radians
tan(x)	Tangent, argument in radians
exp(x)	Exponential
exp10(x)	Exponential base 10
pow(x,a)	Raise *x* to the power *a*
log(x)	Natural logarithm
log10(x)	Base 10 logarithm
sqrt(x)	Square root
srand(x)	Set new seed for random number generator
rand()	Return random integer
frand()	Return random real value in interval 0-1

FORMATTED INPUT AND OUTPUT

C includes several standard functions for formatted input and output:

Name	*Description*
printf()	Formatted print to standard output device
fprintf()	Formatted print to file
sprint()	Formatted output to string
scanf()	Formatted input from standard input device
fscanf()	Formatted input from file
sscan()	Formatted input from string

DISK I/O ROUTINES

C includes many functions related to disk file input and output. The following functions are typical:

Name	*Description*
creat(f)	Create file and assign file name
open(f)	Open existing file
close(f)	Close file
fopen()	Alternate routine for file open
fclose()	Alternate routine for file close
fgetc(f)	Get next character
fputc(f)	Put next character
fgets(f)	Get string from file
fputs(f)	Put string

CHARACTER ROUTINES

The character functions accept a character argument and return a result which may be character, integer, or Boolean (true = 1 and false = 0). The common character functions follow:

Name	*Description*
isalnum()	Is argument alphanumeric?
isalpha()	Is argument alphabetic?
iscntrl()	Is argument control symbol?

isdigit()	Is argument numeric digit?
islower()	Is argument lowercase?
isupper()	Is argument uppercase?
isspace()	Is argument blank, tab, LF, or CR?
tolower()	Convert to lowercase
toupper()	Convert to uppercase

STRING ROUTINES

The string routines operate on character strings. Common string functions follow:

Name	*Description*
atoi(s)	Convert string to integer
atof(s)	Convert string to double precision
atol(s)	Convert string to long integer
index(s,c)	Return pointer to first occurrence of *c* in *s*
rindex(s,c)	Return pointer to last occurrence
strcat(a,b)	Concatenate *b* to end of *a*
strcmp(a,b)	Compare two strings
strlen(s)	Length of string

OTHER FUNCTIONS

Sorting arrays into order is a common process. Many implementations of C include a function qsort which uses the efficient quicksort algorithm for performing an internal sort. There may be a group of functions for controlling the cursor on the video screen and using the screen in modes other than one-line-at-a-time scrolling.

ABSOLUTE VALUE

The following program uses the abs() function to illustrate the use of standard functions:

```
main()      /* Integer absolute value function */
  {
      int
         arg,        /* Argument for function */
         value;      /* Value returned by function */
```

```
    arg = -12;
    value = abs(arg);
    printf("Absolute value of %d is %d\n", arg, value);

    arg = 29;
    value = abs(arg);
    printf("Absolute value of %d is %d\n", arg, value);
}
```

The output follows:

```
Absolute value of -12 is 12
Absolute value of 29 is 29
```

Negative numbers are changed to positive numbers and positive numbers remain unchanged.

SINGLE-PRECISION FLOATING POINT

The standard math functions assume double precision arguments and results. Single precision variables defined using the keyword "float" can also use these standard functions. The following program illustrates this by calculating the natural logarithm for the values .075, 1.5, and 32.75:

```
#include      <math.h>

main()      /* Floating point variables */
  {
    float
      value,      /* Argument for function */
      nlog;       /* Value returned by function */
      printf("Value      Natural log\n");

    value = 0.075;
    nlog  = log(value);
    printf("%7.2f %12.8f\n", value, nlog);

    value = 1.5;
    nlog  = log(value);
    printf("7.2f %12.8f\n", value, nlog);
```

```
        value = 32.75;
        nlog  = log(value);
        print("%7.2f %12.8f\n", value, nlog);
  }
```

The output follows:

```
Value       Natural log
   .08      -2.59026718
  1.50        .40546510
 32.75       3.48890305
```

Because of the format code %7.2f, the value .075 was rounded to .08 for output.

DOUBLE PRECISION

The following program uses double precision variables for the natural log function:

```
#include     <math.h>

main()     /* Floating point variables */
  {
        double
          value,      /* Argument for function */
          nlog;       /* Value returned by function */

        printf("   Value      Natural log\n");

        value = 0.075;
        nlog  = log(value);
        printf("7.3lf %16.121f\n", value, nlog);

        value = 1.5;
        nlog  = log(value);
        printf("%7.3lf %16.121f\n", value, nlog);

        value = 32.75;
        nlog  = log(value);
        printf("%7.3lf %16.121f\n", value, nlog);
  }
```

The output follows:

```
Value            Natural log
  .075      -2.590267165440
 1.500        .405465108108
32.750       3.488902962080
```

The format codes %7.31f and %16.121f include the letter l, indicating that long floating point—or double precision—values are involved.

ISDIGIT FUNCTION

The following program demonstrates the isdigit function:

```
main()      /* Is character a digit? */
  {
    char
      symbol;           /* Characterer to test */
    int
      result;           /* Logical result */

    printf("Symbol Result\n");

    symbol = '4';
    result  = isdigit(symbol);
    printf("%c          %d\n", symbol, result);

    symbol = 'E';
    result  = isdigit(symbol);
    printf("%c          %d\n", symbol, result);

    symbol = 'a';
    printf("%c          %d\n", symbol, isdigit(symbol));

    print("%c           %d\n", '7', isdigit('7'));
  }
```

The output follows:

```
Symbol    Result
4         1
E         0
```

```
a           0
7           1
```

The function returns the result 1 (true) if the argument is a numeric digit. It returns the result 0 (false) if it is not a digit.

TOLOWER FUNCTION

The following program demonstrates the function that converts uppercase letters to lowercase while leaving other symbols unchanged:

```
main()      /* Convert uppercase to lowercase */
  {
        char
          symbol,          /* Character to convert */
          result;          /* Resulting character */

        printf("Symbol Result\n");

        symbol = 'E';
        result  = tolower(symbol);
        printf("%c          %c\n", symbol, result);

        symbol = 'a';
        result  = tolower(symbol);
        printf("%c          %c\n", symbol, result);

        symbol = 'G';
        printf("%c          %c\n", symbol, tolower(symbol));

        printf("%c          %c\n", '7', tolower('7'));
  }
```

The output follows:

```
Symbol   Result
E        e
a        a
G        g
7        7
```

Exercises

1. Find the list of standard functions available for your system.

2. Write a program to generate a table of natural logarithms for the values 1, 2, . . . , 10.

3. Write a program to generate a table of cosines for the values 0, .1, .2, . . . , 3.0.

4. Write a program to convert the character string "125" to its corresponding internal integer form.

5. Write a program to convert the integer 125 to its corresponding character string form.

5.2 Function Definitions

A function is a subprogram identified by name. The function heading

```
florida()
```

assigns the name florida to the subprogram when used as a heading. The statement

```
florida()
```

calls the function.

Every program has at least one function, and one of the functions must have the name main() identifying it as the root function. The root, called the main routine, calls functions which in turn may call lower-level functions.

EXAMPLE PROGRAM WITH ONE LEVEL OF FUNCTIONS

The following program illustrates the flow of control from the main routine to subroutines and back to the main routine:

```
main()      /* Main routine calling subroutines */
  {
      printf("Start main\n");
      ohio();
```

```
        florida();
        nevada();
        printf("Finish main\n");
  }

ohio()
  {
        printf("I'm in Ohio\n");
  }

florida()
  {
        printf("I'm in Florida\n");
  }

nevada()
  {
        printf("I'm in Nevada\n");
  }
```

The function main() calls three functions ohio, florida, and nevada. Each function displays an identifying message. Running the program shows the flow of control.

The output follows:

```
Start main
I'm in Ohio
I'm in Florida
I'm in Nevada
Finish main
```

HIERARCHICAL PROGRAM

Organize large programs into a hierarchical tree of functions. The main routine forms the root. Each upper-level function controls a set of subsidiary functions. Keep each function small enough to be easily debugged.

The following indented list shows the organization of the functions which are given names of states and names of cities within states:

```
main()
   ohio()
      akron()
      toledo()
   florida
      miami()
      orlando()
      tampa()
   nevada()
      reno()
```

The following program displays messages for each function tracing the flow of control through the program as it runs:

```
main()      /* Nested function calls *
  {
        printf("Starting main\n");
        ohio();
        florida();
        nevada();
        printf("Finish main\n");
  }

ohio()
  {
        printf("Enter Ohio\n");
        akron();
        toledo();
        printf("Leave Ohio\n");
  }

florida()
  {
        printf("Enter Florida\n");
        miami();
        orlando();
        tampa();
        printf("Leave Florida\n");
  }

nevada()
```

```
  {
      printf("Enter Nevada\n");
      reno();
      printf("Leave Nevada\n");
  }

akron()
  {
      printf("I'm in Akron\n");
  }

toledo()
  {
      printf("I'm in Toledo\n");
  }

miami()
  {
      printf("I'm in Miami\n");
  }

orlando()
  {
      printf("I'm in Orlando\n");
  }

tampa()
  {
      printf("I'm in Tampa\n");
  }

reno()
  {
      printf("I'm in Reno\n");
  }
```

The output follows:

```
Starting main
Enter Ohio
I'm in Akron
I'm in Toledo
```

```
Leave Ohio
Enter Florida
I'm in Miami
I'm in Orlando
I'm in Tampa
Leave Florida
Enter Nevada
I'm in Reno
Leave Nevada
Finish main
```

FORMAT OF FUNCTION DEFINITIONS

Each function definition is of the form

```
name()
  {
  }
```

with the header giving the name of the function and arguments, if any. The body of the function definition is contained within the braces. The terminating brace completes the function definition.

Exercises

1. Define the functions alaska, indiana and iowa to be called by main(). Include appropriate messages to aid in tracing the flow of control.

2. Define a hierarchical set of functions using three states and at least two cities for each state. Include a message within each function for tracing the flow of control.

5.3 Arguments

Some functions have arguments, many do not. The mathematical function $f(x)$ in the statement

$$y = f(x)$$

receives the argument *x* and returns the result which is placed in *y*. C functions are similar.

The C function sqrt (x) returns the square root of the argument. The argument may be a variable

```
y = sqrt(value)
```

constant

```
y = sqrt(25.0)
```

or expression

```
y = sqrt(0.5 * (a + b)).
```

The result of the function sqrt(x) may be assigned to a variable

```
y = sqrt(value)
```

used in an expression

```
y = z / sqrt(value)
```

or may be used as an argument to another function

```
y = log(sqrt(value) / 2).
```

FUNCTIONS HAVING NEITHER ARGUMENTS NOR RESULTS

Some functions do not have arguments or results. The following function defines the function ohio() which has neither:

```
ohio()
  {
     printf("I'm in Ohio\n");
  }
```

Some functions of this nature do not need to communicate with other functions. C permits the defining of external variables accessible to all functions. They may allow communication among functions.

FUNCTION RESULTS

Functions that return results must be typed according to the form of the result. Character functions return results of type char. Floating point functions return results of type float. Other types of functions include double, int, and long. Functions of type int are so common that any function not explicitly typed is assumed to be integer.

Functions that return results to the calling program use the keyword return to designate the value returned. The function

```
sum5()
  {
       int a;
       a = 1 + 2 + 3 + 4 + 5;
       return (a);
  }
```

returns the sum of the first five integers.

A call to this function would be

```
answer = sum5()
```

with the parentheses identifying sum5() as a function requiring no arguments. The function result is placed in answer.

EXAMPLE FUNCTION WITH RESULT BUT NO ARGUMENTS

The following program consists of the function main() calling the function product() which requires no arguments since it always returns the product of the first five integers:

```
main()      /* product of first 5 integers */
  {
       int
          answer;      /* Product of integers */
```

```
        answer = product5();
        printf("Product of first 5 integers is %d\n", answer);
  }

product5()
  {
      int
        product,      /* Product of integers */
        counter;      /* Counter for loop */

      product = 1;
      for(counter = 1; counter <= 5; counter++)
        product *= counter;

      return(product);
  }
```

The output follows:

```
Product of first 5 integers is 120
```

The function product() is of type integer since it returns an integer value. Integer functions do not have to be explicitly typed.

FUNCTIONS HAVING ARGUMENTS

Arguments to functions must be typed as part of the function definition before the braces defining the function body. The function definition

```
sumsqr(a, b)
  int a, b
  {
      int c;
      c = a * a + b * b;
      return (c);
  }
```

has two integer arguments and returns an integer result.

Many C programmers perform the calculation within the

return statement and eliminate the declaration of variable c. The function definition

```
sumsqr(a, b)
  int a, b;
  {
      return (a*a + b*b);
  }
```

is shorter and still readable.

EXAMPLE PROGRAM HAVING INTEGER ARGUMENT AND INTEGER RESULT

The following program sends an argument to the function product() which returns the sum of the integers up to and including the argument:

```
main()      /* product of first n integers */
  {
      int
        number,     /* Number of integers */
        answer;     /* Product of integers */

        number = 5;
        answer = product(number);
        printf("Product of first %d integers is %d\n",
                number, answer);
  }

product(n)
  int n;                  /* Number of integers */
  {
      int
        prod,             /* Product of integers */
        c;                /* Counter for loop */

      prod = 1;
      for(c = 1; c <= n; c++)
        prod *= c;
      return(prod);
  }
```

The output follows:

```
Product of first 5 integers is 120
```

FUNCTIONS RETURNING NONINTEGER RESULTS

Functions returning noninteger results must be explicitly typed in both the function heading and in the calling program. Let the function sqr() accept a double precision floating point argument and return the square as a double precision result. The function definition follows:

```
double sqr(value)
  double value;
  {
      return (value * value);
  }
```

The calling program uses a statement of the form

```
answer = sqr(amount);
```

to use the function. The declaration statement

```
double
  amount, sqr();
```

declares both the variable amount and the function sqr() to be double precision.

EXAMPLE DOUBLE PRECISION FUNCTION

The following program uses the function diagonal() to compute the length of the diagonal of a rectangle as the square root of the sum of the squares of the lengths of the two sides:

```
#include    <math.h>

main()    /* Length of diagonal */
```

```
{
      double
         side1,
         side2,
         length,
         diagonal();

      side1 = 3.0;
      side2 = 4.0;
      length = diagonal(side1, side2);

      printf("Side 1        %7.2lf\n", side 1);
      printf("Side 2        %7.2lf\n", side 2);
      printf("Diagonal      %7.2lf\n", length);
}
double diagonal(a, b)
   double a, b;
   {
      double c;

      c = sqrt(a * a + b * b);
      return(c);
   }
```

The output follows:

```
Side 1       3.00
Side 2       4.00
Diagonal     5.00
```

A rectangle is 3 feet long and 4 feet wide. The length of the diagonal is 5 feet.

Exercises

1. Write a program that uses a subsidiary function to calculate the sum of the first *n* integers for argument *n*.

2. Write a double precision function to calculate the value of n! factorial for *n* up to 30 for an integer argument. Have the main program use that argument to calculate the value of 25!.

3. Write a function that accepts a character argument and returns the value 1 if it is a vowel and the value 0 otherwise.

4. Write a double precision function that accepts two double precision arguments and computes their average. Write a program that uses this function to calculate the average of the values 12.5 and 17.1.

5.4 Array Elements

There are two methods for passing arguments to functions. The most common one passes the actual value of the parameter to the function. The output of the function consists of an actual value returned to the calling routine. The less common method passes the address of a variable and is required when referencing arrays in an argument list.

ADDRESS OF A VARIABLE

If vector is the name of an array, the name &name gives its address. The symbol & preceding a variable designates its address. This is the base address of the array and corresponds to vector[0] for a one-dimensional array, or table[0][0] for a two-dimensional array.

USING THE ADDRESS OF A VARIABLE

C uses the term pointer to refer to the address of a variable. If the variable ptr is a pointer for the array vector, the symbol *ptr references the first element vector[0]. The symbol *(ptr+1) references the second element vector[1]. Chapter 7 discusses pointers in greater depth.

FORMAT FOR ARRAY ARGUMENTS

Let x be an array having *n* double precision elements. Let the function sum accept the size *n* as a value parameter and the array x as reference parameter giving the base address of the array. The calling routine uses a statement of the form

```
s = sum(n, &x)
```

to call the function, give it the parameters, and save the result.

The function definition heading is:

```
double sum(n, x)
  int n;
  double x[];
  {
  }
```

indicating that the function returns a double precision result. The first argument is an integer passed as an actual parameter, and the second argument is a double precision one-dimensional array.

EXAMPLE PROGRAM FORMING THE SUM

The following program includes a subroutine to calculate the sum of the elements of a double precision array. It is used to calculate the average:

```
main()      /* Sum values in vector */
  {
       int
         number = 3;
       static double
         vector[] = {27.5, 15.6, 21.7};
       double
         avg,
         sum();

       avg = sum(number, &vector) / 3.0;
       printf("Average        %7.2lf\n", avg);
  }

double sum(n, x)
  int
       n;              /* Number of values */
  double
```

```
    x[ ];           /* Dummy vector */
{
    double
      sumx;         /* Sum of values */
    int
      i;            /* Index for array */

    sumx = 0.0;
    for (i = 0; i < n; i++)
      sumx += x[i];
    return (sumx);
}
```

The output follows:

```
Average     21.60
```

SYSTEM OF FUNCTIONS

It is easier to program, debug, and maintain a program that is organized as a system of functions. Some of the functions are of general interest and can be reused by other programs. Each organization develops a local library of functions for its programmers.

The following program uses separate functions to input the data vector, compute the average, compute the minimum, and compute the maximum:

```
main()      /* Functions for vector */
{
    double
      vector[200],
      average(),
      minimum(),
      maximum(),
      avg,
      min,
      max;
    int
      number;
    getdata(&number, &vector);
```

```
      avg  = average(number, &vector);
      min  = minimum(number, &vector);
      max = maximum(number, &vector);

      printf("Average        %9.2lf\n", avg);
      printf("Minimum        %9.2lf\n", min);
      printf("Maximum        %9.2lf\n", max);
  }

getdata(number, vector)
  int *number;
  double vector[];
  {
      int i, n;
      double value;

      scanf("%d", &n);
      *number = n;
      for (i = 0; i < n; i++)
        scanf("%lf", &vector[i]);
  }

double average(number, vector)
  int number;
  double vector[];
  {
      int i;
      double sum;

      sum = 0.0;
      for (i = 0; i < number; i++)
        sum += vector[i];
      return (sum / number);
  }

double minimum(number, vector)
  int number;
  double vector[ ];
  {
      int i;
      double min;
```

```
        min = vector[0];
        for (i = 1; i < number; i++)
            if (vector[i] < min)
                min = vector[i];
        return (min);
    }

double maximum(number, vector)
    int number;
    double vector[ ];
    {
        int i;
        double max;

        max = vector[0];
        for (i = 1; i < number; i++)
            if (vector[i] > max)
                max = vector[i];
        return (max);
    }
```

The first element of the input file must contain an integer value designating the number of values, followed by the data values. The following lists the contents of a data file containing three values:

```
3
27.5
15.6
21.7
```

Redirecting the standard input device to read from the file gives the following output:

```
Average     21.60
Minimum     15.60
Maximum     27.50
```

The function getdata() requires reference parameters for both the size and the array. The calling program uses the statement

```
getdata(&number, &vector)
```

sending the addresses of the variables to the subroutine.

The function definition header

```
getdata(number, vector)
  int *number;
  double vector[ ];
  {
  }
```

uses the symbol *number to tell the compiler that the parameter will be an address (pointer) to the variable rather than the actual value.

TWO-WAY COMMUNICATION

Actual value parameters are a one-way street from the calling routine to the subroutine. Reference parameters giving the address of the variable provide two-way communication. The subroutine uses the address to reach back into the calling routine's data area to modify one of its variable values.

The getdata() function must return both the size and the data values to the calling routine. The other functions do not modify the size parameters; they access the size parameter as an actual value parameter.

Exercises

1. Write a program that uses one subroutine to read in a set of integer values and another subroutine to compute their sum.

2. Write a program that uses one subroutine to read in a set of double precision values and another to compute the sum of the squares of the values.

3. Write a program that reads a text file into an array and uses a subroutine to calculate the frequencies for the vowels a, e, i, o, u. Count both uppercase and lowercase as the same letter.

5.5 Scope

A variable is normally defined only within its function. The value of a variable may be passed to a function as an actual parameter. When its address is passed as a reference paramater, the subroutine may change the value of a variable in the calling routine.

GLOBAL VARIABLES

A program may contain global, or external, variables accessible to all of its subroutines. External variables are not usually defined within a function, but rather immediately before the main() routine.

C permits the separate compilation of subroutines. A subroutine that is compiled separately uses a statement extern

```
double x;
```

to tell the compiler that the variable x is an externally defined global variable.

Functions that reference global variables should designate that with extern declarations. For small programs containing the function main() and all subsidiary functions, the extern statements are rarely included in the subroutines.

BLOCK STRUCTURED LANGUAGES

PL/I, ALGOL, and Pascal are block-structured languages with nested function definitions. Variables defined within a subroutine are global to all nested subsidiary functions. C is not block structured; a variable is either local to the function or global to all functions.

C does have a limited form of block structuring defined using the braces { and }. A variable defined within the brace is local to that section of the program. The variable disappears when control leaves the section defined by the pair of braces.

EXAMPLE OF LOCAL BLOCK DEFINITION

The following program illustrates the definition of a variable in a block of the program defined within braces:

```
main()
  {
       int a, b;
       a = 13;
       b = 15;
       printf("%d      %d\n", a, b);

       {
            int a, b;
            a = 23;
            b = 25;
            printf("%d      %d\n", a, b);
       }
         printf("%d      %d\n", a, b);
  }
```

The output follows:

```
13    15
23    25
13    15
```

The main program defines two variables and assigns values to them. The inner block defines variables with the same names and assigns different values to its local variables. After control returns to the main program, its variables remain untouched.

SUBROUTINE WITH LOCAL VARIABLES

Local variables defined within a subroutine do not interfere with those of similar names in other functions. The following program illustrates this principle:

```
main()
  {
       int a, b;
       a = 13;
```

```
        b = 15;
        printf("%d     %d\n", a, b);

        sub();

        printf("%d     %d\n", a, b);
  }
sub();
  {
        int a, b;
        a = 23;
        b = 25;
        printf("%d     %d\n", a, b);
  }
```

The output follows:

```
13    15
23    25
13    15
```

EXAMPLE HAVING GLOBAL VARIABLES

The following program defines two global variables, initializes them within the main routine, updates them within the subroutine, and displays the updated values from the main routine:

```
int a, b;      /* External variables */

main()
  {
        a = 13;
        b = 15;
        printf("%d     %d\n", a, b);

        sub();

        printf("%d     %d\n", a, b);
  }
```

```
sub()
  {
      printf("%d     %d\n", a, b);
      a += 10;
      b += 10;
      printf("%d     %d\n", a, b);
  }
```

The output follows:

```
13    15
13    15
23    25
23    25
```

ACTUAL VALUE PARAMETERS

The following program passes arguments to a subroutine as actual parameters, updates them within the subroutine, but does not update the original variables in main():

```
main()
  {
      int a, b;
      a = 13;
      b = 15;
      printf("%d     %d\n", a, b);

      sub(a, b);

      printf("%d     %d\n", a, b);
  }

sub(a, b)
  int a, b;
  {
      printf("%d     %d\n", a, b);
      a += 10;
      b += 10;
      printf("%d     %d\n", a, b);
  }
```

The output follows:

```
13    15
13    15
23    25
13    15
```

Exercises

1. Write a program that uses subroutines to read a data vector and computes the average, minimum and maximum. Define the data vector and size parameter as global variables. Do not include them as subroutine arguments.

2. Write a program to compute the gross pay for several employees. Include a subroutine that accepts the pay rate and hours worked and returns the gross pay, giving time-and-a-half for overtime.

5.6 Recursion

C permits recursive functions that call themselves. Recursive functions require value parameters for their argument lists. When a function is called, the value parameters are saved by that subroutine. Changes to those parameters will not be carried back to the calling routine.

When a function calls itself, the new value parameters are saved in a new save area which includes the value parameters and local variables for each function call. The save areas form a push-down stack that follows a last-in-first-out policy.

NESTED RECURSIVE CALLS

Successive recursive calls of a procedure to itself result in a deeper and deeper nesting of calls. Memory requirements of the parameter save area will exceed available memory unless there is a well-defined stopping point. The recursive call is often part of an IF or WHILE statement which eventually forces the recursive calls to stop.

Once the recursive calls have stopped, the program will extricate itself from the deepest level, working its way level by level to the top. The C system automatically manages the stack of save areas. (One of the main applications of recursion in list management is the maintenance of stacks.)

LOOPING AND RECURSION

Looping and recursion have some similarities. Many simple problems requiring repetition have looping and recursive solutions. Looping is done within the procedure; recursion has the function calling itself. Looping is under the control of a test at the beginning or end of the loop. Recursion also requires a test before the recursive call. Recursion automaticlly maintains a stack of save areas.

EXAMPLE USING LOOPING

The symbol n! is the value 1 for *n* = 0 and the product of the first *n* integers for *n* = 1, 2, . . . The function factorial() in the following program uses a FOR loop to calculate the product of the first *n* integers:

```
main()      /* Compute factorial */
  {
        int number;
        float fact, factorial();

        number = 5;
        fact = factorial(number);
        printf("n =              %d\n", number);
        printf("Factorial  =  %7.2f\n", fact);
  }

float factorial(n)
  int n;
  {
        int i, p;
        p = 1;
        for (i = 1; i <= n; i++)
```

```
        p *= i;
      return (p);
  }
```

The output follows:

```
n =          5
Factorial = 120.00
```

EXAMPLE USING RECURSION

The recursive definition of n! is

```
          1       for n = 0
    n*(n-1)!      for n > 1.
```

The following program uses a recursive definition of the function factorial() to compute n!:

```
main()      /* Compute factorial */
  {
      int number;
      float fact, factorial();

      number = 5;
      fact = factorial(number);
      printf("n =          %d\n", number);
      printf("Factorial = %7.2f\n", fact);
  }

float factorial(n)
  int n;
  {
      if (n <= 0)
        return (1);
      else
        return(n * factorial(n-1));
  }
```

The output is the same as before. The following illustrate the recursive calls made to calculate 5!:

```
factorial(5)
  factorial(4)
    factorial(3)
      factorial(2)
        factorial(1)
          factorial(0)
          return(1)
        return(1)
      return(2)
    return(6)
  return(24)
return(120)
```

EFFICIENCY AND CLARITY

The looping method of calculating factorials is the most efficient and the easiest to understand. Recursive methods are often slower than corresponding iterative methods.

Problems requiring the use of a push-down stack may be easier to understand when using recursive methods because the system does the stack management. Even these programs may not execute as quickly as corresonding iterative programs that require detailed handling.

Exercises

1. Write an iterative (looping) program that computes the sum of the first *n* integers.

2. Write a program using a recursive function to compute the sum of the first *n* integers.

3. Write a recursive program that prints in ascending order all of the Fibonacci numbers less than the value 1,000. The first few numbers are 1, 1, 2, 3, 5, 8. The next term is the sum of the previous two terms.

4. Write a recursive program that prints all of the Fibonacci numbers less than the value 1,000 in descending order.

6

Program Flow Revisited

Primary program flow statements include IF . . . ELSE, FOR, WHILE, and DO . . . WHILE. This chapter covers several additional flow-of-control statements that are used less frequently. These include SWITCH, BREAK, CONTINUE, and GOTO.

6.1 Switch

The switch construct controls the selection of statements for execution from a list of alternatives. The form of the statement follows:

```
switch (expression)
  {
     case constant 1:
       statements;
     case constant 2:
       statements;
     case constant 3:
       statements;
     default:
       statements;
  }
```

The expression consists of an integer, character, or an expression whose result is an integer or character. The constants identifying the cases are integer or character constants. If none of the listed cases is satisfied, control passes to the default statements.

FLOW OF CONTROL

The switch expression controls the beginning point for executing statements. The statements from the selected case to the default are executed unless the flow is broken with the BREAK statement covered in Section 6.2. Many other languages have similar case selection statements which execute only the statement corresponding to the case.

The following example program illustrates the SWITCH statement:

```
main()      /* Illustrate switch */
  {
      int
        code;      /* Code for switch */

      code = 3;
      switch(code)
        {
          case1: printf("First line\n");
          case 2: printf("Second line\n");
          case 3: printf("Third line\n");
          case 4: printf("Fourth line\n");
          case 5: printf("Fifth line\n");
          default: printf("Default line\n");
        }
  }
```

The output follows:

```
Third line
Fourth line
Fifth line
Default line
```

The value 3 for the switch control sets the starting execution point to case 3. The statements for the first two cases are skipped.

Exercises

1. Write a program that accepts an integer in the range 0-4 and counts the number of values greater than or equal to 0 (default), greater than or equal to 1 (last case), greater than or equal to 2 (next to last case), etc.

2. Write a program that accepts the letters A, B, C, D, or F from the standard input device. For each input letter print the letter and a series of asterisks corresponding to that letter. Print four asterisks after the letter A, three after the letter B, two for C, and one asterisk after the letter D. Print nothing following an F. Use a switch statement with each case adding an asterisk and the default statement putting in the final new-line symbol.

6.2 Break

The BREAK statement is contained within a loop. It passes control to the statement immediately following the loop. The loop may consist of a FOR, WHILE, or DO . . . WHILE construct.

The following form shows the BREAK statement:

```
while (condition)
  {
     statements;
     if (condition) break;
     statements;
  }
statements;
```

The break statement provides a means of breaking out of the loop. This is in addition to the loop test provided by the FOR or WHILE tests.

PRIME NUMBERS

A prime number is an integer evenly divisible by itself and the number 1. The number 2 is prime since it is evenly divisible by the numbers 1 and 2. The value 4 is not prime since it is evenly divisible by 1, 2, and 4.

The C modulo operator % gives the integer remainder after dividing the righthand value into the lefthand value. If the remainder is zero, the righthand value is a divisor. If the remainder is not zero, the righthand is not a divisor of the lefthand value.

The expression (n % d) gives the remainder after dividing the integer d into the integer n. The logical expression

(n % d) = = 0

returns the value 1 (true) if the remainder is zero and 1 (false) otherwise.

PROGRAM TESTING PRIME NUMBERS

The following program accepts a set of numbers and tests whether or not they are prime:

```
main()      /* Test for prime number */
  {
       int
         d,      /* Integer divisor */
         n;      /* integer to test*/

       scanf("%d", &n);
       while (n > 0)
         {

              for (d = 2; d < n; d++)
                if ((n % d) == 0)
                  {
                   printf("%d      is not prime\n", n);
                   break;
                  }

              if (d == n)
                printf("%d      is prime\n", n);
```

```
            scanf("%d", &n);
        }
}
```

For a number *n*, the program tests each of the numbers 2, 3, . . . , *n* to see if it divides evenly into *n*. The program breaks out of the loop after finding the first divisor. Every integer number is evenly divisible by 1; therefore, the program does not test that case. If the program does not find a divisor until it reaches the number *n*, the number is prime.

The program accepts numbers for testing one at a time. Use the number zero to terminate the program. For the test file

```
11
123
317
23
119
0
```

the output follows:

```
11 is prime
123 is not prime
317 is prime
23 is prime
119 is not prime
```

SWITCH WITH BREAK

If a BREAK statement is included as part of each case statement group, the SWITCH statement of C functions like the CASE constructs of other languages. The statement form follows:

```
switch (expression)
  {
     case constant 1:
       statements;
       break;
```

```
        case constant 2:
          statements;
          break;
        case constant 3:
          statements;
          break;
        default:
          statements;
      }
```

PROGRAM ASSIGNING LETTER GRADES

The following program uses the SWITCH construct to assign letter grades to a series of numerical scores:

```
main()      /* Assign letter grade */
  {
     char
       grade;      /* Letter grade */
     int
       score;      /* Score for letter grade */

     scanf("%d", &score);
     while (score > 0)
       {

          switch (score / 10)
            {
               case 10:
               case 9:
                 grade = 'A';
                 break;
               case 8:
                 grade = 'B';
                 break;
               case 7:
                 grade = 'C';
                 break;
               case 6:
                 grade = 'D';
                 break;
```

```
            default:
              grade = 'F';
          }

        printf("%d     %c\n", score, grade);
        scantf("%d", &score);
      }
}
```

The program processes a series of scores, terminating when it comes to the trailer value −1 signaling the end of the file. The file

```
87
69
75
93
51
-1
```

results in the following output:

```
87    B
69    D
75    C
93    A
51    F
```

Exercises

1. Write a program that reads a text file of characters and counts the frequency of each vowel. Use the SWITCH statement.

2. Write a program that reads a file containing a product code and quantity like the following:

```
B 4
A 1
D 6
A 24
C 1
```

and prints an output file like:

B	4	2.95	11.80
A	1	7.69	7.69
D	6	4.99	29.94
A	24	1.97	47.28
C	1	24.95	24.95

containing the code, number of units, unit price, and dollar amount of purchase computed as number of units times the per-unit price. Use the SWITCH statement with the product code to determine the unit price.

6.3 Continue

The CONTINUE statement is similar to the BREAK statement. The BREAK transfers control to the statement immediately following the loop. The CONTINUE terminates the current loop iteration and continues with the next. The BREAK exits the loop, the CONTINUE passes to the next iteration of the loop.

ASSIGNING LETTER GRADES TO SCORES

Letter grades are to be assigned to test scores according to the following scheme:

90 - 100	A
80 - 89	B
70 - 79	C
60 - 69	D
0 - 59	F

Dividing the test score by 10 using integer division results in one of the integer results 0, 1, . . . , 10. The scores 90-99 become 9 while a perfect score of 100 becomes 10.

Define a character array "grades" containing the letters F, D, C, B, A in that order. The expression

(score − 50) / 10

gives the subscript of the letter grade for scores in the interval 50-99. Scores less than 60 are assigned F. The score 100 is an A.

PROGRAM ASSIGNING LETTER GRADES

The following program assigns letter grades to test scores:

```
main()      /* Assign letter grades */
  {
        char
          grade;      /* Assigned letter grade */
        static char
          grades[ ] = {'F', 'D', 'C', 'B', 'A', 'A'};
        int
          index,      /* Subscript for letter grade */
          score;      /* Score used for assigning grade */

        scanf("%d", &score);
        while (score > 0)
          {

              if (score < 60)
        {
          printf("%d      %c\n", score, 'F');
          scanf("%d",   &score);
          continue;
        }
                index = (score - 50) / 10;
                grade = grades[index];
                printf("%d      %c\n", score, grade);

                scanf("%d",   &score);
          }
}
```

The program handles an F differently from the other letter grades. After assigning the F and reading the next score, it continues with the next iteration. A appears twice in the array of letter grades. One location is for the scores 90-99, the other for the perfect score of 100.

The program uses the score −1 to signal the end of the file. The file of scores

```
87
69
75
93
51
-1
```

results in the following output:

```
87   B
69   D
75   C
93   A
51   F
```

Exercises

1. Modify the program of this section; do not use the CONTINUE statement.

2. Write a program that uses getchar() and putchar() to copy one file to another. Use the CONTINUE statement to prevent copying characters that fall outside the decimal ASCII codes 31-127.

6.4 GOTO

The GOTO statement is controversial; it branches to a labeled statement. The looping constructs FOR, WHILE, and DO . . . WHILE statements transfer control from the end to the beginning of the loop; the flow is predictable and controlled. The SWITCH also provides transfer of control in a very restricted way. The BREAK and CONTINUE transfer control to another area of the program, but they are also restricted in their transfer of control.

The GOTO statement is completely unbridled in its transfer control. The statement

```
goto target;
```

or

```
if (condition) goto target;
```

transfers control to a labeled program location.The target location is identified by the label and a terminating colon as in:

```
target:
   statements;
```

Programs are hard to understand if they include many GOTO statements. A GOTO statement is helpful with a deeply nested loop with fatal errors which prevent the program from continuing.

The following illustrates this:

```
while (condition)
   {
      while (condition)
         {
            for ()
               {
                  for ()
                     {
                        if (condition hopeless)
                        goto help;
                        statements;
                     }
               }
         }
   }
statements;
exit;
help:
   statements;     /* Clean up the pieces or give up entirely */
```

EXAMPLE SHOWING MISUSE OF GOTO

It is possible to use GOTO and IF . . . GOTO statements to implement loops. The following program uses GOTO statements to control the loop computing the value of n! (factorial) as the product of the first *n* integers:

```
main()      /* Illustrate labels and goto */
  {
       int
          n,      /* Value of n for n! */
          i,      /* Current integer */
          p;      /* Product */

       n = 5;
       p = 1;
       i  = 0;

       loop: ++i;
       if (i > n)
          goto finish;
       p *= i;
       goto loop;

       finish: printf("%d factorial is %d\n", n, p);
}
```

The label "loop" identifies the beginning of the loop. The label "finish" identifies the statement following the end of the loop. The output follows:

```
5 factorial is 120
```

PROGRAM USING STANDARD LOOP CONSTRUCT

Programs using standard loop constructs are easier to understand. The following program calculates n! as the product of the first *n* integers using the WHILE statement:

```
main()      /* Illustrate labels and goto */
  {
       int
```

```
        n,     /* Value of n for n! */
        i,     /* Current integer */
        p;     /* Product */

    n = 5;
    p = 1;
    i  = 0;

    while (++i <= n)
        p *= i;

    printf("%d factorial is %d\n", n, p);
}
```

The output is the same as before; but this program is easier to understand than one using labels and GOTO statements.

Exercises

1. Write a program using GOTO and IF . . . GOTO statements to implement loops for reading a set of values into an array. Compute the average, minimum and maximum values, and print the results.

2. Rewrite the program of exercise 1 using one of the standard looping constructs.

7

Pointers

A pointer is a variable that points to another variable. Each variable has an address and a value. A pointer gives the address of a variable. Pointers and arrays are related. The array variable is really a pointer. Programmers may use subscripts or pointers when accessing arrays. Proper use of pointers can improve the execution of programs that use arrays extensively.

7.1 Pointers and Addresses

A source program uses symbols (+ − * / . . .) to designate operations and symbolic names to represent functions and variables. The compiler translates the operator symbols to appropriate machine language instructions. It translates the symbolic names to memory address references.

SYMBOLIC NAMES AND ADDRESSES

The declaration

```
int var1, var2:
```

defines two integer variables. The compiler develops a symbol table containing the variable name, memory address, and type specification. The compiler substitutes memory addresses for symbolic names when generating object program machine language code.

The source program statement

```
var2 = var1;
```

moves the contents of var1 to the contents of var2. The compiler fills the memory address portion of the symbol table as it assigns memory locations to variables. The variables var1 and var2 are of type int (16-bit on microcomputers and minicomputers, 32-bit on mainframes). Assume that the addresses are E72C for var1 and E72E for var2.

Many computers are single-address, with most instructions revolving around one or more central accumulators. The symbolic machine language instructions

```
LOAD 2,var1
STORE 2,var2
```

perform the data movement by loading accumulator 2 from var1, then storing the loaded value in var2.

Assume that the machine language instructions contain an 8-bit operation code with the code 4A representing a load and the code 4B representing a store. Each instruction consists of an 8-bit operation code, a 4-bit accumulator reference, and a 20-bit address reference. The compiler generates the absolute machine language statements

```
4A20E72C
4B20E72E
```

to move the contents of var1 to var2.

POINTERS CONTAIN ADDRESSES

The address of var1 remains E7C2 regardless of its contents. If changes are made to the program and it is recompiled, the new address may be different from other compilations. C provides pointer variables to contain variable addresses

The statement

```
ptr1 = &var1;
```

places the address of the variable var1 in the pointer variable ptr. The symbol & tells the compiler to provide the address of the variable rather than its contents.

POINTER VARIABLE TYPES

Pointer variables are unsigned and not necessarily the same length as integer variables. Pointer variable references to arrays require knowledge of the type of variable referenced.

The declaration

```
int var1, var2, *ptr1, *ptr2;
```

defines two integer variables var1 and var2. These may be 16-bit integers. The variables ptr1 and ptr2 are pointers to integer variables. The symbol * preceding a variable name in a declaration statement designates a pointer to a variable of the indicated type.

INDIRECT ADDRESSING

C permits indirect addressing through its pointer variables. The expression

```
var1 = var2 + var3;
```

directly references the variables, and the compiler substitutes the address from the symbol table into the machine code.

The symbol *ptr1 is an indirect reference using the address contained in the pointer variable ptr1. The sequence

```
ptr2 = &var2;
ptr3 = &var3;
```

places the addresses of var2 and var3 into the pointer variables. The statement

```
var1 = *ptr2 + *ptr3;
```

references the variables var2 and var3 through their pointers.

The indirect reference may for the variable on the left of the assignment statement. If the pointer ptr1 points to var1, the statement

```
*ptr1 = *ptr2 + *ptr3;
```

places the result into the variable addressed by ptr1.

EXAMPLE USING INDIRECT REFERENCE

The following program assigns the value 12 to the integer variable var1, places its address into the pointer variable ptr1, and uses indirect reference to access var1:

```
main()      /* Pointer and indirect addressing */
  {
      int var1, var2, *ptr1;

      var1 = 12;
      ptr1 = &var1;
      var2 = *ptr1;

      printf("Variable 1    %d\n", var1);
      printf("Variable 2    %d\n", var2);
  }
```

The output follows:

```
Variable 1    12
Variable 2    12
```

INDIRECT REFERENCE TO TARGET OF ASSIGNMENT

The following program uses indirect referencing to the target of the assignment statement:

```
main()      /* Pointer and indirect addressing */
  {
      int var1, var2, *ptr1, *ptr2;
```

```
        var1  = 12;
        ptr1  = &var1;
        ptr2  = &var2;
        *ptr2 = *ptr1;

        printf("Variable 1      %d\n", var1);
        printf("Variable 2      %d\n", var2);
        printf("Indirect 1      %d\n", *ptr1);
        printf("Indirect 2      %d\n", *ptr2);
    }
```

The output follows:

```
Variable 1    12
Variable 2    12
Indirect 1    12
Indirect 2    12
```

The printf statements contrast direct and indirect references within output statements.

VARIABLE ADDRESSES

Variable addresses contained in pointers are available for display or calculation. Most computer systems use hexadecimal or octal codes for internal binary information, including memory addresses. The printf conversion code %6x specifies hexadecimal output up to six digits, with zero suppression of leading zeros.

The following program defines four variables of different types with corresponding pointers, assigns values to the variables, assigns addresses to the pointers, and displays both the address and contents of each variable:

```
main()     /* Variable values and addresses */
  {
        int var1, *ptr1;
        char var2, *ptr2;
        float var3, *ptr3;
        double var4, *ptr4;

        var1 = 12;
        var2 = 'E';
```

```
    var3 = 2.5;
    var4 = 2.0 / 3.0;

    ptr1 = &var1;
    ptr2 = &var2;
    ptr3 = &var3;
    ptr4 = &var4;
    printf("Variable Address Value\n");
    printf("              Hex\n");
    printf("Var 1     %6x     %d\n", ptr1, var1);
    printf("Var 2     %6x     %c\n", ptr2, var2);
    printf("Var 3     %6x     %5.2f\n", ptr3, var3);
    printf("Var 4     %6x     %14.11f\n", ptr4, var4);
}
```

The output follows:

```
Variable    Address    Value
            Hex
Var1        FFE2       12
Var2        FFDF       E
Var3        FFD8         2.50
Var4        FFCE          .66666666667
```

Other computer systems and C compilers will not assign the same locations. The variable contents, however, are similar.

Exercises

1. Write a program to compute the area and circumference of a 40-foot by 30-foot rectangle. Use pointer variables and indirect addressing to reference the variables' length, width, area and circumference.

2. Write a program that defines several variables with corresponding pointers, assigns values to the variables, and lists the values and variable addresses.

7.2 Pointers and Functions

The variable *x* in the expression

$$y = f(x)$$

is an argument to the function *f*. The two major types of arguments in programming languages are called value parameters (most common) and variable (or reference) parameters.

Value parameters send the value of the argument to the function and do not permit the function to access the arguments. Output from the function is a returned result. A reference parameter sends the address of the argument to the function which accesses and modifies its contents.

EXAMPLE USING VALUE PARAMETERS

The following program computes the area and circumference of a rectangle using one function to calculate the area and another function to calculate the circumference:

```
main()      /* Area and circumference */
  {
      float length, width, area, circum,
      areaf(), circumf();

      length  = 12.5;
      width   =  7.5;

      area    = areaf(length, width);
      circum  = circumf(length, width);

      printf("Length             %9.2f\n", length);
      printf("Width              %9.2f\n", width);
      printf("Area               %9.2f\n", area);
      printf("Circumference      %9.2f\n", circum);
  }

float areaf(length, width)
  float length, width;
  {
      float area;
      area = length * width;
      return (area);
  }

float circumf(length, width)
  float length, width;
```

```
{
    float circum;
    circum = 2.0 * (length + width);
    return (circum);
}
```

The output follows:

```
Length                                  12.50
Width                                    7.50
Area                                    93.75
Circumference                           40.00
```

VALUE PARAMETERS RECOMMENDED

Value parameters are usually recommended because the function will not have unexpected side effects. Each function can return one result using the RETURN statement.

Since a function cannot return more than one result, the previous program needed two functions—one to calculate the area and the other to calculate the circumference. Combining these calculations in one function requires reference parameters. This increases the vulnerability of the calling program to actions taken by the function.

REFERENCE PARAMETERS

Reference parameters pass the memory addresses of the variables to the function. The function can modify the variables indirectly through their addresses; this allows more than one output value per function call. The following program uses one function and passes the addresses of the area and circumference variables for its output:

```
main()      /* Area and length */
  {
    float length, width, area, circum;

    length  =  12.5;
    width   =   7.5;
```

```
        measures(length, width, &area, &circum);

        printf("Length          %9.2f\n", length);
        printf("Width           %9.2f\n", width);
        printf("Area            %9.2f\n", area);
        printf("Circumference   %9.2f\n", circum);
    }

measures(length, width, area, circum)
    float length, width, *area, *circum;
    {
        *area   = length * width;
        *circum = 2.0 * (length + width);
    }
```

The output is the same as before. There is only one function call rather than two. The variables' length and width are value parameters which the function cannot change. The function call passes the addresses of the variables area and circumference for the function to use, and indirectly places the results.

FUNCTION TO SWAP CONTENTS OF VARIABLES

Writing a function to swap the contents of two variables is an entertaining exercise for the unwary. The following program using value parameters pretends to swap the contents of the two arguments:

```
main()      /* Swap values */
    {
        int var1, var2;

        var1 = 12;
        var2 = 39;
        printf("Var 1     Var 2\n");
        printf("%5d     %5d     before swapping\n", var1, var2);

        swap(var1, var2);
        printf("%5d     %5d     after swapping\n", var1, var2);
    }
```

```
swap(var1, var2)
  int var1, var2;
  {
      int temp;

      temp = var1;
      var1  = var2;
      var2  = temp;
      printf("%5d     %5d     within function\n", var1, var2);
  }
```

The output follows:

```
Var 1     Var 2
   12        39     before swapping
   39        12     within function
   12        39     after swapping
```

It looks as if the swap is accomplished, but the function does not change the values of the variables used as arguments because they are value parameters. The function maintains its own private copy of the variables and swaps its private copies.

SWAP FUNCTION USING REFERENCE PARAMETERS

The swap takes place in the calling program's data area using the addresses given by the reference parameters. The function uses indirect addressing to reference the variables. The following program actually makes the swap:

```
main()      /* Swap values */
  {
      int var1, var2;
      var1 = 12;
      var2 = 39;
      printf("Var 1      Var 2\n");
      printf("%5d     %5d     before swapping\n", var1, var2);

      swap(&var1, &var2);
      printf("%5d     %5d     after swapping\n", var1, var2);
  }
```

```
swap(var1, var2)
  int *var1, *var2;
  {
     int temp

     temp  = *var1;
     *var1 = *var2;
     *var2 = temp;
     printf("%5d    %5d    within function\n", *var1, *var2);
  }
```

The output follows:

```
Var 1   Var 2
  12      39    before swapping
  39      12    within function
  39      12    after swapping
```

Exercises

1. Write a program using one function that accepts two input values and computes the sum and sum of squares of the two vaues.

2. Write a program using reference parameters that accepts three values and arranges them in ascending order.

7.3 Pointers and Arrays

Pointers are rarely used with simple objects like integers or characters. They provide a more efficient method of accessing array elements.

COMPARING SUBSCRIPTS AND POINTERS

The declaration

```
float vector[20];
```

declares a floating point array of 20 elements. The array name is a pointer variable giving the base address of the array. The statement

```
value = vector[0];
```

references the first element of the array, and

```
value = vector[19];
```

references the last.

Since the array name is a pointer variable, the statement

```
value = *vector;
```

references the first element of the array. The statement

```
value = *(vector+1);
```

references the second element, and

```
value = *(vector+19);
```

references the last.

Both vector[i] and *(vector+i) reference the *i*th element of the array. Notice that *(vector+i) adds the value *i* to the base address. C automatically adjusts the value of *i* to reflect the width of the data type elements of the array. Floating point variables are 32-bits wide. The reference *(vector +10) accesses the eleventh element of the array which is at the base address plus 40 bytes.

The reference *(vector+10) gives the eleventh element which is at the base plus 80 bytes for a double precision array having 64-bit elements. The eleventh element of a 16-bit integer is at the base address plus 20 bytes. The eleventh character is at the base plus 10 bytes.

INCREMENTING AND DECREMENTING

C permits incrementing or decrementing pointers in the same manner as subscripts. If i is the subscript, the operation ++i preincrements i and i++ postincrements it. When preincrements the subscript before using it. The computer uses the subscript first, then increments it when postincrementing.

The increment or decrement operation can take place within the subscript. The statement

```
value = vector[i++];
```

accesses the value of vector[i], then increments the subscript. The statement

```
value = vector[++i];
```

increments the index first. The result is as if the statement

```
value = vector[i+1];
```

uses preincrementing

The similar statement

```
value = *(vector + i++);
```

uses a pointer with postincremeting, and

```
value = *(vector + ++i);
```

uses preincrementing. There is no computational advantage to using pointers in this manner.

EFFICIENT USE OF POINTERS

The declaration

```
float vector[20], *ptr;
```

declares a floating point array of 20 elements and a floating point pointer. The statement

```
ptr = &vector[0];
```

or

```
ptr = vector;
```

assigns the base address of the array to the pointer.

The statement

```
value = *ptr;
```

is equivalent to the statement

```
value = vector[0];
```

which uses subscripts. Similarly, the statements

```
value = vector[i];
```

and

```
value = *(ptr+i);
```

are equivalent.

Incrementing or decrementing pointer variables is often more efficient that incrementing or decrementing subscripts. The statement

```
value = *ptr++;
```

uses the current value of the pointer in an indirect access, then increments the pointer according to the width of the data type for the pointer variable. The base address is taken care of with the initialization of the pointer.

The statement

```
value = vector[i++];
```

accesses the same element and uses the same postincrementing. The computer must add the subscript to the base address with each subscripted reference. Proper use of pointers eliminates the addition of the base address for each iteration.

EXAMPLE COMPARING POINTER AND SUBSCRIPT

The following program declares an integer array and lists its values in two columns using a pointer for the first column accesses and a subscript for the second:

```
main()      /* Pointers and arrays */
  {
       static int
         vector[] = {12, 11, 19, 14, 15, -1};
       int
         i,          /* Index */
         *ptr;       /* Pointer to vector */

       ptr = &vector[0];
       i   = 0;

       while (vector[i] != -1)
         printf("%2d     %5d     %5d\n",
           i, *ptr++, vector[i++]);
  }
```

The output follows:

```
1   12   12
2   11   11
3   19   19
4   14   14
5   15   15
```

This program uses the statement

```
ptr = &vector[0];
```

to establish the pointer's base address. The starting point could have been any element. The statement

```
ptr = &vector[2];
```

sets the starting address to the third element.

ALTERNATE STATEMENT INITIALIZING POINTER

Since the name of the array is a pointer variable, the statement

```
ptr = vector;
```

initializes the pointer to the base address corresponding to the element vector[0].

The following program uses this form of initialization:

```
main()      /* Pointers and arrays */
  {
      static int
        vector[] = {12, 11, 19, 14, 15, -1};
      int
        i,          /* Index */
        *ptr;       /* Pointer to vector */

      ptr = vector;
      i   = 0;

      while (vector[i] != -1)
        printf("%2d     %5d     %5d\n",
          i, *ptr++, vector[i++]);
  }
```

The output is the same as before.

SUM THE ELEMENTS OF AN ARRAY

The statement

```
sum += *ptr++;
```

sums the elements of the array. It corresponds to the two statements

```
sum = sum + vector[i];
i   = i + 1;
```

but is more efficient.

The following program uses the method of incrementing a pointer variable to compute the sum of the elements of an array:

```
main()      /* Pointers and arrays */
  {
       static int
         vector[ ] = {12, 11, 19, 14, 15, -1};
       int
         sum;

       sum = sumf(vector);
       printf("Sum is %5d\n", sum);
  }

int sumf(vector)
  int vector[ ];
  {
       int
         sum,        /* Sum of values of vector */
         *ptr;       /* Pointer to vector */

       ptr = vector;

       sum = 0;
       while (*ptr != -1)
         sum += *ptr++;

       return (sum);
  }
```

The output follows:

```
Sum is    71
```

POINTER VARIABLE TYPES

A pointer references a specified variable type. When incrementing pointers, the variable type controls the incrementing. The increment is one byte for character arrays, two bytes for 16-bit integers, and four bytes for floating point arrays.

LIST VALUES OF ARRAYS

The following lists the elements of arrays of character, integer, and double precision type:

```
main()      /* Pointer increment size */
  {
      static char
        letter[ ]   = {'a', 'b' 'c', 'd', 'e'};
      static int
        number[ ] = {12, 11, 19, 14, 15};
      static double
        amount[ ] = {2.5, 1.2, 3.9, 2.4, 4,1};

      int counter, *iptr;
      char *cptr;
      double *dptr;

      iptr  = &number[0];
      cptr = &letter[0];
      dptr = &amount[0];

      for (counter = 1; counter <= 5; counter++)
        printf("%c     %2d     %5.21f\n",
          *cptr++, *iptr++, *dptr++);
  }
```

The output follows:

```
a    12    2.50
b    11    1.20
c    19    3.90
d    14    2.40
e    15    4.00
```

LISTING LOCATIONS OF ARRAY ELEMENTS

The system must increment the pointers by an amount corresponding to the data type. The following program lists the locations of the elements of the arrays. It prints the contents of the pointers instead of the contents of the locations that they reference:

```
main()      /* Point increment size */
  {
        static char
          letter[ ]    = {'a', 'b', 'c', 'd', 'e'};
        static int
          number[ ] = {12, 11, 19, 14, 15};
        static double
          amount[ ] = {2.5, 1.2, 3.9, 2.4, 4,1};

        int counter, *iptr;
        char *cptr;
        double *dptr;

        iptr  = &number[0];
        cptr = &letter[0];
        dptr = &amount[0];

        for (counter = 1; counter <= 5; counter++)
          printf("%6x      %6x      %6x\n",
            cptr++, iptr++, dptr++);
  }
```

The output follows:

```
4      9     13
5      B     1B
6      D     23
7      F     2B
8     11     33
```

Exercises

1. Write a program using subscripts to read a set of values from the standard input device into an array, and compute the average, minimum and maximum values.

2. Write a program using pointers to read a set of values into an array, and compute the average, minimum and maximum values.

3. Write a program that reads a text file into a character array and sets a subscript to reference the first occurrence of the letter e.

4. Write a program that reads a text file into a character array and sets a pointer to reference the first occurrence of the letter e.

7.4 Pointer Arrays

Pointers are variables of a different type than char, int, float, or double. Pointers are similar to unsigned integers, but may not have the same number of bits. A computer that has 16-bit or 32-bit standard integers may have 20-bit or 24-bit addresses.

C allows arrays of pointers. Of what value are pointer arrays? One primary use is to access an array, element by element, in an order different from its physical order.

One pointer array may give the location of customer records alphabetically by name. Another may reference the records in zip code order. A third may access the records by customer ID number.

INDEX ARRAY

The following program defines an array and establishes an array of subscripts indexing the array values in ascending order:

```
main()      /* Array of indices */
  {
      static int
        vector[ ] = {12, 11, 19, 14, 15};
      int
        indices[5],      /* Array of indices */
        index,           /* Index to array of indices */
        number;          /* Number of values */

      number = 5;
      indices[0] = 1;
      indices[1] = 0;
      indices[2] = 3;
      indices[3] = 4;
      indices[4] = 2;
```

```
        index = 0;
        while (index < number)
            printf("%d\n", vector[indices[index++]]);
    }
```

The output follows:

```
11
12
14
15
19
```

POINTER ARRAY

The following program uses an array of pointers to access the array elements in ascending order:

```
main()      /* Array of pointers */
    {
        static int
            vector[ ] = {12, 11, 19, 14, 15};
        int
            *pointers[5],     /* Array of indices */
            index,            /* Index to array of indices */
            number;           /* Number of values */

        number = 5;
        pointers[0] = &vector[1];
        pointers[1] = &vector[0];
        pointers[2] = &vector[3];
        pointers[3] = &vector[4];
        pointers[4] = &vector[2];

        index = 0;
        while (index < number)
            printf("%d\n", *pointers[index++]);
    }
```

The output is the same as before. The printf statement makes an indirect reference to the element referenced by the subscripted pointer element.

Exercises

1. Place the characters FAHGTE in a character array. Establish a pointer array that references the characters in ascending alphabetic sequence.

2. Read a series of character strings from the standard input device using the scanf function. Place the strings head-to-tail in a character array. Use a pointer array specifying the beginning locations of the character strings. The first pointer locates the first string, the second pointer locates the second string, etc.

8

Program Flow Revisited

C includes structures, bit fields, unions, and disk files, subjects not discussed in the earlier chapters. Structures correspond to records in Pascal and COBOL. Bit fields are a special type of structure allowing subdivision of an integer variable into named fields. Unions permit the use of the same data area for more than one data type.

Section 8.5 will discuss disk files. The standard I/O redirection feature of UNIX is gaining popularity with other operating systems, including Microsoft's PC DOS and MS DOS. There is much less need for special disk file handling facilities for systems having I/O redirection. Programs having more than one input or output require more than standard I/O facilities.

8.1 Structures

A structure groups related items under one named type. The components can be any previously named type including structures. The structure

```
struct date
  {
     int month;
     int day;
     int year;
  }
```

defines the structure date as containing the three integer variables month, day, and year.

The variable declarations:

```
struct date
   birthday,
   startday,
   payday;
```

declare the variables birthday, startday, and payday to be of type date having the three integers month, day, and year.

The reference birthday.month is to the month element within the structured variable birthday. The statement

```
birthday.month = 4;
```

assigns the value 4 to the month field of birthday. The statement

```
printf("Day = %d\n", payday.day);
```

prints the day field of the structured variable payday.

GROSS PAY FOR ONE EMPLOYEE

Employee information for a simple payroll application consists of employee ID number, hourly pay rate, and number of hours worked. The purpose of the program is to compute the gross pay giving time-and-a-half for overtime.

The declaration

```
struct list
   {
       int idnumber;
       float rate;
       float hours;
       float gross;
   } payroll;
```

defines the type list and declares the structured variable payroll to be of that type.

The following program illustrates the declaration and use of the structured variable payroll:

```
main()      /* Define structure */
  {
       struct list
         {
            int idnumber;
            float rate;
            float hours;
            float gross;
         } payroll;

       payroll.idnumber  = 103;
       payroll.rate      = 8.25;
       payroll.hours     = 35.6;
       payroll.gross     = payroll.rate * payroll.hours;

       printf("ID number        %5d\n", payroll.idnumber);
       printf("Pay rate         %8.2f\n", payroll.rate);
       printf("Hours worked     %8.2f\n", payroll.hours);
       printf("Gross pay        %8.2f\n", payroll.gross);
  }
```

The output follows:

```
ID number       103
Pay rate          8.25
Hours worked     35.60
Gross pay       293.70
```

The reference payroll.rate refers to the element rate of the structured variable payroll. A period separates the parts of the name. One structured variable may include another structured variable as one of its elements. Such hierarchical structures require more than one period for some of their references.

STRUCTURED VARIABLE ARRAY

A structured variable may include an array as one of its elements. C also allows arrays of structured variables. The declaration

```
struct list
  {
    int idnumber;
    float rate;
    float hours;
    float gross;
  } payroll[20];
```

declares the variable payroll to be an array of 20 elements, each containing an ID number, pay rate, hours worked, and gross pay.

The following program reads an ID number, pay rate and hours worked for each of several employees into the array, calculates the gross pay, and displays the result:

```
main()      /* Define structure */
  {
      struct list
        {
          int idnumber;
          float rate;
          float hours;
          float gross;
        } payroll[20];
      int
        number,
        counter;
      float
        calc();

      scanf("%d", &number);
      for (counter = 0; counter < number; counter++)
        scanf("%d %f %f", &payroll[counter].idnumber,
          &payroll[counter].rate, &payroll[counter].hours);

      for (counter = 0; counter < number; counter++)
        payroll[counter].gross =
          calc(payroll[counter].rate, payroll[counter].hours);

      for (counter = 0; counter < number; counter++)
        printf("%5d     %8.2f     %8.2f     %8.2f\n",
```

```
            payroll[counter].idnumber, payroll[counter].rate,
            payroll[counter].hours, payroll[counter].gross);
  }

float calc(rate, hours)
  float
      rate,
      hours;
  {
      float
        gross;

      if (hours <= 40.0)
        gross = rate * hours;
      else
        gross = rate * hours + 0.5 * rate * (hours - 40.0);
      return (gross);
  }
```

The function calc() accepts a pay rate and hours worked, and returns the gross pay. The subroutine requires value parameters. The data file

```
3
103 8.25 35.6
112 6.75 50.3
117 7.60 42.8
```

includes the number of employees as the first item. The data for each employee follows. I/O redirection permits assigning the data file to the standard input file.

The output follows:

```
103    8.25    35.60    293.70
112    6.75    50.30    374.29
117    7.60    42.80    335.92
```

STANDARD POINTER USAGE

Most C compilers do not permit passing a structured variable as an actual value parameter. Pointers must be used to pass the beginning location of the structure. Defining the structure type outside the main() routine makes its definition available to all functions. A higher-level function passes the address (pointer) to a subsidiary function which declares the pointer to be of the global structured type.

The following program defines the global structure type payinfo which it uses within the main routine in an array and in the function calc() which accepts one element of the array:

```
struct payinfo      /* Template for functions */
  {
      int idnumber;
      float rate;
      float hours;
      float gross;
  };

main()
  {
      Struct payinfo
        payroll[20];
      int
        number,
        counter;
      float
        calc();

      scanf("%d", &number);
      for (counter = 0; counter < number; counter++)
        scanf("%d %f %f", &payroll[counter].idnumber,
          &payroll[counter].rate, &payroll[counter].hours);

      for (counter = 0; counter < number; counter++)
        payroll[counter].gross =
          calc(&payroll[counter]);

      for (counter = 0; counter < number; counter++)
        printf("%5d     %8.2f     %8.2f     %8.2f\n",
          payroll[counter].idnumber, payroll[counter].rate,
          payroll[counter].hours, payroll[counter].gross);
  }
```

```
float calc(payptr)
  struct payinfo
    *payptr;
  {
      float
        gross;

      if ((*payptr).hours <= 40.0)
        gross = (*payptr).rate * (*payptr).hours;
      else
        gross = (*payptr).rate * (*payptr).hours
          + 0.5 * (*payptr).rate * ((*payptr).hours - 40.0);
      return (gross);
  {
```

This program is functionally equivalent to the previous program. The expression (*payptr) is the pointer to the current subscripted element of the structured array payroll.

STRUCTURED POINTER SYMBOL

Pointers to structured variables are common. C includes a shorthand notation for them. The references

```
(*payptr).rate
```

and

```
payptr->rate
```

are equivalent. The hyphen followed by the "greater than" symbol gives the impression of a right arrow. The variable payptr is a pointer specifying which pay rate.

The following program substitutes the shorthand pointer notation for the standard pointer notation:

```
struct payinfo      /* Template for functions */
  {
      int idnumber;
      float rate;
```

```
        float hours;
        float gross;
    }

main()
    {
        struct payinfo
            payroll[20];
        int
            number,
            counter;
        float
            calc();

        scanf("%d", &number);
        for (counter = 0; counter < number; counter++)
            scanf("%d %f %f", &payroll[counter].idnumber,
                &payroll[counter].rate, &payroll[counter].hours);

        for (counter = 0; counter < number; counter++)
            payroll[counter].gross =
                calc(&payroll[counter]);

        for (counter = 0; counter < number; counter++)
            printf("%5d      %8.2f      %8.2f      %8.2f\n",
                payroll[counter].idnumber, payroll[counter].rate,
                payroll[counter].hours, payroll[counter].gross);
    }

float calc(payptr)
    struct payinfo
        *payptr;
    {
        float
            gross;

        if (payptr->hours <= 40.0)
            gross = payptr->rate * payptr->hours;
        else
            gross = payptr->rate * payptr->hours
                + 0.5 * payptr->rate * (payptr->hours - 40.0);
        return (gross);
    }
```

Exercises

1. Define a structured variable to contain the length, width, area and circumference of a rectangle. Use it in a program which computes the area and circumference of a rectangle 40-feet long by 30-feet wide.

2. Extend the program of exercise 1 to include an array of structured variables containing the length, width, area and circumference for the following rectangle dimensions:

40	30
35	35
65	20

8.2 Unions

A union is a variable that may hold different sizes and types of values at different times. The compiler keeps track of size requirements and alignment. One of the major purposes of this facility is to reuse the same memory area for more than one purpose, thus fitting large programs into computers having small memory capacities. Inexpensive memory reduces the significance of this factor.

A second application of unions is the definition of variant records for external files. A specified field may contain an integer variable for some records, and a character variable for others. The C program needs the type of the current record. Another variable identifies which type is involved, and an IF . . . ELSE statement selects the appropriate form for referencing the correct type.

EXAMPLE PROGRAM WITH UNION

The following program contains the union variable uvalue defining the variable names cvalue for character type, ivalue for integer type, and fvalue for floating point:

```
main()     /* Example of union */
 {
     union uname
       {
```

```
            char cvalue;
            int ivalue;
            float fvalue;
        }  uvalue

      uvalue.cvalue = 'E';
      printf("Character    %c\n", uvalue.cvalue);
      uvalue.ivalue = 12;
      printf("Integer    %d\n", uvalue.ivalue);

      uvalue.fvalue = 3.14159;
      printf("Float      %f\n", uvalue.fvalue);
}
```

The output follows:

```
Character   E
Integer     12
Float       3.141590
```

The three variables use the same memory area. The size of the allocated space is the size required by the largest defined variable. If character variables require 8 bits, integers require 16 bits, and floating point variables require 32 bits, the compiler allocates 32 bits for the union variable uvalue.

Exercises

1. Write a program that uses a union variable to reuse the same memory area for a long integer and a floating point variable.

2. Write a program that uses pointers to indirectly reference character, integer, and double precision variables. Place the pointer variables in a union variable so that they share the same memory area.

8.3 Fields

Some applications require packing several small bit strings into one computer word. Many C compilers include the bit-field structure definition needed to accomplish this task. The structure

```
struct
  {
      unsigned field1 : 1;
      unsigned field2 : 1;
      unsigned field3 : 3;
  } bvalue;
```

defines the structured variable bvalue containing two 1-bit fields followed by a 3-bit field.

The fields use the unsigned integer type; they cannot include negative quantities. The fields containing one bit only can assume one of the values 0 or 1. The 3-bit field corresponds to an octal digit and can assume one of the values 0 through 7 corresponding to the binary numbers 000 through 111. The values assigned may be decimal, octal, or hexadecimal, but must fit in the specified field.

PROGRAM USING BIT FIELDS

The following program defines three bit fields and illustrates their use:

```
main()      /* Bit fields */
  {
      struct
        {
            unsigned    field1 : 1;
            unsigned    field2 : 1;
            unsigned    field3 : 3;
        }   bvalue;

      bvalue.field1 = 1;
      bvalue.field2 = 0;
      bvalue.field3 = 5;

      printf("Field1     %2x\n", bvalue.field1);
      printf("Field2     %2x\n", bvalue.field2);
      printf("Field3     %2x\n", bvalue.field3);
```

```
}
```

The output follows

```
Field1    1
Field2    0
Field3    5
```

This program illustrates packing several variables into one internal computer word. Many systems use the standard integer of 16 bits for minicomputers and microcomputers or 32 bits for larger systems. Since the packing and word alignments fit the internal requirements of the computer, bit fields may not be consistently handled by all systems. The use of bit fields may reduce the portability of programs among systems.

BITFIELDS WITH DECIMAL AND HEXADECIMAL OUTPUT

The following program defines three 4-bit fields and illustrates both decimal and hexadecimal assignments and decimal and hexadecimal output:

```
main()      /* Bit fields */
  {
       struct
         {
             unsigned     field1 : 4;
             unsigned     field2 : 4;
             unsigned     field3 : 4;
         }   hvalue;

       hvalue.field1 = Oxe;
       hvalue.field2 = 12;
       hvalue.field3 = 5;

       printf("Decimal\n");
       printf("Field1     %2d\n", hvalue.field1);
       printf("Field2     %2d\n", hvalue.field2);
       printf("Field3     %2d\n", hvalue.field3);
```

```
        printf("\nHexadecimal\n");
        printf("Field1      %2x\n", hvalue.field1);
        printf("Field2      %2x\n", hvalue.field2);
        printf("Field3      %2x\n", hvalue.field3);
  }
```

The output follows:

```
Decimal
Field1    14
Field2    12
Field3     5

Hexadecimal
Field1    E
Field2    C
Field3    5
```

DECIMAL, OCTAL, AND HEXADECIMAL CONSTANTS

An octal integer is designated by adding a leading zero to an integer constant. The prefix Ox or OX designates a hexadecimal constant. The assignment statement

```
var1 = 27;
```

assigns a 2-digit decimal quantity to var1.

The statement

```
var1 = 027;
```

assigns the octal integer 27. The digits 8 and 9 are not permitted for octal constants.

The statement

```
var1 = Oxf7;
```

is equivalent to the statement

```
var1 = OXF7;
```

which assigns the hexadecimal constant F7 to var1. This constant allows the digits 0-9 and the symbols A-F. The lowercase a-f symbols are equivalent to the corresponding uppercase symbols A-F.

Exercises

1. Write a program using four 1-bit fields.

2. Write a program using four 3-bit fields.

3. Write a program using two 6-bit fields with octal constants.

4. Write a program using two 8-bit fields with hexadecimal constants.

8.4 Miscellaneous

This section discusses C features not covered in previous chapters, including the comma operator, the TYPEDEF facility, register variables, and the C precompiler.

COMMA OPERATOR

The C comma operator is most commonly used within the FOR statement. A pair of expressions separated by a comma are evaluated. The FOR statement

```
for (i = 0, j = n - 1; i < n; i++ j--)
```

generates the values 0, 1, . . . , $n - 1$ for *i* while generating the corresponding values $n - 1, n - 2, \ldots, 0$ for *j*.

The following program illustrates the comma operator with the FOR statement

```
for (i = 0, j = n; i < j; i++, j--)
```

and outputs the values for *i* and *j* each time through the loop:

```
main()      /* Comma operator */
  {
      int i, j, n;

      n = 8;
      for (i = 0, j = n; i < j; i++, j--)
        printf("%2d     %2d\n", i, j);
  }
```

The output follows:

```
0   8
1   7
2   6
3   5
```

TYPEDEF

The TYPEDEF facility creates new data type names for existing types. The TYPEDEF statements

```
typedef int INTEGER;
typedef float REAL;
```

allow the type name INTEGER for int variables and REAL for floating point variables. Many programmers use uppercase for TYPEDEF and constant definition names.

The following program illustrates the use of TYPEDEF:

```
typedef int INTEGER;
typedef float REAL;

main()      /* Example of typedef */
  {
      INTEGER
        length,
        width,
        rarea;
      REAL
        diameter,
        carea;
```

```
    length   = 40;
    width    = 30;
    rarea    = length * width;
    printf("Area of rectangle     %5d\n", rarea);

    diameter = 25.0;
    carea    = 3.14159 * diameter * diameter / 4.0;
    printf("Area of circle   %8.2f\n", carea);
}
```

The output follows:

```
Area of rectangle     1200
Area of circle          490.87
```

REGISTER VARIABLES

Register variables are a special class of frequently used variables. By defining the variables as register variables, the C programmer suggests to the compiler that they be assigned to general-purpose registers. This is a suggestion, not a mandate. The register declaration is local within a function. Most compilers would ignore an attempt to define a global variable as a register variable.

The statement

```
sum = sum + x;
```

or its equivalent statement

```
sum += x;
```

adds the contents of x to the contents of sum.

The symbolic machine language sequence

```
LOAD 2,SUM
ADD 2,X
STORE 2,SUM
```

loads the contents of SUM into the accumulator, adds the contents of X, and stores the result in SUM.

If the C compiler reserves general-purpose register 2 for the variable SUM, the single machine language instruction

ADD SUM,X

adds the contents of X to the variable SUM which has been assigned to register 2. The LOAD and STORE instructions are no longer needed.

The following program illustrates the use of the register storage class:

```
main()      /* Example register variable */
  {
      int
        vector[20],
        number,
        *pointer;
      register int
        sum,
        counter;
      number = 3;
      vector[0] = 12;
      vector[1] = 11;
      vector[2] = 19;

      counter = number
      sum     = 0;
      pointer = &vector[0];

      while (--counter >= 0)
        sum += *(pointer++);

      printf("Sum = %3d\n", sum);
  }
```

The output follows:

```
Sum = 42
```

Inappropriate register definitions will not help program performance. Many minicomputers and microcomputers do not have floating point accumulators; they use software routines to simulate floating point hardware. Computers without floating point hardware do not gain in performance from placing floating point variables in the register storage class. Larger systems that have several floating point registers may have improved performance from the judicious assignment of variables to floating point registers.

C PREPROCESSOR

The C compiler contains a preprocessor. Communication with the preprocessor is through the lines beginning with the symbol #. The preprocessor does macro substitution (#define), inclusion of named files (#include), and conditional compilation (#if, #ifdef, #ifundef, #else, and #endif).

Exercises

1. Write a program that places the values

11 12 14 15 19

into an array. Use the comma operator with a FOR loop to increment i and decrement j, swapping the *i*th and *j*th values so that the array is reversed. Swap the values in positions 0 and $n - 1$ first. Then swap the values in position 1 and $n - 2$. Continue swapping while the first subscript is less than the second.

2. Study the machine language architecture and registers defined for your computer. What kinds of variables make good candidates for the register storage class?

8.5 Disk Files

The standard I/O facilities satisfy the needs of many programs because of I/O redirection with UNIX and the popular microcomputer operating systems. The standard C I/O library includes functions for creating, deleting, reading from and writing to disk files.

COPY PROGRAM USING STANDARD I/O

The file FILE11.DAT on drive B contains the following character data:

I came, I saw, I conquered.

The function getchar() brings one character from the standard input file and returns the character as its result. The integer value −1 signals the end of input for many systems. Some systems use the integer value 0 to signal the end of file. The statement

```
#define EOF -1
```

defines the name EOF to designate the end of file signal.

Both putchar() and printf() send results to the standard output device. The function putchar() sends one character. The function printf() sends a formatted string. The following program reads a file of characters, places them in an array, and sends the contents of the character to the standard output device, using putchar() first and printf() second:

```
#define    EOF    -1

main()     /* Standard character I/O */
  {
     int
       vector[80],      /* Character array */
       c,               /* Character variable */
       i,               /* Subscript */
       n;               /* Number of characters */

     /* Get character array */
     i = 0;
     while ((c = getchar()) != EOF)
       vector[i++] = c;
     n = i - 1;

     /* Put character array */
     for (i = 0; i < n; i++)
       putchar(vector[i]);
```

```
    /* Print character array */
    for (i = 0; i < n; i++)
      printf("%c", vector[i]);
    printf("\n");
}
```

The output follows:

```
I came, I saw, I conquered.
I came, I saw, I conquered.
```

DISK FILE USAGE

The primary functions for disk files include fopen(), fclose(), getc() (which is equivalent to fgetc()), putc() (which is equivalent to fputc()), fprintf(), and fscanf(). The standard I/O library <STDIO.H> contains the disk file functions. Many compilers require its inclusion using the #include statement.

C compilers differ in their definition and use of files. The fopen() function

```
file1 = fopen("B:FILE1.DAT, "r")
```

will return an integer file unit number for some systems and a pointer to a file control block in others. The function fopen() returns an integer result in the first case and a pointer (memory address) in the second.

Those systems using an integer unit number let the integer 0 or −1 represent an error message. For systems using file pointers, a null pointer represents an error condition. The second parameter of the fopen() function is "r" for read and update, "w" for write, and "a" for append. If the file does not exist, the function fopen() will return an error code if an attempt is made to open it for read operations.

The following program reads a file of characters from the data file B:FILE12A.DAT into an array, writes them to the file B:FILE12B.DAT, and displays them on the standard output device:

```
#include      <STDIO.H>
#define       EOF     -1
```

```
main()      /* File copy */
  {
      FILE
        file1,
        file2;
      int
        vector[80],     /* Character array */
        c,              /* Character variable */
        i,              /* Subscript */
        n;              /* Number of characters */

      /* Get character array */
      file1 = fopen("B:FILE12A.DAT", "r");
      i = 0;
      while ((c = getc(file1)) != EOF)
        vector[i++] = c;
      n = i - 1;
      fclose(file1);

      /* Put character array */
      file 2 = fopen("B:FILE12B.DAT", "w");
      for (i = 0; i < n; i++)
        fputc(vector[i], file2);
      fclose(file2);

      /* Print character array */
      for (i = 0; i < n; i++)
        printf("%c", vector[i]);
      printf("\n");
  }
```

The contents of the input file are sent to both the standard output device and the defined output disk file.

SCANF() AND PRINTF() FOR STANDARD I/O

A data file contains the length and width for each of several rectangles. The first element of the file specifies the number of rectangles involved. The data file FILE13.DAT contains the data

```
4
40 30
```

```
35 35
65 20
50 25
```

giving the lengths and widths for four rectangles.

The following program obtains the input information from the standard input file. It sends the length, width, area and circumference measures to the standard output file:

```
main()      /* Formatted standard input */
  {
       int
          number,
          counter,
          length,
          width,
          area,
          circum;

       scanf("%d", &number);
       for (counter = 1; counter <= number; counter++)
          {
             scanf("%d %d", &length, &width);
             area   = length * width;
             circum = 2 * (length + width);
             printf("%5d %5d %5d %5d\n",
                length, width, area, circum);
          }
  }
```

The following output results from redirecting the standard input file to the disk file FILE13.DAT:

```
40    30  1200    140
35    35  1225    140
65    20  1300    170
50    25  1250    150
```

Input to the program may come from the keyboard or a disk file. The output may go to the display or to another disk file. I/O redirection has great flexibility potential.

FSCANF() AND FPRINTF() FOR DISK FILES

The fscanf() and fprintf() functions for disk files correspond to the scanf() and printf() for standard input and output. The following program illustrates this; it reads the input from the data file B:FILE14A.DAT, sends the summary output to the file B:FILE14B.DAT, and sends the labeled output with column headings to the standard output device:

```
#include      <STDIO.H>
#define           EOF. – 1

main()      /* Formatted standard input */
  {
      FILE
        file1,
        file2;
      int
        number,
        counter,
        length,
        width,
        area,
        circum;

      file1 = fopen("B:FILE14A.DAT", "r");
      file2 = fopen("B:FILE14B.DAT", "w");
      printf("Length     Width     Area     Circumference\n");

      fscanf(file1, "%d", &number);
      for (counter = 1; counter <= number; counter++)
        {
          fscanf(file1, "%d %d", &length, &width);
          area   = length * width;
          circum = 2 * (length + width);
          fprintf(file2, "%5d %5d %5d %5d\n",
            length, width, area, circum);
          printf("%5d     %5d     %5d     %5d\n",
            length, width, area, circum);
        }
      fclose(file1);
      fclose(file2);
  }
```

The contents of the input data file B:FILE14A.DAT follows:

```
4
40 30
35 35
65 20
50 25
```

The following lists the contents of the output file B:FILE-14B.DAT generated by the program:

```
40   30  1200   140
35   35  1225   140
65   20  1300   170
50   25  1250   150
```

The standard output including column headings follows:

```
Length   Width   Area   Circumference
40       30      1200   140
35       35      1225   140
65       20      1300   170
50       25      1250   150
```

Exercises

1. List the disk I/O functions defined for your implementation of C. If your system has one set for stream I/O and another for record I/O, explore the stream I/O set first as they operate like standard I/O.

2. Write a program that accepts a set of floating point numbers in formatted form from a disk file and computes the average.

3. Write a program that accepts an ID number, pay rate, and hours worked for each of several employees. Create an output disk file containing the ID number, pay rate, hours worked, and gross pay for each employee. Send the same output to the standard output device and include appropriate column headings.

PART II

Applications

9

Mathematics

Calculus is the mathematical study of movement and change with applications in science and economics. Applications include finding the slope of the tangent line of a curve and calculating the area bounded by a curve.

The basic calculus operations are differentiation and integration. Differential calculus involves finding the rate of change of a function. Integral calculus concerns the inverse problem of finding the function that has a given rate of change.

Sequences and series are important in calculus. A sequence is an ordered set of terms calculated by using a specified rule. A series is the sum of a sequence of terms. Calculus approximations use sequences, series, and limits. A limit is a troublesome concept from the perspective of both theory and practice.

A matrix is a two-dimensional table of numbers. Matrix algebra applications include the solution of simultaneous linear equations.

9.1 Series and Sequences

A sequence is an ordered set of values derived using a specified rule. The sequence of values

$$1 \quad 2 \quad 3 \quad 4 \quad 5 \quad \ldots$$

consists of the set of integers. The rule

$$x_1 = i \text{ for } i = 1, 2, \ldots$$

describes the sequence. The rule

$$x_1 = 1/i^2 \text{ for } i = 1, 2, \ldots$$

describes another sequence. The values

$$1 \ 1/4 \ 1/9 \ 1/16 \ldots$$

are the terms of this sequence. Both of these are infinite sequences.

A sequence may have a limit, but many do not have finite limits. A sequence has a limit if its larger numbered terms converge to a finite value. The first sequence does not converge. The second sequence converges to the value 0. As n approaches infinity, the term $1/n^2$ approaches 0.

SEQUENCE ESTIMATE OF EXP(X)

The limit of the sequence defined by $(1 + x/n)^n$ *is* e^x as n approaches infinity. The following program computes the nth term of the sequence for a given value of x:

```
#include     <math.h>

main()     /* SEQ1 -- nth term of sequence */
  {
      double
        rn,        /* Real value of n */
        x,         /* Value of x */
        y;         /* Value of nth term */
      int
        n;         /* Number of term */

      printf("\nProgram SEQ1\n");
      printf("\nCompute the value (1 + 1/x)\n/");
      printf("raised to the nth power as\n");
      printf("estimate of exp(x)\n");

      printf("\nValue for x ? ");
      scanf("%lf", & x);
      printf("\nValue for n ? ");
      scanf("%d", &n);
```

```
    while (n > 0)
      {
         rn = n;
    y = pow(1.0 + x / rn, rn);
    printf("Result = %lf\n", y);
    printf("\nValue for n ? ");
    scanf("%d", &n);
      }

    printf("\nEnd of program SEQ1\n");
}
```

The test run computes the terms of the sequence for $x = 1$ and several values of n:

```
Program SEQ1

Compute the value (1 + 1/x)
raised to the nth power as
estimate fo exp(x)

Value for x ? 1.0

Value for n ? 1
Result = 2.000000

Value for n ? 2
Result = 2.250000

Value for n ? 3
Result = 2.370370

Value for n ? 4
Result = 2.441406

Value for n ? 10
Result = 2.593742

Value for n ? 100
Result = 2.704814

Value for n ? 1000
Result = 2.716924
```

```
Value for n ? 0

End of program SEQ1
```

The value $n = 0$ terminates the program.

INTEREST RATE COMPOUNDING

A savings institution compounding interest quarterly has a higher effective interest rate than another institution offering the same rate but compounding annually. An institution offering monthly compounding has an even better effective rate. Some savings institutions offer daily compounding. How much better is daily compounding than annual compounding? What about continuous compounding?

The expression

$$p(1 + r/n)^n$$

gives the value at the end of the year of the present amount p earning interest at $100r$ percent interest compounded n times per year. The term

$$(1 + r/n)^n$$

is the multiplier of p giving the value at the end of the year. Subtracting this multiplier from 1 gives the effective interest rate as a fraction. The multiplier is the sequence $(1 + x/n)^n$ which has $\exp(x)$ as its limit. Continuous compounding gives the multiplier $\exp(r)$ for the interest rate r given as a fraction.

The following program asks for an interest rate and computes the annual effective interest rates for annual, quarterly, monthly, daily, and continuous compounding:

```
#include    <math.h>

main()  /* SEQ2 -- Interest compounding frequency */
  {
      double
         interest,         /* Nominal interest rate */
         effective,        /* Effective interest rate */
         compound();       /* Compute effective rate */
```

```
    /* Initial message */
    printf("\nProgram SEQ2\n");
    printf("\nCompare effective interest\n");
    printf("rates for several different\n");
    printf("compounding frequencies\n");

    /* Get data */
    printf("\nInterest rate (per cent) ? ");
    scanf("%lf", &interest);
    interest = interest / 100.00;

    /* Compare compounding frequencies */
    printf("\nCompounding    Effective\n");
    printf("periods     rate\n);
    effective = 100.0 * interest;
    printf("        1     %10.5lf\n", effective);
    effective = compound(interest, 4);
    printf("        4     %10.5lf\n", effective);
    effective = compound(interest, 12);
    printf("       12     %10.5lf\n", effective);
    effective = compound(interest, 365);
    printf("      365     %10.5lf\n", effective);
    effective = 100.0 * (exp(interest) - 1.0);
    printf("continuous %10.5lf\n", effective);

    printf("\nEnd of program SEQ2\n");
  }

double compound(interest, number)
  double
    interest;           /* Nominal interest rate */
  int
    number;             /* Number of compounding periods */
  {
    double
      effective;          /* Effective interest rate (per cent) */

    effective = 100.0 * (-1.0 +
      exp(number * log(1.0 + interest / number)));
    return (effective);
  }
```

A sample test run follows:

```
Program SEQ2

Compare effective interest
rates for several different
compounding frequencies

Interest rate (per cent) ? 12.5
Compounding      Effective
periods          rate
        1        12.50000
        4        13.09824
       12        13.24160
      365        13.31242
continuous       13.31485

End of program SEQ2
```

LIMITS AT POINT HAVING UNDEFINED VALUE

The expression $(x^2 - 4)/(x - 2)$ is undefined at the point $x = 2$ since the denominator $x - 2$ becomes 0. The limit as x approaches 2 is defined. The following program estimates this limit by trying values successive to the value 2.0:

```
main()      /* SEQ3 -- Limit at undefined point */
  {
     float
        fnc(),       /* Function f(x) */
        width,       /* Width of limit */
        left,        /* Evaluation of left limit */
        right;       /* Evaluation of right limit */
     int
        counter;     /* Loop control variable */

     /* Initial message */
     printf("\nProgram SEQ3\n");
     printf("\nEvaluate function\n");
     printf("(x*x - 4) / (x - 2)\n");
     printf("at the limit x = 2\n");

     /* Generate table */
     printf("\nError     Left limit     Right limit\n");
```

```
        width = 1.0;
        for (counter = 1; counter <= 8; counter++)
          {
             width = width / 10.0;
             left  = fnc(2.0 - width);
             right = fnc(2.0 + width);
             printf("%12.6e %12.8f %12.8f\n", width, left, right);
          }

        /* Final message */
        printf("\nEnd of program SEQ3\n");
    }

float fnc(x)
  float
     x;
  {
     float
       y;

     y = (x * x - 4.0) / (x - 2.0);
     return (y);
  }
```

The test run follows:

```
Program SEQ3

Evaluate function
(x*x - 4) / (x - 2)
at the limit x = 2

Error         Left limit    Right limit
1.000000E-1   3.90000010    4.09999990
9.999999E-3   3.99000001    4.01000023
9.999999E-4   3.99900007    4.00099993
9.999999E-5   3.99990010    4.00010014
9.999998E-6   3.99998999    4.00001001
9.999998E-7   3.99999905    4.00000095
9.999998E-8   4.00000000    4.00000000
9.999999E-9   4.00000000    4.00000000

End of program SEQ3
```

Roundoff errors are a potential problem. The single precision real number representation for many computers cannot distinguish between the value 2.0 and 1.9999999. Subtracting .0000001 from 2.0 results in 2.0. Similarly, adding the value .0000001 to 2.0 gives 2.0. The denominator eventually goes to 0, causing a divide by 0 error.

LIMIT OF AN INFINITE SEQUENCE

Determine the limit of

$$(x + 1/x)/(2x - 1/x)$$

as x approaches infinity. The following program evaluates this limit for $x = 1, 10, 100$, etc.:

```
main()      /* SEQ4 -- Limit of infinite sequence */
  {
      double
        x,          /* Argument of function */
        y;          /* Result y = f(x) */
      int
        i;          /* Loop control variable */

      /* Initial message */
      printf("\nProgram SEQ4\n");
      printf("\nEstimate the limit\n");
      printf("of the function\n");
      printf("(x+1/x)/(2x-1/x)\n");
      printf("as x approaches infinity.\n");

      /* Generate table */
      printf("\nx      f(x)\n");
      x = 1.0;
      for (i = 1; i <= 8; i++)
        {
            y = (x + 1.0 / x) / (2.0 * x - 1.0 / x);
            printf("%12.6le %12.7lf\n", x, y);
            x = x * 10.0;
        }

      /* Final message */
      printf("\nEnd of program SEQ4\n");
  }
```

The test run follows:

```
Program SEQ4

Estimate the limit
of the function
(x+1/x)/(2x-1/x)
as x approaches infinity.

x               f(x)
   1.000000E0   2.0000000
   1.000000E1    .5075377
   1.000000E2    .5000750
   1.000000E3    .5000008
   1.000000E4    .5000000
   1.000000E5    .5000000
   1.000000E6    .5000000
   1.000000E7    .5000000

End of program SEQ4
```

SERIES

A sequence is a succession of terms formed by a fixed rule. A series is the sum of the terms of a sequence. The sum of the sequence 1, 2, . . . , 5 is the series

$$1 + 2 + 3 + 4 + 5 = 15.$$

The sum of the infinite series

$$1 + 1/2 + 1/4 + 1/8 + \ldots$$

is 2.0. In this case the infinite series converges to a finite value. Not all infinite series have a finite limit. The infinite series

$$1 + 2 + 3 + 4 + \ldots$$

does not have a finite limit.

FINITE SERIES

The simple series giving the sum of the successive integers has the value 15 for its first five terms. The following program evaluates this finite series:

```
main()      /* SERIES1 -- Sum of first few integers */
  {
      int
        number,  /* Upper limit */
        value,   /* Current limit */
        sum;     /* Sum of the integers */

      /* Initial message */
      printf("\nProgram SERIES1\n");
      printf("\nCompute the sum\n");
      printf("of the first\n");
      printf("few integers.\n");

      /* Generate table */
      printf("\nTerm    Sum\n");
      number = 5;
      sum    = 0;
      for (value = 1; value <= number; value++)
        {
          sum += value;
          printf("%3d    %5d\n", value, sum);
        }

      /* Final message */
      printf("\n End of program SERIES1\n");
        }
```

The test run follows:

```
Program SERIES1

Compute the sum
of the first
few integers.

Term    Sum
  1       1
  2       3
  3       6
  4      10
  5      15

End of program SERIES1
```

FUTURE VALUE OF REGULAR DEPOSITS

Many pension plans consist of regular deposits by employers or employees into a savings account held in trust until retirement. One question concerns the future value at the end of a specified number of years. What will the future accumulated value be at the end of 20 years if an employee deposits $50.00 monthly? Assume an interest rate of 12.5 percent compounded monthly at the time of deposit.

The following program evaluates plans consisting of regular deposits:

```
main()      /* SERIES2 -- Future value of annuity */
  {
      double
        interest,               /* Annual interest rate */
        rate,                   /* Monthly interest multiplier */
        deposit,                /* Monthly deposit */
        future;                 /* Future value of annuity */
      int
        number,                 /* Number of monthly deposits */
        current;                /* Current month*/

      /* Initial message */
      printf("\nProgram SERIES2\n");
      printf("\nCompute the future value\n");
      printf("of regular deposits into\n");
      printf("a savings account.\n");

      /* Problem parameters */
      printf("\nSize of regular monthly deposit ? ");
      scanf("%lf", &deposit);
      printf("Number of monthly deposits     ? ");
      scanf("%d", &number);
      printf("Interest rate (per cent)       ? ");
      scanf("%lf", &interest);

      /* Process */
      rate   = 1.0 + interest / 1200.0;
      future = 0.0;
      for (current = 1; current <= number; current++)
        future = (future + deposit) * rate;
      printf("\nFuture value    %12.2lf\n", future);
```

```
    /* Final message */
    printf("\nEnd of program SERIES2\n");
}
```

A sample test run follows:

```
Program SERIES2

Compute the future value
of regular deposits into
a savings account.

Size of regular monthly deposit ? 50.00
Number of monthly deposits      ? 240
Interest rate (per cent)        ? 12.5

Future value                53475.98

End of program SERIES2
```

INFINITE SERIES

Consider the infinite series

$$1 + 1/2 + 1/4 + 1/8 \ldots$$

which has $1/2^n$ as its nth term (assuming 1 is the 0th term). Does this infinite series have a finite value? If so, what is its value? The following program computes the sum of the terms of the series for the first few terms:

```
main()      /* SERIES3 -- Infinite series */
  {
     int
       number,            /* Number of terms */
       counter;           /* Loop control variable */
     double
       value,             /* Value of the current term */
       sum;               /* Sum of the terms */

     /* Initial message */
     printf("\nProgram SERIES3\n");
```

```
    printf("\nEstimate the value of the infinite\n");
    printf("series 1 + 1/2 + 1/4 + 1/8 + . . .\n");
    printf("for the first few terms.\n");

    /* Process */
    printf("\nTerm     Sum\n");
    number = 10;
    value  = 2.0;
    sum    = 0.0;
    for (counter = 1; counter <= number; counter++)
      {
         value = value / 2.0;
         sum += value;
         printf("%3d     %12.8lf\n", counter, sum);
      }

    /* Final message */
    printf("\nEnd of program SERIES3\n");
}
```

A sample test run follows:

```
Program SERIES3

     Estimate the value of the infinite
     series 1 + 1/2 + 1/4 + 1/8 + . . .
     for the first few terms.

     Term     Sum
       1        1.00000000
       2        1.50000000
       3        1.75000000
       4        1.87500000
       5        1.93750000
       6        1.96875000
       7        1.98437500
       8        1.99218750
       9        1.99609375
      10        1.99804688

     End of program SERIES3
```

The limit of the infinite series appers to converge to 2.0.

POWER SERIES ESTIMATE OF EXP (*X*)

The series 1 + 1/2 + 1/4 + 1/8 + . . . is an example of a power series. The *n*th term $1/2^n$ contains a power of 2. The series

$$1 + x + x^2/2 + x^3/3! + x^4/4! + \dots$$

converges to the value e^x. *The* *n*th term $x^n/n!$ is the ratio *x* to the *n*th power divided by n! The value of n! is the product of the first *n* integers.

Recursive formulas simplify the calculation of the successive terms of the series. Multiplying the previous term by the ratio *x*/*n* gives the new term. The value of the series for the first *n* terms is the sum of those terms. The following program uses this recursive method to calculate the individual terms of the series:

```
main()     /* SERIES4 -- Power series estimate of exp(x) */
  {
      int
        number,       /* Number of terms */
        counter;      /* Loop control variable */
      double
        x,            /* Value of x */
        term,         /* Current term in the series */
        sum;          /* Sum of the terms */

      /* Initial message */
      printf("\nProgram SERIES4\n");
      printf("\nEstimate exp(x) using \n");
      printf("power series expansion.\n");

      /* Problem parameters */
      printf("\nMaximum number of terms ? ");
      scanf("%d", &number);
      printf("Value of x     ?");
      scanf("%lf", &x);
```

```
/* Generate table */
printf("\nTerm      Value      Sum\n");
term = 1.0;
sum = 1.0;
for (counter = 1; counter <= number; counter++)
  {
     term *= x / counter;
     sum += term;
     printf("%4d %15.8lf %15.8lf\n",
       counter, term, sum);
  }

/* Final message */
printf("\nEnd of program SERIES4\n/");
  }
```

The following test run estimates e^2:

```
Program SERIES4

Estimate exp(x) using
power series expansion.

Maximum number of terms ? 10
Value of x              ? 2.0
Term      Value          Sum
   1   2.00000000   3.00000000
   2   2.00000000   5.00000000
   3   1.33333333   6.33333333
   4    .66666667   7.00000000
   5    .26666667   7.26666667
   6    .08888889   7.35555556
   7    .02539683   7.38095238
   8    .00634921   7.38730159
   9    .00141093   7.38871252
  10    .00028219   7.38899471

End of program SERIES4
```

The series converges to the value 7.38899 by the tenth term.

Exercises

1. Write a program that computes the first ten terms of the sequence $1/2^n$ for $n = 1, 2, \ldots, 10$.

2. Write a program to estimate the limit of $1/2n$ as n approaches infinity.

3. Write a program to compute the limit of the term

$$(3x^2 - 5x + 4)/(x^2 + 2)$$

as x approaches infinity.

4. Write a program to estimate the limit of the term

$$(x^2 - 16)/(x - 4)^2$$

as x approaches 4.

5. Write a program to determine the limit, if it exists, of the infinite series

$$1/2 - 3/4 + 5/8 - 7/16 + \ldots$$

6. Write a program to estimate the limit, if it exists, of the infinite series

$$x + x/1.15 + x/1.15^2\ x/1.15^3 + \ldots$$

and test using $x = 100.00$.

7. Write a program to estimate the limit, if it exists, of the infinite series

$$1/2 - 4/4 + 9/8 - 16/16 + 25/32 - 36/64 + \ldots$$

The signs alternate and the expression $n^2/2^n$ gives the magnitude of the nth term.

9.2 Numerical Calculus

Differential calculus estimates the slope of the tangent line to a function $f(x)$. Calculus analytically determines the derivative function $f'(x)$, giving the slope of $f(x)$ for every defined value of x.

One of the major applications of integral calculus is finding the area under a curve within a stated interval. Numerical integration divides the interval in a large number of subintervals, estimates the area of each subinterval, and sums the estimated areas.

ESTIMATING THE SLOPE—NUMERICAL DIFFERENTIATION

The computer is a powerful tool for estimating the slope of a function at a point. To estimate the slope of $f(x)$ at the point $x = a$, select two points $x1$ and $x2$ close to the point "a" and evaluate $y1 = f(x1)$ and $y2 = f(x2)$. The equation

$$b = (y1 - y2)/(x1 - x2)$$

is approximately equal to the slope.

Let w be a small incremental value. The equation

$$b = (f(a + w) - f(a))/w$$

is an equivalent approximation of the slope at the point $x = a$. The limit as w approaches 0 is the derivative (slope of tangent line) at that point. This is the righthand limit as the limit $x + a$ approaches x from the right. The equation

$$b = (f(a - w) - f(a))/(-w)$$

gives the lefthand limit as w approaches 0 as it approaches $x = a$ from the left.

The derivative may not always be defined. The function must be defined and continuous at the point in question. The lefthand and righthand limits for the derivative must be equal and finite.

The natural logarithm $ln(x)$ has a derivative $1/x$. The derivative of $ln(x)$ at the point $x = 3$ is 1/3. The program of this section estimates this slope. Estimating the slope of a function is difficult with the computer because it involves the subtraction of values that are almost equal.

Subtracting the value 3.754689 from the value 3.754713 gives the difference .000024. The single precision floating point representation has seven to twelve significant digits, depending on the system. Normalization for addition and subtraction requires aligning the decimal points. In this simple example, each term in the subtraction has seven significant digits. The result has only two significant digits.

Be careful when selecting the interval width for use in estimating the slope of the function. Too broad an interval does not give an accurate estimate of the slope. Too narrow an interval will result in roundoff errors caused by the subtraction of nearly equal quantities.

DEFINITIONAL FORMULA $(Y1 - Y2)/(X1 - X2)$

The following program estimates the derivatives of $ln(x)$ using the definitional formula $(f(x + w) - f(x))/((x + w) - x)$:

```
#include     <math.h>

main()    /* SLOPE1 -- Estimate slope of a function */
  {
      float
        fnc()t,          /* Function f(x) */
        x,               /* Argument x for y = f (x) */
        width,           /* Interval width for estimate */
        value1,          /* Value of f(x) at x */
        value2,          /* Value of f(x+width) */
        slope;           /* Estimated slope of f(x) at x */
      int
        number,          /* Number of interval widths to try */
        counter;         /* Loop control variable */

      /* Initial message */
      printf("\nProgram SLOPE1\n");
      printf("\nEstimate the slope of f(x)\n");
      printf("at a point x using the\n");
      printf("following formula.\n");
      printf("(f(x+w)-f(x))/((x+w)-x)\n");

      /* Problem parameters */
      printf("\nEstimate slope at point x = ? ");
      scanf("%f", &x);
      printf("Number of interval widths     ? ");
      scanf("%d", &number);
```

```
        /* Generate table */
        printf("\nInterval      Estimated\n");
        printf("width        slope\n");
        width  = 1.0;
        value1 = fnc(x);
        for (counter = 1; counter <= number; counter++)
          {
             width  = width / 10.0;
             value2 = fnc(x + width);
             slope  = (value2 - value1) / ((x + width) - x);
        printf("%e     %15.8f\n", width, slope);
          }

        /* Final message */
        printf("\nEnd of program SLOPE1\n");
    }

float fnc(x)               /* Function f(x) */
    float
                x;         /* Argument x for f(x) */

    {
          float
                y;         /* Value y = f(x) */

          y = log(x);
          return (y);
    }
```

A sample test run follows:

```
Program SLOPE1

Estimate the slope of f(x)
at a point x using the
following formula.
(f(x+w)-f(x))/((x+w)-x)

Estimate slope at point x = ? 3.0
Number of interval widths   ? 10
```

Interval width	Estimated slope
1.000000E-1	.32789826
9.999999E-3	.33277273
9.999999E-4	.33330920
9.999999E-5	.33259395
9.999998E-6	.33378604
9.999998E-7	.35762795

Run time error

The value of *w* will eventually approach the value 0 so closely that 3.0 + *w* will give 3.0 exactly because of the finite nature of the computer's floating point number representation. When that happens the denominator $(x + w) - x$ becomes 0 and a divide-by-zero error will result.

ALTERNATE DEFINITIONAL FORMULA

The alternate definitional formula $(f(x + w) - f(x))/w$ avoids dividing by zero, but $x + w$ and x will eventually be equal in a machine that has a finite level of precision. The following program uses this formula:

```
#include     <math.h>

main()      /* SLOPE2 -- Estimate slope of a function */
  {
      float
        fnc(),          /* Function f(x) */
        x,              /* Argument x for y = f (x) */
        width,          /* Interval width for estimate */
        value1,         /* Value of f(x) at x */
        value2,         /* Value of f(x+width) */
        slope;          /* Estimated slope of f(x) at x */
      int
        number,         /* Number of interval widths to try */
        counter;        /* Loop control variable */

      /* Initial message */
      printf("\nProgram SLOPE2\n");
```

```
        printf("\nEstimate the slope of f(x)\n");
        printf("at a point x using the\n");
        printf("following formula.\n");
        printf("(f(x+w)-f(x))/w\n");

        /* Problem parameters */
        printf("\nEstimate slope at point x = ? ");
        scanf("%f", &x);
        printf("Number of interval widths     ? ");
        scanf("%d", &number);

        /* Generate table */
        printf("\nInterval     Estimated\n");
        printf("width        slope\n");
        width  = 1.0;
        value1 = fnc(x);
        for (counter = 1; counter <= number; counter++)
          {
             width  = width / 10.0;
             value2 = fnc(x + width);
             slope  = (value2 - value1) / width;
        printf("%e     %15.8f\n", width, slope);
          }

        /* Final message */
        printf("\nEnd of program SLOPE2\n");
  }

float fnc(x)              /* Function f(x) */
  float
      x;                  /* Argument x for f(x) */
  {
      float
        y;                /* Value y = f(x) */

      y = log(x);
      return  (y);
  }
```

A sample test run follows:

Program SLOPE2

```
Estimate the slope of f(x)
at a point x using the
following formula.
(f(x+w)-f(x))/w

Estimate slope at point x = ? 3.0
Number of interval widths   ? 10

Interval         Estimated
width            slope
1.000000E-1       .32789826
9.999999E-3       .33277273
9.999999E-4       .33330920
9.999999E-5       .33259395
9.999998E-6       .33378604
9.999998E-7       .35762790
9.999998E-8      0.00000000
9.999999E-9      0.00000000
9.999998E-10     0.00000000
9.999998E-11     0.00000000

End of program SLOPE2
```

The interval width becomes successively smaller and the estimate of the slope will eventually become zero.

SINGLE PRECISION ESTIMATE OF SLOPE

The function $f(x) = x^2$ has a derivative function $f'(x) = 2x$. The derivative of $f(x)$ at the point $x = 2$ is $f'(x = 2) = 4$. The following program uses standard precision real numbers with seven significant digits to estimate the slope:

```
#include     <math.h>

main()     /* SLOPE3 -- Estimate slope of a function */
  {
      float
        fnc(),        /* Function f(x) */
        x,            /* Argument x for y = f(x) */
        width,        /* Interval width for estimate */
```

```
        value1,      /* Value of f(x) at x */
        value2,      /* Value of f(x+width) */
        slope;       /* Estimated slope of f(x) at x */
    int
        number,      /* Number of interval widths to try */
        counter;     /* Loop control variable */

    /* Initial message */
    printf("\nProgram SLOPE3\n");
    printf("\nEstimate the slope of f(x)\n");
    printf("at a point x using the\n");
    printf("following formula.\n");
    printf("(f(x+w)-f(x))/w\n");

    /* Problem parameters */
    printf("\nEstimate slope at point x = ? ");
    scanf("%f", &x);
    printf("Number of interval widths    ? ");
    scanf("%d", &number);

    /* Generate table */
    printf("\nInterval      Estimated\n");
    printf("width           slope\n");
    width  = 1.0;
    value1 = fnc(x);
    for (counter = 1; counter <= number; counter++)
      {
        width  = width / 10.0;
        value2 = fnc(x + width);
        slope  = (value2 - value1) / width;
        printf("%e     %15.8f\n", width, slope);
      }

    /* Final message */
    printf("\nEnd of program SLOPE3\n");
}

float fnc(x)     /* Function f(x) */
  float
    x;           /* Argument x for f(x) */
  {
    float
      y;     /* Value y = f(x) */
```

```
        y = x * x;
        return (y);
}
```

The test run follows:

```
Program SLOPE3

Estimate the slope of f(x)
at a point x using the
following formula.
(f(x+w)-f(x))/w

Estimate slope at point x = ? 2.0
Number of interval widths   ? 10

Interval          Estimated
width             slope
1.000000E-1       4.09999847
9.999999E-3       4.01000977
9.999999E-4       4.00114107
9.999999E-5       4.00066423
9.999998E-6       4.00543261
9.999998E-7       3.81469774
9.999998E-8       4.76837206
9.999999E-9       0.00000000
9.999998E-10       0.00000000
9.999998E-11       0.00000000

End of program SLOPE3
```

The best estimate of the slope results from using *w* = .0001.

DOUBLE PRECISION

Double precision floating point provides 16 significant digits for most systems. Many programmers use double precision almost exclusively for scientific applications. The following program uses double precision:

```
#include    <math.h>
```

```
main()      /* SLOPE4 -- Estimate slope of a function */
  {
      double
        fnc(),         /* Function f(x) */
        x,             /* Argument x for y = f(x) */
        width,         /* Interval width for estimate */
        value1,        /* Value of f(x) at x */
        value2,        /* Value of f(x+width) */
        slope;         /* Estimated slope of f(x) at x */
      int
        number,        /* Number of interval widths to try */
        counter;       /* Loop control variable */

      /* Initial message */
      printf("\nProgram SLOPE4\n");
      printf("\nEstimate the slope of f(x)\n");
      printf("at a point x using the\n");
      printf("following formula.\n");
      printf("(f(x+w)-f(x))/w\n");

      /* Problem parameters */
      printf("\nEstimate slope at point x = ? ");
      scanf("%lf", &x);
      printf("Number of interval widths      ? ");
      scanf("%d", &number);

      /* Generate table */
      printf("\nInterval        Estimated\n");
      printf("width           slope\n");
      width  = 1.0;
      value1 = fnc(x);
      for (counter = 1; counter <= number; counter++)
        {
            width  = width / 10.0;
            value2 = fnc(x + width);
            slope  = (value2 - value1) / width;
            printf("%10.5le     %15.8lf\n", width, slope);
        }

      /* Final message */
      printf("\nEnd of program SLOPE4\n");
  }
```

```
double fnc(x)  /* Function f(x) */
  double
      x;        /* Argument x for f(x) */
  {
      double
          y;    /* Value y = f(x) */

      y = x * x;
      return (y);
  }
```

A sample output from this program follows:

```
Program SLOPE4

Estimate the slope of f(x)
at a point x using the
following formula.
(f(x+w)-f(x))/w

Estimate slope at point x = ? 2.0
Number of interval widths   ? 20

Interval        Estimated
width           slope
1.00000E-1      4.10000000
1.00000E-2      4.01000000
1.00000E-3      4.00100000
1.00000E-4      4.00010000
1.00000E-5      4.00001000
1.00000E-6      4.00000100
1.00000E-7      4.00000009
1.00000E-8      3.99999998
1.00000E-9      4.00000033
1.00000E-10       4.00000033
1.00000E-11       4.00000033
1.00000E-12       4.00035560
1.00000E-13       3.99680289
1.00000E-14       4.08562073
1.00000E-15       3.55271368
1.00000E-16       0.00000000
1.00000E-17       0.00000000
```

```
1.00000E-18      0.00000000
1.00000E-19      0.00000000
1.00000E-20      0.00000000

End of program SLOPE4
```

AREA UNDER A CURVE

Integration and differentiation are inverse operations in a similar manner to the inverse operations of multiplication and division. The indefinite integral of the function $f(x)$ is that function which has $f(x)$ as its derivative. There may be a family of functions from which to choose. For example, the functions

$$3x^2 - 2x + 4$$

and

$$3x^2 - 2x + 12$$

both have

$$6x - 2$$

as their derivative function. The constant term is always involved since the derivative of that constant drops out.

A definite integral corresponds to the area under a curve if $f(x)$ is positive throughout the region of interest. Numerical integration requires dividing the region into subintervals and estimating the integral as the sum of the areas of the subintervals. Two approaches commonly introduced in elementary calculus are the trapezoid method and Simpson's method.

The function

$$f(x) = x^2 - 3x + 7$$

has

$$(1/3)x^3 - (3/2)^2 + 7X + C$$

as its integral. The definite integral between the limits 1 and 2 is 4.83333333. The two programs of this section use numerical methods to estimate this definite integral.

TRAPEZOID METHOD

A trapezoid has two sides of unequal length. The area of the trapezoid is the width times the average length. Dividing the region of interest into n subintervals results in n trapezoids having a total of $n + 1$ boundaries. The function $f(x)$ gives the lengths of the sides of the trapezoids. Each trapezoid has the same width.

If $f1$ is the length of the lefthand side, $f2$ is the length of the righthand side, and w is the subinterval width, the formula $w(f1 + f2)/2$ gives the area of the trapezoid. The righthand boundary of one trapezoid is also the lefthand boundary of the following trapezoid. All except the leftmost and rightmost boundaries appear twice.

It is more efficient to multiply by the width after forming the sums of the sides of the trapezoids. The following program uses this more efficient computational procedure:

```
main()     /* AREA1 -- Trapezoid rule */
  {
     double
       fnc(),        /* Function f(x) */
       lower,        /* Lefthand boundary */
       upper,        /* Righthand boundary */
       width,        /* Subinterval width */
       x,            /* Value of x for f(x) */
       sum,          /* Sum of the ordinates f(x) */
       area;         /* Estimated area */
     int
       number,       /* Number of subintervals */
       counter;      /* Loop control variable */

     /* Initial message */
     printf("\nProgram AREA1\n");
     printf("\nEstimate area under f(x)\n");
     printf("using trapezoid method.\n");

     /* Problem parameters */
     printf("\nLower limit for x          ? ");
     scanf("%lf", &lower);
     printf("Upper limit for x          ? ");
```

```
        scanf("%lf", &upper);
        printf("Number of subintervals ? ");
        scanf("%d", &number);

        /* Process */
        width = (upper - lower) / number;
        sum   = 0.0;
        x     = lower;
        for (counter = 1; counter < number; counter++)
          {
             x += width;
             sum += fnc(x);
          }
        sum += 0.5 * (fnc(lower) + fnc(upper));
        area = sum * width;
        printf("\nEstimated area = %15.9lf\n", area);

        /* Final message */
        printf("\nEnd of program AREA1\n");
  }

double fnc(x)  /* Function f(x) */
  double
        x;       /* Argument x */
  {
        double
            y;  /* Result y = f(x) */

        y = x * x - 3.0 * x + 7.0;
        return (y);
  }
```

The test run follows:

```
Program AREA1

Estimate area under f(x)
using trapezoid method.

Lower limit for x        ? 1.0
Upper limit for x        ? 2.0
Number of subintervals ? 100
```

```
Estimated area =       4.833350000

End of program AREA1
```

The integral of 4.83335 agrees closely with the known solution.

SIMPSON'S METHOD

Simpson's method provides a more refined method of numerically estimating the definite integral. The method involves fitting a parabolic curve to the three points defined by the midpoint and the two boundaries.

Let *w* be the width between the midpoint and either of the two boundaries. The formula

$$(f(L) + 4f(M) + f(U))w/3$$

gives the area of one of the trapezoids. *L* is the first side, *U* is the upper side, and *M* is the midpoint.

The following program uses Simpson's method for numerical integration:

```
main()     /* AREA2 -- Simpson's rule */
  {
       double
         fnc(),          /* Function f(x) */
         lower,          /* Lefthand boundary */
         upper,          /* Righthand boundary */
         width,          /* Subinterval width */
         x,              /* Value of x for f(x) */
         sum,            /* Sum of the ordinates f(x) */
         area;           /* Estimated area */
       int
         number,         /* Number of subintervals */
         counter;        /* Loop control variable */

       /* Initial message */
       printf("\nProgram AREA2\n);
       printf("\nEstimate area under f(x)\n");
       printf("using Simpson's method.\n");
```

```
        /* Problem parameters */
        printf("\nLower limit for x           ? ");
        scanf("%lf", &lower);
        printf("Upper limit for x           ? ");
        scanf("%lf", &upper);
        printf("Number of subintervals ? ");
        scanf("%d", &number);

        /* Process */
        width = 0.5 * (upper - lower) / number;
        sum   = 0.0;
        x     = lower - width;
        for (counter = 1; counter <= number; counter++)
          {
            x += 2.0 width;
            sum += fnc(x - width) + 4.0 * fnc(x)
                        + fnc(x + width);
          }
        area = sum * width / 3.0;
        printf("\nEstimated area = %15.9lf\n", area);

        /* Final message */
        printf("\nEnd of program AREA2\n");
    }

double fnc(x)        /* Function f(x) */
  double
        x;           /* Argument x */
  {
        double
            y;       /* Result y = f(x) */

      y = x * x - 3.0 * x + 7.0;
      return (y);
  }
```

The test run follows:

```
Program AREA2

Estimate area under f(x)
using Simpson's method.
```

```
Lower limit for x          ? 1.0
Upper limit for x          ? 2.0
Number of subintervals ? 10

Estimated area =        4.833333333

End of program AREA2
```

Exercises

1. Write a program to estimate the derivative of the function

$$3/(1 + 2x^2)$$

at the point $x = 2$.

2. Write a program to estimate the derivative of the function

$$26 - 2x + 4x^2$$

at the point $x = 1.5$.

3. Write a program using the trapezoid method to integrate the following function in the interval $-2 \leq x \leq 2$:

$$x(2x + x^2)$$

4. Write a program using Simpson's method to integrate the function of exercise 3.

9.3 Matrix Operations

A matrix is a table of numeric values. Common matrix operations include matrix transposition, multiplication, and inversion. The matrix

1	2	3
4	5	6

contains two rows and three columns.

MATRIX TRANSPOSITION

Transposition exchanges columns with rows of the matrix. The first row becomes the first column of the transpose, the second row becomes the second column, etc. The matrix

1	4
2	5
3	6

is the transpose of the previous matrix.

MATRIX PROGRAMS USING STANDARD FILES

The programs of this section accept matrices defined in a standard manner. The first elements are of two integers giving the number of rows and the number of columns contained in the matrix. The floating point values of the matrix follow on a row-by-row basis.

The matrix

1	2	3
4	5	6

is stored in a file in the following manner:

```
2 6
1.0
2.0
3.0
4.0
5.0
6.0
```

PROGRAM TO TRANSPOSE A MATRIX

The following program transposes a matrix obtained from the standard input device and sends the result to the standard output device:

```
main()     /* MATRIX1 -- Matrix transposition */
  {
     double
       matrix[50][50];
     int
       nrows,      /* Number of rows */
       ncols,      /* Number of columns */
       i,          /* Subscript */
       j;          /* Subscript */
```

```
/* Load matrix */
scanf("%d %d", &nrows; &ncols);
for (i = 0; i < nrows; i++)
        for (j = 0; j < ncols; j++)
          scanf("%lf", &matrix[i]
        [j];

        /* Store transpose */
        printf("%2d %2d\n", ncols, nrows);
        for (j = 0; j < ncols; j++)
           for (i = 0; i < nrows; i++)
              printf("%lf\n", matrix[i][j]);
  }
```

The disk file contents

```
2 3
27.5
15.8
21.3
24.9
12.3
18.4
```

represent the following matrix:

27.5	15.8	21.3
24.9	12.3	18.4

Output from the matrix transposition program follows:

```
 3  2
27.500000
24.900000
15.800000
12.300000
21.300000
18.400000
```

The output represents the matrix:

27.5	24.9
15.8	12.3
21.3	18.4

IDENTITY MATRIX

A square matrix has the same number of columns as rows. An identity matrix is a square matrix having the value 1.0 for each main diagonal element and 0.0 elsewhere. The matrix

$$\begin{matrix} 1.0 & 0.0 & 0.0 \\ 0.0 & 1.0 & 0.0 \\ 0.0 & 0.0 & 1.0 \end{matrix}$$

is an identity matrix having three rows and three columns.

The following program requests the size of the square matrix and generates a file of values representing the identity matrix:

```
main()     /* MATRIX2 -- Identity matrix */
 {
      int
         nrows,
         i,
         j;

 scanf("%d", &nrows);
 printf("%2d %2d\n", nrows, nrows);
 for (i = 0; i < nrows; i++)
      for (j = 0; j < nrows; j++)
         if (i == j)
            printf("%4.1f\n", 1.0);
         else
            printf("%4.1f\n", 0.0);
 }
```

An identity matrix has an equal number of rows and columns. The only input is the size of the square matrix. The output includes parameters for the number of rows and the number of columns to maintain compatibility with the other programs of this section.

The following output represents a three-row by three-column identity matrix:

```
3  3
1.0
0.0
```

0.0
0.0
1.0
0.0
0.0
0.0
1.0

MATRIX MULTIPLICATION

Matrix multiplication computes the value x_{ij} for the product matrix as the sum of the products of the *i*th row of the first matrix and the *j*th column of the second. The number of columns of the first matrix must equal the number of rows of the second. The product matrix has the same number of rows as the first matrix and the same number of columns as the second.

Let

1	2	3
4	5	6

be the first matrix and

1	4
2	5
3	6

the second.

The matrix

14	32
32	77

results from the matrix multiplication.

MATRIX MULTIPLICATION PROGRAM

The matrix multiplication program accepts the first and second matrices from the standard input device. Most operating systems include the ability to concatenate files. Concatenating the first two matrices gives the following data file contents:

```
2 3
1.0
2.0
3.0
4.0
5.0
6.0
3 2
1.0
4.0
2.0
5.0
3.0
6.0
```

The following program accepts two matrices from the standard input device and places their product on the standard output device:

```
main()      /* MATRIX3 -- Matrix multiplication */
  {
     double
       first[50][50],         /* First matrix */
       second[50][50],        /* Second matrix */
       sum;                   /* Sum of products */
     int
       nrowsf,                /* Number of rows of first */
       ncolsf,                /* Number of columns of first */
       nrowss,                /* Number of rows of second */
       ncolss,                /* Number of columns of second */
       i, j, k;               /* Subscripts */

     /* Load first matrix */
     scanf("%d %d", &nrowsf, &ncolsf);
     for (i = 0; i < nrowsf; i++)
       for (j = 0; j < ncolsf; j++)
         scanf("%lf", &first[i][j]);

     /* Load second matrix */
     scanf("%d %d", &nrowss, &ncolss);
     for (i = 0; i < nrowss; i++)
       for (j = 0; j < ncolss; j++)
         scanf("%lf", &second[i][j]);
```

```
        /* Matrix multiplication */
        if (ncolsf != nrowss)
          printf("Nonconformable matrices\n");
        else
          {
            printf("%2d %2d\n", nrowsf, ncolss);
            for (i = 0; i < nrowsf; i++)
              for (j = 0; j < ncolss; j++)
                {
                  sum = 0.0;
                  for (k = 0; k < ncolsf; k++)
                    sum += first[i][k] * second[k][j];
                  printf("%lf\n", sum);
                }
          }
}
```

The output follows:

```
 2  2
14.000000
32.000000
32.000000
77.000000
```

MATRIX INVERSION

The inverse of the square matrix A is matrix A' for which the identity matrix I results. The matrix products AA' and A'A both give the identity matrix. Some square matrices do not have an inverse and are said to be singular. A determinant of zero signifies a singular matrix, and a determinant that is very close to zero warns of possible singularity. Problems having determinants near zero have the greatest roundoff errors.

The operations of transposition and multiplication are straightforward, but inverting a matrix is not. The matrix inversion program of this chapter uses the well-known Gaussian elimination method. The program uses several adjustments from the textbook methods to improve computational efficiency.

The program uses double precision values for the matrix, giving 16 significant digits of precision. The program selects the remaining row having the largest potential pivot element as the next pivot row. The swapping of rows takes place logically within a vector of row indices. Picking the best pivot row for each iteration reduces the roundoff error problem.

Many textbooks illustrating the Gaussian elimination procedure keep an identity matrix with the matrix being inverted. The identity matrix is excess baggage; it requires unnecessary memory and increases the computational effort required to invert the matrix. The matrix inversion program does not use memory for the identity matrix.

MATRIX INVERSION PROGRAM

The following program accepts a square matrix from the standard input device and inverts it:

```
main()      /* MATRIX4 -- Matrix inversion */
  {
     double
       fabs(),
       matrix[50][50],
       row[50],            /* Pivot row elements */
       col[50],            /* Pivot column elements */
       det,                /* Determinant */
       pivot,              /* Pivot value */
       temp;               /* Temporary value */
     int
       lrow[50],           /* Location vector for rows */
       size,               /* Size of matrix, rows = columns */
       ltemp,              /* Temporary value */
       ipivot,             /* Pivot row and column index */
       lpivot,             /* Location of pivot row */
       irow,               /* Row index */
       jcol,               /* Row index */
       i,                  /* Subscript */
       j;                  /* Subscript */

     /* Load matrix */
     scanf("%d", &size);
```

```
for (i = 0; i < size; i++)
   for (j = 0; j < size; j++)
      scanf("%lf", &matrix[i][j]);

/* Initialize row index */
for (i = 0; i < size; i++)
      lrow[i] = i;

/* Gaussian elimination */
det = 1.0;
for (ipivot = 0; ipivot < size; ipivot++)
   {

      /* Select pivot row */
      pivot = 0.0;
      for (i = ipivot; < size; i++)
         {
            j      = lrow[i];
            temp = matrix[j][ipivot];
            if (fabs(temp) > fabs(pivot))
               {
                  irow  = i;
                  pivot = temp;
               }
         }
      lpivot = lrow[irow];

      /* Save pivot column */
      for (i = 0; i < size; i++)
         }
            col[i] = matrix[i][ipivot];
            matrix[i][ipivot] = 0.0;
         }
      matrix[lpivot][ipivot] = 1.0;

      /* Check for singularity */
      det *= pivot;
      if (fabs(det) < 1.0e-14)
         break;

      /* Transform pivot row */
      ltemp       = lrow[ipivot];
```

```
            lrow[ipivot] = lrow[irow];
            lrow[irow]   = ltemp;
            for (j = 0; j < size; j++)
              {
                row[j] = matrix[lpivot][j] / pivot;
                matrix[lpivot][j] = row[j];
              }

            /* Sweep matrix */
            for (i = 0; i < size; i++)
              {
                if (i != lpivot)
                  {
                    temp = col[i];
                    for (j = 0; j < size; j++)
                      matrix[i][j] += -temp * row[j];
                  }
              }
  }     /* End of Gaussian elimination */

        /* Output inverse matrix */
        if (fabs(det) <= 1.0e-14)
          printf("Singular matrix\n");
        else
          {
            printf("%2d %2d\n", size, size);
            for (i = 0; i < size; i++)
              {
                irow = lrow[i];
                for (j = 0; j < size; j++)
                  {
                    jcol = lrow[j];
                    printf("%lf\n", matrix[irow][jcol]);
                  }
              }
            printf("Determinant = %lf\n", det);
          }
  }
```

The file

```
2 2
4.0
```

```
2.0
2.0
4.0
```

represents the following matrix:

4.0	2.0
2.0	4.0

The matrix inversion program gives the output file

```
2  2
.333333
-.166667
-.166667
.333333
Determinant = 12.000000
```

representing the inverse matrix:

.333333	−.166667
−.166667	.333333

The determinant is 12.0. Roundoff errors should not be a problem unless the determinant is a fractional number close to zero.

MATRIX OUTPUT IN TABLE FORM

The following program accepts a matrix from the standard input device and formats it for output in the appropriate table form:

```
main()     /* MATRIX5 -- List contents of matrix */
  {
     double
       value;                    /* Current value */
     int
       nrows,                    /* Number of rows */
       ncols,                    /* Number of columns */
       i,                        /* Subscript */
       j;                        /* Subscript */
```

```
       scanf("%d %d", &nrows, &ncols);
       for (i = 0; i < nrows; i++)
         {
           for (j = 0; j < ncols; j++)
             {
               scanf("%lf", &value);
               printf("%15.8lf", value);
             }
           printf("\n");
         }
}
```

The file

```
2  3
27.3425
15.9215
21.4561
19.2349
17.2167
25.2163
```

represents a matrix having two rows and three columns. The program formats the matrix as follows:

```
    27.34250000    15.92150000    21.45610000
    19.23490000    17.21670000    25.21630000
```

Exercises

1. Implement a matrix multiplication program and use it to multiply the matrix

12.0	15.0	11.0
19.0	14.0	12.0

by the matrix

71.0
55.0
89.0

2. Implement the matrix inversion program of this section to invert the matrix

16.7	19.1	25.4
27.5	22.8	19.3
30.4	26.2	17.5

9.4 Simultaneous Linear Equations

The following is an example of a simple linear equation:

$$2x = 50.$$

The solution is $x = 25$. The following is a set of two simultaneous linear equations in two unknowns:

$$4x + 2y = 60$$
$$2x + 4y = 48.$$

The solution is the value for x and the value for y which jointly satisfy both equations. If the solution exists, it is unique. There will be no more than one set of solution values.

Elementary linear algebra presents a step-by-step procedure for solving sets of linear simultaneous equations. The first step is to place the coefficients into a matrix exactly as they appear in the equations. The matrix

4	2	60
2	4	48

contains the coefficients.

An identity matrix has the values 1 down the diagonal and zeros off the diagonal. The matrix

1	0
0	1

is an identity matrix. Multiplying any row by a constant gives an equivalent matrix with the same solution values. Subtracting a constant multiple of one row from another row also gives a matrix having the same solution values. Exchanging two rows leaves the solution values unchanged.

The step-by-step procedure uses these three row operations to generate an identity matrix in the first n columns.

When completed, the righthand column will contain the solution values for the unknowns.

Divide the first row by 4 to place the value 1 in the upper lefthand corner. The matrix

$$\begin{matrix} 1 & .5 & 15 \\ 2 & 4 & 48 \end{matrix}$$

results. Subtract 2 times the first row from the second row to force a 0 in the lower lefthand corner. The matrix

$$\begin{matrix} 1 & .5 & 15 \\ 0 & 3 & 18 \end{matrix}$$

results. The first column is the desired first column of the identity matrix.

Divide the second row by 3 to place the 1 in its appropriate position in the identity matrix. The matrix

$$\begin{matrix} 1 & .5 & 15 \\ 0 & 1 & 6 \end{matrix}$$

results. Subtract 2 times the second row from the first row to place a 0 in its appropriate position in the second column. The matrix

$$\begin{matrix} 1 & 0 & 12 \\ 0 & 1 & 6 \end{matrix}$$

results. The identity matrix is complete; the first solution value is $x = 12$ and the second is $y = 6$.

Substituting these values in the original equations gives

$$4x + 2y = 4 \times 12 + 2 \times 6 = 60$$

and

$$2x + 4y = 2 \times 12 + 4 \times 6 = 48$$

The solution values are $x = 12$ and $y = 6$.

During the identity matrix development, there may be a 0 where a 1 belongs. Exchanging that row with another row farther down in the matrix is required if a row can be found which has a nonzero value in the needed column. If no such row is available, the system of equations has no solution.

The pivot value is that value used as a divisor to force the value 1 where it should be. The determinant of the matrix is the product of the pivot values. If a nonzero pivot is not available, the determinant is 0, indicating that there is no solution. A determinant almost equal to zero may indicate roundoff error problems.

PROGRAM FOR SOLVING SIMUTANEOUS LINEAR EQUATIONS

The following program uses the step-by-step procedure to solve systems of simultaneous liner equations:

```
/* Matrix 6 -- Simultaneous equations */
double
  matrix[50][51],          /* Problem coefficients */
  det;                     /* Determinant */
int
  size;                    /* Number of equations */
char
  singular;                /* Flag indicating singularity */

main()     /* Main routine */
  {
     parameters();         /* Load problem parameters */
     solve();              /* Solve equations */
     if (singular == 'N')
       output();
  }

parameters()               /* Load problem parameters */
  {
     int
       row,                /* Row subscript */
       col;                /* Column subscript */

     scanf("%d", &size);
     for (row = 0; row < size; row++)
       for (col = 0; col <= size; col++)
         scanf("%lf", &matrix[row][col]);
  }
```

```
solve()                      /* Solve equations */
  {
     double
        fabs(),              /* Absolute value function */
        temp,                /* Temporary value for exchange */
        pivot                /* Pivot element */
        mult;                /* Multiplier for sweep */
     int
        loc,                 /* Location of largest coefficient */
        i,                   /* Subscript */
        j,                   /* Subscript */
        k;                   /* Subscript */

     det = 1.0;
     singular = 'N';
     k = 0;

     while ((k < size) && (singular == 'N'))
        {
           /* Search for largest magnitude */
           loc = k;
           for (i = k; i < size; i++)
              if (fabs(matrix[i][k] > fabs(matrix[loc][k]))
                 loc = i;

           /* Exchange rows */
           for (j = k; j < size; j++)
              {
                 temp = matrix[k][j];
                 matrix[k][j] = matrix[loc][j];
                 matrix[loc][j] = temp;
              }

           /* Calculate determinant */
           pivot = Matrix[k][k];
           det *= pivot;
           if (fabs(det) < 1.0e-14)
              {
                 printf("No solution\n");
                 singular = 'Y':
                 break;
              }
```

```
            /* Transform augmented matrix */
            for (j = k; j <= size; j++)
              matrix[k][j] *= 1 / pivot;
            for (i = 0; i < size; i++)
              {
                if (i != k)
                  {
                      mult = matrix[i][k];
                      for (j = k; j <= size; j++)
                        matrix[i][j] += -mult * matrix[k][j];
                  }
              }

            /* Update pivot column */
            k++;
          }
  }
output()                        /* Output results */
  {
      int
        row;                    /* Row subscript */

      printf("%2d %2d\n", size, 1);
      for (row = 0; row < size; row++)
        printf("lf\n", matrix[row][size]);
      printf("Determinant     %lf\n", det);
  }
```

The following file contains the problem coefficients:

```
2 3
4.0
2.0
60.0
2.0
4.0
48.0
```

The following output results:

```
 2  1
12.000000
```

6.000000
Determinant 12.000000

The value for the first unknown is 12.0 and the value for the second is 6.0. The determinant of 12.0 suggests the absence of significant roundoff errors.

Exercises

1. Use the program of this section to solve the following system of equations:

$$\begin{aligned} 6x + 5y - 4z &= 124 \\ x - 4y + 2z &= 200 \\ 3x + y + 3z &= 125. \end{aligned}$$

2. Use the program of this section to solve the following system of equations:

$$\begin{aligned} 12x + 19y &= 2520 \\ 24x + 11y &= 3186. \end{aligned}$$

10

Data Analysis

The computer is a powerful tool for data analysis. Summary measures describe important characteristics, and frequency distributions show the shape of the data. The primary goal of data analysis is the prediction of values of one variable on the basis of its association with another variable.

Many programs are interactive, with data entry from the keyboard at run time. Other programs process data contained in disk data files. The C programming language provides standard input from the keyboard which can be redirected to a disk file. Standard output can be the video screen, printer, or another disk file. The programs of this section use standard I/O.

10.1 Summary Measures

Summary measures include the mean and the standard deviation. The arithmetic mean is the average. The mean of the set of values

$$12 \quad 11 \quad 19 \quad 14 \quad 15$$

is the sum

$$71 = 12 + 11 + 19 + 14 + 15$$

divided by the number of values. The expression

$$14.2 = 71/5$$

gives the mean.

The mean divides the total equally among the parts. Five commune members pool their resources of \$12, \$11, \$19, \$14, and \$15, respectively. Their total resources amount to \$71.00. Dividing the total \$71.00 equally among the five members nets \$14.20 each.

The variance of a set of data is the average squared deviation of the values around the mean. The standard deviation is the square root of the variance. Statisticians define two variances and two standard deviations. The population variance for a finite population of size N uses the divisor N for computing the average squared deviation. For a sample of size n, the sample variance requires the divisor $n - 1$.

FORMULAS

For a finite population of size N, the formula

$$\mu = (\Sigma x)/N$$

gives the population mean μ, and the formula

$$\sigma^2 = \Sigma(x - \mu)^2/N$$

gives the population variance. The standard deviation σ is the square root of the variance.

For a sample of size n, the formula

$$m = (\Sigma x)/n$$

gives the sample mean m, and the formula

$$s^2 = \Sigma(X - m)^2/(n - 1)$$

gives the sample variance. Again, the sample standard deviation is the square root of the variance.

The two variance formulas are not in a convenient form. The alternate formula

$$\sigma^2 = (\Sigma x^2)/N - \mu^2$$

gives the population variance. The similar alternate formula

$$s^2 = (\Sigma x^2 - (\Sigma x)^2/n)/(n - 1)$$

gives the sample variance.

SAMPLE MEAN AND STANDARD DEVIATION

Five batteries give the following hours of service:

12 11 19 14 15.

Compute the sample mean and standard deviation for the hours of service. The following program computes the sample mean and sample standard deviation:

```
#include     <math.h>

main()     /* STAT1 -- Sample mean and std dev */
  {
      int
        number,        /* Number of observations */
        counter;       /* Loop control variable */
      double
        value,         /* Current value */
        sum,           /* Sum of the values */
        sumsqr,        /* Sum of the squares */
        mean,          /* Arithmetic mean */
        std;           /* Standard deviation */

      /* Process */
      scanf("%d", &number);
      sum    = 0.0;
      sumsqr = 0.0;
      for (counter = 1; counter <= number; counter++)
        {
           scanf("%lf", &value);
           sum    += value;
           sumsqr += value * value;
        }

      /* Compute measures */
      mean = sum / number;
      std = sqrt((sumsqr - sum * / number)
                / (number - 1.0));

      /* Output */
      printf("\nNumber of values     %4d\n", number);
      printf("Mean      %15.8lf\n", mean);
      printf("Standard deviation     %15.8lf\n", std);
  }
```

The data file contains an integer value giving the number of items followed by the floating point values. The test data follows:

```
5
12.1
11.3
19.5
14.2
15.8
```

The output follows:

```
Number of values      5
Mean                   14.58000000
Standard deviation      3.26909773
```

The sample mean is 14.58 and the sample standard deviation is 3.269.

INTERPRETATION OF STANDARD DEVIATION

The mean is an average which divides the total equally. The mean is the "center of gravity" of the data. The variance is the average squared deviation around the center of gravity. The variance is the "moment of inertia" of the data. If most of the data is close to the center of gravity, it has low inertia. If most of the data is at the extreme limits, it has high inertia, like a flywheel with a heavily weighted rim.

The largest concentration of values for most problems is around the center of gravity. For such bell-shaped distributions, 68 percent of the values will fall within one standard deviation of the mean and 95 percent within two standard deviations.

If, for example, battery service life means and standard deviations are representative, then about 68 percent of the batteries should last within 3.27 hours of the mean of 14.6 hours. About 95 percent of the batteries should last 14.6 ± 6.54 hours.

SAMPLE AND POPULATION MEASURES

The purpose of statistical analysis is usually to generalize from a small sample to a larger population. It is to draw valid conclusions on the basis of sample evidence. A census consists of the entire population; population measures are appropriate for census data.

A statistician may interpret a set of data as a sample in one study and a population in another. At times, the sample standard deviation is required, while at other times the population standard deviation is needed. For large sets of data, there is no practical numerical difference between the two measures.

The following program computes the minimum and maximum values, the mean, population variance, population standard deviation, sample variance, and sample standard deviation for a set of data:

```
#include     <math.h>

main()     /* STAT2--Summary measures */
  {
      int
         number,         /* Number of values */
         counter;        /* Loop control variable */
      double
         value,          /* Current value */
         minimum,        /* Minimum value */
         maximum,        /* Maximum value */
         sum,            /* Sum of the values */
         sumsqr,         /* Sum of the squares */
         mean,           /* Arithmetic mean */
         popvar,         /* Population variance */
         popstd,         /* Population standard deviation */
         samvar,         /* Sample variance */
         samstd;         /* Samle standard deviation */

      /* Initial message */
      printf("\nProgram STAT2\n");
      printf("\nCompute summary measures\n");
      printf("for a set of data.\n");
```

```
    /* Initialize */
    scanf("%d", &number);
    sum       = 0.0;
    sumsqr    = 0.0;
    minimum   = 1.0e30;
    maximum   = -1.0e30;

    /* Process */
    for (counter = 1; counter <= number; counter++)
      {
         scanf("%lf", &value);
         sum     += value;
         sumsqr  += value * value;
         if (value < minimum)
           minimum = value;
         if (value > maximum)
           maximum = value;
      }

    /* Compute measures */
    mean    = sum / number;
    popvar  = sumsqr / number - mean * mean;
    popstd  = sqrt(popvar);
    samvar  = (sumsqr - sum * sum / number) / (number - 1.0);
    samstd  = sqrt(samvar);

    /* Output */
    printf("\nNumber of values      %4d\n", number);
    printf("Minimum               %15.8lf\n", minimum);
    printf("Maximum               %15.8lf\n", maximum);
    printf("Sample\n");
    printf("Variance              %15.8lf\n", samvar);
    printf("Std dev               %15.8lf\n", samstd);
    printf("Population\n");
    printf("Variance              %15.8lf\n", popvar);
    printf("Std dev               %15.8lf\n", popstd);
    printf("\nEnd of program STAT2\n");
}
```

A test file follows:

```
5
12.0
```

11.0
19.0
14.0
15.0

The output follows:

Program STAT2

Compute summary measures
for a set of data.

Number of values	5
Minimum	11.00000000
Maximum	19.00000000
Sample	
Variance	9.70000000
Std dev	3.11448230
Population	
Variance	7.76000000
Std dev	2.78567766

End of program STAT2

TABULATING FREQUENCIES

A frequency distribution gives the distribution of the data values. Where do most of the values fall? How many fall to the far right and to the far left?

The first step is to divide the range of values into classes. The second step is to tally the frequencies by counting the number of values that fall into each class. Class boundaries separate the classes, and if possible, they should uniquely separate the classes. Use boundaries similar to 9.5, 19.5, 29.5 for values recorded to the nearest whole number. Use boundaries such as 24.995 and 29.995 for data recorded to the nearest hundredth. Class widths should be equal.

FREQUENCY DISTRIBUTION

The following program forms a frequency distribution for a set of data:

```
main()     /* Tabulate frequency distribution */
  {
      int
        table[50],         /* Tale of frequencies */
        class,             /* Class index */
        lower,             /* Lowest class index */
        upper,             /* Highest class index */
        sum,               /* Cumulative frequency */
        number,            /* Number of values */
        counter;           /* Loop control variable */
      double
        value,             /* Current value */
        lowest,            /* Value of lowest boundary */
        width,             /* Class width */
        bound;             /* Boundary of current class */

      /* Initial message */
      printf("\nProgram STAT3\n");
      printf("\nForm frequency distribution\n");
      printf("for a set of data using the\n");
      printf("standard input device.\n");

      /* Initialize */
      scanf("%lf, %lf", &lowest, &width);
      scanf("%d", &number);
      for (class = 0; class < 50; class++)
        table[class] = 0;

      /* Process */
      for (counter = 1; counter <= number; counter++)
        {
           scanf("%lf", &value);
           class = (value - lowest) / width;
           table[class] += 1;
        }

      /* Determine classes utilized */
      lower = 49;
      upper = 0;
      for (class = 0; class < 50; class++)
        {
           if (table[class] == 0)
```

```
                continue;
            if (class < lower)
                lower = class;
            if (class > upper)
                upper = class;
        }

    /* Output */
    printf("\nLowest bound     Frequency   Cumulative\n");
    sum = 0;
    for (class = lower; class <= upper; class++)
        {
            bound = lowest + class * width;
            sum += table[class];
            printf("%l5.8lf      %5d      %5d\n",
                bound, table[class], sum);
        }

    /* Final message */
    printf("\nEnd of program STAT3\n");
        }
```

The input data includes the lefthand boundary of the first class, the interval width, and the number of values in the file. The test file follows:

```
9.5  2.0
5
12.0
11.0
19.0
14.0
15.0
```

The test run follows:

```
Program STAT3

Form frequency distribution
for a set of data using the
standard input service.
```

Lowest bound	Frequency	Cumulative
9.50000000	1	1
11.50000000	1	2
13.50000000	2	4
15.50000000	0	4
17.50000000	1	5

End of program STAT3

HISTOGRAM

A histogram is a bar chart representing the frequencies of a frequency distribution. It gives a graphic picture of the distribution of the data values. The simplest charts consist of lines of asterisks or other characters. The Pascal

```
WRITE('*')
```

command forms the line of asterisks one symbol at a time. The following program generates three lines per frequency class and makes the longest bar 40 column positions in length:

```
main()      /* STAT4 -- Tabulate frequency distribution */
  {
      int
        table[50],         /* Table of frequencies */
        class,             /* Class index */
        lower,             /* Lowest class index */
        upper,             /* Highest class index */
        sum,               /* Cumulative frequency */
        freq,              /* Class frequency */
        max,               /* Maximum frequency */
        length,            /* Length of longest bar */
        barwidth,          /* Width of histogram bar */
        columns,           /* Length of current bar */
        pos,               /* Current column position */
        number,            /* Number of values */
        counter;           /* Loop control variable */
      double
        value,             /* Current value */
```

```
  lowest,          /* Value of lowest boundary */
  width,           /* Class width */
  bound;           /* Boundary of current class */

/* Initial message */
printf("\nProgram STAT4\n");
printf("\nForm frequency distribution\n");
printf("and histogram bar chart\n");
printf("for a set of data using the\n");
printf("standard input device.\n");

/* Initialize */
scanf("%lf, %lf", &lowest, &width);
scanf("%d, %d", &length, &barwidth);
scanf("%d", &number);
for (class = 0; class < 50; class++)
  table[class] = 0;

/* Process */
for (counter = 1; counter <= number; counter++)
  {
     scanf("%lf", &value);
     class = (value - lowest) / width;
     table[class] += 1;
  }

/* Determine classes utilized */
lower  = 49;
upper  = 0;
max    = 0;
for (class = 0; class < 50; class++)
  {
     freq = table[class];
     if (freq == 0)
       continue;
     if (class < lower)
       lower = class;
     if (class > upper)
       upper = class;
     if (freq > max)
       max = freq;
  }
```

```
    /* Output */
    printf("\nLowest bound      Frequency    Cumulative\n");
    sum = 0;
    for (class = lower; class <= upper; class++)
      {
          bound = lowest + class * width;
          sum += table[class];
          printf("%15.8lf     %5d     %5d\n",
               bound, table[class], sum);
      }

    /* Histogram */
    printf("\n");
    for (class = lower; class <= upper; class++)
      {
          columns = (length * table[class]) / max;
          for (counter = 1; counter <= barwidth; counter++)
            {
                  for (pos = 1; pos <= columns; pos++)
                    printf("*");
                  printf("\n");
            }
      }

    /* Final message */
    printf("\nEnd of program STAT4\n");
}
```

The input includes the lowest class boundary, the class width, the number of values, and the values. The test file follows:

```
9.5 2.0
40 3
5
12.0
11.0
19.0
14.0
15.0
```

The output follows:

Program STAT4

Form a frequency distribution
and histogram bar chart
for a set of data using the
standard input device.

Lowest bound	Frequency	Cumulative
9.50000000	1	1
11.50000000	1	2
13.50000000	2	4
15.50000000	0	4
17.50000000	1	5

```
********************
********************
********************
********************
********************
********************
****************************************
****************************************
****************************************



********************
********************
********************

End of program STAT4
```

Exercises

1. Write a program to compute the sample mean and standard deviation. Make the program interactive, with prompt messages for input from the keyboard.

2. Write a program to compute the population mean and standard deviation using the definitional formulas. Load the values into an array and calculate the mean before using the definitional formula to calculate the variance.

3. Write a program that computes the sample mean and standard deviation, and that forms a frequency distribution.

4. Write a program that computes the minimum, maximum, mean and standard deviation, that forms a frequency distribution, and that displays a histogram.

10.2 Sorting

Sorting data into order is an important task assigned to the computer; it brings order out of chaos. This section discusses several sorting algorithms that are adequate for small sets of data. Large sets of data require more complex algorithms.

SORT BY INSERTION INTO AN ORDERED LIST

The first method is appropriate for programs using interactive data entry. Each data item is placed in its proper position relative to the other values. The new value is inserted into the list in its proper location. Values within the list are moved to make room for the new value.

Sort by insertion uses the bubble sort algorithm for each value as it is read. When used interactively, the set of data can grow quite large before the user senses that the program response is slowing down because of the insertion activity. The following program uses the sort by insertion method:

```
main()      /* SORT1 - Sort by insertion */
  {
      float
        vector[5000],      /* Vector of data values */
        value;             /* Value for insertion */
      int
        number,            /* Number of values */
        index,             /* Index for vector */
        counter;           /* Loop control variable */

      /* Initialize */
      scanf("%d", &number);
      vector[0] = -1.0e30;
```

```
     /* Read and insert */
     for (counter = 1; counter <= number; counter++)
       {
             scanf("%f", &value);
             index = counter - 1;
             while (value < vector[index])
               {
                 vector[index+1] = vector[index];
                 --index;
               }
             vector[index+1] = value;
       }

     /* Output */
     printf("%d\n", number);
     for (index = 1; index <= number; index++)
       printf("%15.8f\n", vector[index]);
  }
```

The input test file follows:

```
5
12.0
11.0
19.0
14.0
15.0
```

The output follows:

```
5
     11.00000000
     12.00000000
     14.00000000
     15.00000000
     19.00000000
```

SORT BY SELECTION AND EXCHANGE

Sort by selection and exchange is one of the easiest sorting methods to understand. The first task is to place the smallest value in the first location. The program searches the entire list for the smallest value and exchanges places between the smallest value and the value in the first position. The next task is to place the next smallest value in the second position. The program searches the remaining $n - 1$ items for the second smallest value and exchanges that with the value in the second position. This process continues until the list is sorted.

The following program uses the sort by selection and exchange:

```
main()     /* SORT2 -- Sort by selection and exchange */
  {
      float
        vector[5000],        /* Vector of data values */
        vector[5000],        /* Vector of data values */
        temp,                /* Temporary value for exchange */
        value;               /* Value for insertion */
      int
        number,              /* Number of values */
        counter,             /* Loop control variable */
        last,                /* Number - 1 */
        index,               /* Index for vector */
        location;            /* Location of next smallest */

      /* Load data */
      scanf("%f", &value);
      index = -1;
      while (value > -998.0)
        {
           ++index;
           vector[index] = value;
           scanf("%f", &value);
        }
      number = index + 1;

      /* Sort */
      last = number - 1;
      for (counter = 0; counter < last; counter++)
        {
           location = counter;
           for (index = counter + 1; index < number; index++)
```

```
            if (vector[index] < vector[location])
              location = index;
      temp = vector[counter];
      vector[counter] = vector[location];
      vector[location] = temp;
        }

      /* Output */
      for (index = 0; index < number; index++)
        printf("%15.8f\n", vector[index]);
      printf("%6.1f", -999.0);
  }
```

This program uses the value −999.0 to signal the end of the data. The test file follows:

```
12.0
11.0
19.0
14.0
15.0
-999.0
```

The output follows:

```
      11.00000000
      12.00000000
      14.00000000
      15.00000000
      19.00000000
-999.0
```

QUICKSORT

Quicksort is harder to understand than either the bubble sort or the sort by selection and exchange, but it is much faster for large sets of values which are in random order. Quicksort is a recursive procedure which selects one value in the sublist and places that value in its proper location with all smaller values to its left and all larger values to its right. The lefthand and righthand sublists are partitioned in the next iteration.

The quicksort algorithm is easiest to understand when defined recursively. (Subscripts define the endpoints of the sublists.) A recursive function is one which calls itself. The system maintains a pushdown stack containing the values of the local variables and the function arguments.

The following program uses the quicksort algorithm:

```
float
  vector[5000];      /* Vector of data values */

main()      /* SORT3 -- Quicksort */
  {
      int
        number,            /* Number of values */
        index;             /* Index to vector */

      /* Load data */
      scanf("%d", &number);
      for (index = 0; index < number; index++)
        scanf("%f", &vector[index]);

      /* Initiate recursive quicksort */
      sort (0, number - 1);

      /* Output */
      printf("%d\n", number);
      for (index = 0; index < number; index++)
        printf("%15.8f\n", vector[index]);
  }

sort(left, right)     /* Recursive quicksort function */
  int
      left,                  /* Left index of sublist */
      right;                 /* Right index of sublist */
  {
      float
        value,               /* Value to divide sublist */
        temp;                /* Temporary value for exchange */
      int
        i,                   /* Current lefthand position in list */
        j;                   /* Current righthand position */
```

```
        /* Initialize */
        i = left;
        j = right;
        value = vector[(left + right) / 2];

        /* Divide into lefthand and righthand sublists */
        while (i <= j)
          {
            /* Alternate left and right scans */
            while (vector[i] < value)
              i++;
            while (vector[j] > value)
              j--;

            /* Swap and continue search */
            if (i <= j)
              {
                    temp = vector[i];
                    vector[i] = vector[j];
                    vector[j] = temp;
                    i++;
                    j--;
              }

            /* Sort left sublist, then right sublist */
            if (left < j)
              sort(left, j);
            if (right > i)
              sort(i, right);
          }
  }
```

The test file follows:

```
5
12.0
11.0
19.0
14.0
15.0
```

The output follows:

```
5
    11.00000000
    12.00000000
    14.00000000
    15.00000000
    19.00000000
```

ADDRESS CALCULATION SORT

Some sets of data lend themselves to sorting using a method based on frequency distributions. Appropriate address calculation sorts are among the fastest sorting methods.

Given the lowest boundary of the first class and the class width, the formula

$$\text{class} = (\text{value} - \text{boundary})/\text{width}$$

calculates the subscript of the class containing the current value. The frequency distribution class is incremented. The data values should be integer rather than floating point. Two distinct values should not result in the same frequency class if the program is to keep them separate.

The following program uses the frequency distribution approach:

```
main()      /* SORT4 -- Address calculation sort */
  {
     int
        freq[500],        /* Frequency table */
        number,           /* Number of values */
        value,            /* Current value */
        bound,            /* Lowest class boundary */
        width,            /* Class width */
        class,            /* Frequency class */
        counter,          /* Loop control variable */
        minimum,          /* Minimum index */
        maximum;          /* Maximum index */

     /* Clear frequency table */
     for (class = 0; class < 500; class++)
        freq[class] = 0;
```

```
    minimum  = 500;
    maximum = 0;

    /* Parameters */
    scanf("%d %d", &bound, &width);
    scanf("%d", &number);

    /* Process */
    for (counter = 1; counter <= number; counter++)
      {
          scanf("%d", &value);
          class = (value - bound) / width;
          freq[class]++;
          if (class < minimum)
            minimum = class;
          if (class > maximum)
            maximum = class;
      }

    /* Output */
    printf("%d\n", number);
    for (class = minimum; class <= maximum; class++)
      {
          value = class * width + bound;
          counter = freq[class];
          while (0 < counter--)
            printf("%5d\n", value);
      }
}
```

The input file includes the lowest boundary, the class width, the number of values, and the data values, in that order. A sample test file follows:

```
10 1
5
12
11
19
14
15
```

The output follows:

```
5
    11
    12
    14
    15
    19
```

Exercises

1. Write a program that computes the mean, median, and standard deviation for a set of sample data. The median is the middle value or values of a set of data that has been sorted into order. It is the middle value for an odd number of values. It is the average of the two middle values for an even number of values.

2. Write a program that computes the mean and standard deviation for a set of data, sorts the data into order, forms a frequency distribution, and displays a histogram.

3. Implement the quicksort method of program SORT3. The system saves all local variables in a pushdown stack with each recursive call. This requires both memory space and computer time. The floating point variables temp and value do not need to be saved in the pushdown stack. Define them as global variables along with the vector of data values.

4. Write a program using the random number generator to generate a file of 2,000 floating point values. Compare the execution times of the sorting programs of this section.

10.3 Linear Regression

A function of the form

$$y = f(x)$$

computes the value y as a function of the value x. The linear function

$$y = f(x) = a + bx$$

describes a straight line crossing the Y axis at point *a* and having slope *b*.

The function

$$y = f(x) = \text{Log}\,(x)$$

gives *y* as the logarithm of *x*. Other functional representations are quadratic, cubic, exponential, etc.

Regression analysis, also called curve fitting, predicts the dependent variable *y* as a function of the independent variable *x*. The functional relationship is not known beforehand. The analyst tries to determine the appropriate relationship on the basis of the pairs of sample values.

LINEAR REGRESSION

Linear regression attempts to fit a linear function to the data. The Y-intercept *a* and the slope *b* are the two parameters. The formula

$$b = (\Sigma xy - (\Sigma x)(\Sigma y)/n)/(\Sigma x^2 - (\Sigma x^2)/n)$$

gives the slope and

$$a = my - b * mx$$

gives the Y-intercept. The symbol "*my*" gives the mean of *y* and "*mx*" gives the mean of *x*.

The three measures of goodness of fit are the standard error of estimate, the correlation coefficient, and the coefficient of determination. The standard error of estimate is the standard deviation among the residual errors. The errors have a mean of 0. If the errors are normally distributed, 68 percent of the observations fall within one standard error of the regression line and 95 percent fall within two standard errors.

The coefficient of determination is the square of the correlation coefficient. It gives the fraction of the variation of the dependent variable *y* explained by its association with the independent variable *x*. The variation of *y* is the sum of the squares of the deviations of *y* around its mean. The error variation is the sum of the squares of the deviations of *y* around the regression line. The explained variation is the difference between the total variation and the error variation.

The formula

$$SST = \Sigma(y - my)^2$$

gives the total variation. SST stands for Total Sum of Squares. If y' is the predicted value of y, the formula

$$SSE = \Sigma(y - y')^2$$

gives the error variation. SSE stands for Error Sum of Squares. The formula

$$SSR = \Sigma(y' - my)^2$$

gives the explained variation. SSR stands for Regression Sum of Squares. In least squares regression, the slope and Y-intercept are chosen to minimize the error variation. For least squares regression, the relationship

$$SST = SSR + SSE$$

holds.

The ratio

$$SSR/SST$$

gives the coefficient of determination. The correlation coefficient is the square root of the coefficient of determination. The expression

$$1 - r^2$$

gives the fraction of the variation of Y not explained. Multiply by the variation of Y and take the square root to obtain the standard error of estimate.

SUMMARY FORMULAS

The variation of the dependent variable y is

$$\text{Var}(y) = \Sigma(y - my)^2 = \Sigma y^2 - (\Sigma y)^2/n$$

giving the sum of the squares of the deviations of y around its mean.

The variation of the independent variable x is

$$\mathrm{Var}(x) = \Sigma(x - mx)^2 = \Sigma x^2 - (\Sigma x)^2/n$$

giving the sum of the squares of the deviations of x around its mean.

The formula

$$\mathrm{Var}(xy) = \Sigma(y - my)\,(x - mx) = \Sigma xy - (\Sigma x)\,(\Sigma y)/n$$

gives the covariation between x and y.

Using these summary measures, the formula

$$b = \mathrm{Var}(xy)/\mathrm{var}(x)$$

gives the slope and

$$a = my - b * mx$$

gives the Y-intercept.

The standard error of estimate, correlation coefficient, and coefficient of determination are measures of goodness of fit for the regression equation. The formula

$$r = \mathrm{Var}(xy)/\sqrt{(\mathrm{var}(x)} * \sqrt{\ }\mathrm{var}\,(y))$$

gives the correlation coefficient. The coefficient of determination is the square of the correlation coefficient.

The coefficient of determination r^2 gives the fraction of the variation of y explained by its association with x. The term $(1 - r^2)$ gives the fraction not explained. The term $(1 - r^2) * \mathrm{Var}(y)$ gives the square of the standard error of estimate.

PROGRAM GIVING SLOPE AND Y-INTERCEPT

The following program computes the Y-intercept and slope for a linear regression equation estimating the first variable as a function of its association with the second.

```
main()     /* REG1 -- Slope and Y-intercept */
  {
       double
         y,              /* Dependent variable */
         x,              /* Independent variable */
```

```
  b,                 /* Slope */
  a,                 /* Y-intercept */
  sumy,              /* Sum for dependent variable */
  sumx,              /* Sum for independent variable */
  sumyy,             /* Sum of squares for dep var */
  sumxx,             /* Sum of squares for ind var */
  sumxy,             /* Sum of cross products */
  vary,              /* Variation of dependent variable */
  varx,              /* Variation of independent variable */
  varxy;             /* Covariation */
int
  number,            /* Number of observations */
  counter;           /* Loop control variable */

/* Initial message */
printf("\nProgram REG1\n");
printf("\nLinear regression analysis\n");
printf("giving slope and Y-intercept.\n");

/* clear accumulators */
sumy  = 0.0;
sumx  = 0.0;
sumxx = 0.0;
sumyy = 0.0;
sumxy = 0.0;

/* Process data */
scanf("%d", &number);
for (counter = 1; counter <= number; counter++)
  {
     scanf("%lf %lf", &y, &x);
     sumy += y;
     sumx += x;
     sumyy += y * y;
     sumxx += x * x;
     sumxy += x * y;
  }

/* Calculate */
vary  = sumyy - sumy * sumy / number;
varx  = sumxx - sumx * sumx / number;
```

```
    varxy = sumxy - sumx * sumy / number;
    b     = varxy / varx;
    a     = sumy / number - b * sumx / number;

    /* Output */
    printf("\nNumber of obs      %d\n", number);
    printf("Y-intercept       %15.8lf\n", a);
    printf("Slope             %15.8lf\n", b);

    /* Final message */
    printf("\nEnd of program REG1\n");
}
```

The input data for the programs of this section contain the number of paired observations as the first parameter. The program reads each paired observation with one scanf statement. The first value is for the dependent variable and the second is for the independent variable. A sample test file follows:

```
6
9.0  1.0
7.0  1.0
5.0  2.0
4.0  2.0
4.0  3.0
1.0  3.0
```

The output from the test run follows:

```
Program REG1

Linear regression analysis
giving slope and Y-intercept.

Number of obs       6
Y-intercept       10.50000000
Slope             -2.75000000

End of program REG1
```

The regression equation

$$y = a + bx = 10.5 - 2.75x$$

has Y-intercept 10.5 and slope -2.75.

MEASURES OF GOODNESS OF FIT

The following program adds the measures of goodness of fit:

```
#include    <math.h>

main()    /* REG2 -- Goodness of fit */
  {
      double
        y,                /* Dependent variable */
        x,                /* Independent variable */
        b,                /* Slope */
        a,                /* Y-intercept */
        sumy,             /* Sum for dependent variable */
        sumx,             /* Sum for independent variable */
        sumyy,            /* Sum of squares for dep var */
        sumxx,            /* Sum of squares for ind var */
        sumxy,            /* Sum of cross products */
        vary,             /* Variation of dependent variable */
        varx,             /* Variation of independent variable */
        varxy,            /* Covariation */
        stderr,           /* Standard error of estimate */
        r,                /* Correlation coefficient */
        r2;               /* Correlation squared */
      int
        number,           /* Number of observations */
        counter;          /* Loop control variable */

      /* Initial message */
      printf("\nProgram REG2\n");
      printf("\nLinear regression analysis\n");
      printf("giving slope, Y-intercept,\n");
      printf("standard error of estimate,\n");
      printf("and correlation coefficient.\n");
```

```
    /* clear accumulators */
    sumy  = 0.0;
    sumx  = 0.0;
    sumxx = 0.0;
    sumyy = 0.0;
    sumxy = 0.0;

    /* Process data */
    scanf("%d", &number);
    for (counter = 1; counter <= number; counter++)
      {
          scanf("%lf %lf", &y, &x);
          sumy  += y;
          sumx  += x;
          sumyy += y * y;
          sumxx += x * x;
          sumxy += x * y;
      }

    /* Calculate */
    vary  = sumyy - sumy * sumy / number;
    varx  = sumxx - sumx * sumx / number;
    varxy = sumxy - sumx * sumy / number;
    b     = varxy / varx;
    a     = sumy / number - b * sumx / number;
    r     = varxy / sqrt(varx * vary);
    r2    = r * r;
    stderr = sqrt((1.0 - r2) * vary);

    /* Output */
    printf("\nNumber of obs     %d\n", number);
    printf("Y-intercept       %15.8lf\n", a);
    printf("Slope             %15.8lf\n", b);
    printf("Std error             %15.8lf\n", stderr);
    printf("Correlation       %15.8lf\n", r);
    printf("Squared           %15.8lf\n", r2);
    /* Final message */
    printf("\nEnd of program REG2\n");
}
```

The input data is the same as for the previous program. The output for the test file follows:

```
Program REG2

Linear regression analysis
giving slope, Y-intercept,
standard error of estimate,
and correlation coefficient.

Number of obs          6
Y-intercept          10.50000000
Slope                -2.75000000

Std error             2.78388218
Correlation          -.89221782
Squared               .79605263

End of program REG2
```

RESIDUAL ERRORS

The program can calculate predicted values using the regression slope and Y-intercept for each observed value of the independent variable *x*. The residual error for a given value of *x* is the difference between the observed value of *y* for that observation and the predicted value using the value for *x*.

The following program adds the residual errors:

```
#include      <math.h>

main()     /* REG3 -- Goodness of fit */
  {
      double
        dep[1000],         /* Dependent variable values */
        ind[1000],         /* Independent variable values */
        y,                 /* Individual dep variable value */
        x,                 /* Individual ind variable value */
        b,                 /* Slope */
        a,                 /* Y-intercept */
        sumy,              /* Sum for dependent variable */
        sumx,              /* Sum for independent variable */
        sumyy,             /* Sum of squares for dep var */
```

```
    sumxx,          /* Sum of squares for ind var */
    sumxy,          /* Sum of cross products */
    vary,           /* Variation of dependent variable */
    varx,           /* Variation of independent variable */
    varxy,          /* Covariation */
    stderr,         /* Standard error of estimate */
    r,              /* Correlation coefficient */
    r2,             /* Correlation squared */
    p,              /* Predicted value */
    e;              /* Residual error */
int
    number,         /* Number of observations */
    i;              /* Index for data vector */

/* Initial message */
printf("\nProgram REG3\n");
printf("\nLinear regression analysis\n");
printf("giving slope, Y-intercept, \n");
printf("standard error of estimate,\n");
printf("correlation coefficient,\n");
printf("and residual errors.\n");

/* clear accumulators */
sumy  = 0.0;
sumx  = 0.0;
sumxx = 0.0;
sumyy = 0.0;
sumxy = 0.0;

/* Process data */
scanf("%d", &number);
for (i = 0; i < number; i++)
  {
    scanf("%lf %lf", &y, &x);
    sumy  += y;
    sumx  += x;
    sumyy += y * y;
    sumxx += x * x;
    sumxy += x * y;
    dep[i] = y;
    ind[i] = x;
  }
```

```
    /* Calculate */
    vary   = sumyy - sumy * sumy / number;
    varx   = sumxx - sumx * sumx / number;
    varxy  = sumxy - sumx * sumy / number;
    b      = varxy / varx;
    a      = sumy / number - b * sumx / number;
    r      = varxy / sqrt(varx * vary);
    r2     = r * r;
    stderr = sqrt((1.0 - r2) * vary);

    /* Output */
    printf("\nNumber of obs     %d\n", number);
    printf("Y-intercept      %15.8lf\n", a);
    printf("Slope            %15.8lf\n", b);
    printf("\nStd error        %15.8lf\n", stderr);
    printf("Correlation      %15.8llf\n", r);
    printf("Squared          %15.8lf\n", r2);

    /* Residuals */
    printf("\n     Observed     Predicted     Residual\n");
    for (i = 0; i < number; i++)
      {
         p = a + b * ind[i];
         e = dep[i] - p;
         printf("%15.8lf %15.8lf %15.8lf\n",
           dep[i], p, e);
      }

    /* Final message */
    printf("\nEnd of program REG3\n");
}
```

When used with the test file

```
6
9.0  1.0
7.0  1.0
5.0  2.0
4.0  2.0
4.0  3.0
1.0  3.0
```

the following output results:

```
Program REG3

Linear regression analysis
giving slope, Y-intercept,
standard error of estimate,
correlation coefficient,
and residual errors.

Number of obs            6
Y-intercept        10.50000000
Slope              -2.75000000

Std error           2.78388218
Correlation         -.89221782
Squared              .79605263

      Observed        Predicted        Residual
     9.00000000      7.75000000      1.25000000
     7.00000000      7.75000000      -.75000000
     5.00000000      5.00000000      0.00000000
     4.00000000      5.00000000     -1.00000000
     4.00000000      2.25000000      1.75000000
     1.00000000      2.25000000     -1.25000000

End of program REG3
```

INTERACTIVE DATA ENTRY

Programs that regularly accept data interactively from the keyboard should provide prompt messages identifying the data items needed from the user. The following program adds the prompt messages, increasing its usefulness as an interactive program:

```
#include     <math.h>

main()     /* REG4 -- Goodness of fit */
  {
     double
        dep[1000],        /* Dependent variable values */
        ind[1000],        /* Independent variable values */
        y,               /* Individual dep variable value */
```

```
   x,              /* Individual ind variable value */
   b,              /* Slope */
   a,              /* Y-intercept */
   sumy,           /* Sum for dependent variable */
   sumx,           /* Sum for independent variable */
   sumyy,          /* Sum of squares for dep var */
   sumxx,          /* Sum of squares for ind var */
   sumxy,          /* Sum of cross products */
   vary,           /* Variation of dependent variable */
   varx,           /* Variation of independent variable */
   varxy,          /* Covariation */
   stderr,         /* Standard error of estimate */
   r,              /* Correlation coefficient */
   r2,             /* Correlation squared */
   p,              /* Predicted value */
   e;              /* Residual error */
int
   number,         /* Number of observations */
   i;              /* Index for data vector */

/* Initial message */
printf("\nProgram REG4\n");
printf("\nLinear regression analysis\n");
printf("using interactive data entry\n");
printf("giving slope, Y-intercept, \n");
printf("standard error of estimate, \n");
printf("correlation coefficient,\n");
printf("and residual errors.\n");

/* Load data */
printf("\nNumber of observations ? ");
scanf("%d", &number);
printf("\nValue for Dep var and ind var for\n");
for (i = 0; i < number; i++)
   {
      printf("obs %d ? ", i+1);
      scanf("%lf %lf", &dep[i], &ind[i]);
   }
/* clear accumulators */
sumy  = 0.0;
sumx  = 0.0;
sumxx = 0.0;
```

```
sumyy = 0.0;
sumxy = 0.0;

/* Process data */
for (i = 0; i < number; i++)
  {
    y = dep[i];
    x = ind[i];
    sumy  += y;
    sumx  += x;
    sumyy += y * y;
    sumxx += x * x;
    sumxy += x * y;
  }

/* Calculate */
vary   = sumyy - sumy * sumy / number;
varx   = sumxx - sumx * sumx / number;
varxy  = sumxy - sumx * sumy / number;
b      = varxy / varx;
a      = sumy / number - b * sumx / number;
r      = varxy / sqrt(varx * vary);
r2     = r * r;
stderr = sqrt((1.0 - r2) * vary);

/* Output */
printf("\nNumber of obs     %d\n", number);
printf("Y-intercept       %15.8lf\n", a);
printf("Slope             %15.8lf\n", b);
printf("\nStd error         %15.8lf\n", stderr);
printf("Correlation       %15.8llf\n", r);
printf("Squared           %15.8lf\n", r2);

/* Residuals */
printf("\n     Observed     Predicted     Residual\n");
for (i = 0; i < number; i++)
  {
    p = a + b * ind[i];
    e = dep[i] - p;
    printf("%15.8lf %15.8lf %15.8lf\n",
      dep[i], p, e);
  }
```

```
    /* Final message */
    printf("\nEnd of program REG4\n");
}
```

The following output shows the interactive data entry and the computed results:

```
Program REG4

Linear regression analysis
using interactive data entry
giving slope, Y-intercept,
standard error of estimate,
correlation coefficient,
and residual errors.

Number of observations ? 6

Value for Dep var and ind var for
obs 1 ? 9.0 1.0
obs 2 ? 7.0 1.0
obs 3 ? 5.0 2.0
obs 4 ? 4.0 2.0
obs 5 ? 4.0 3.0
obs 6 ? 1.0 3.0

Number of obs           6
Y-intercept          10.50000000
Slope                -2.75000000

Std error             2.78388218
Correlation           -.89221782
Squared                .79605263

        Observed       Predicted       Residual
        9.00000000     7.75000000      1.25000000
        7.00000000     7.75000000      -.75000000
        5.00000000     5.00000000      0.00000000
        4.00000000     5.00000000     -1.00000000
        4.00000000     2.25000000      1.75000000
        1.00000000     2.25000000     -1.25000000

End of program REG4
```

Exercises

1. Write a program to calculate the slope, Y-intercept, and measure of goodness of fit. Include prompt messages for interactive data entry.

2. Write a program to calculate the slope, Y-intercept, and measures of goodness of fit. Obtain the data from a file using the special file functions rather than the standard input.

10.4 Nonlinear Curve Fitting

The world is not always linear; linear regression is not always appropriate. One of the most productive methods of handling nonlinear relationships is to transform the independent variable into a form for which a linear fit is appropriate. Common transformations are square, square root, cube, logarithm, exponential, and reciprocal.

Standard linear regression analysis of the transformed data gives the Y-intercept, slope, and measures of goodness of fit. The Y-intercept and slope apply only for the transformed independent variable. The measures of goodness of fit and the table of residuals aid in choosing an appropriate transformation. The best transformation is the one with the smallest standard error. This is also the one with the correlation coefficient magnitude closest to 1.0.

SCATTER DIAGRAM

The scatter diagram is a cross plot of the paired values of the dependent and independent variables. It is one of the most productive tools for determining whether a linear regression line is appropriate.

The following program generates a scatter diagram for a set of paired observations:

```
main()     /* REG5 -- Scatter diagram */
  {
       char
         plot[66][132];            /* Maximum plot size */
       float
         y[200],                   /* Value of dependent variable */
```

```
  x[200],                    /* Value of independent variable */
  ymin,                      /* Minimum value for y */
  xmin,                      /* Minimum value for x */
  ymax,                      /* Maximum value for y */
  xmax,                      /* Maximum value for x */
  yrange,                    /* Range for y */
  xrange;                    /* Range for x */
int
  number,                    /* Number of observation */
  index,                     /* Index for observation */
  row,                       /* Row index for plotting */
  col,                       /* Column index for plotting */
  nrows,                     /* Number of rows for plot */
  ncols;                     /* Number of columns for plot */

/* Initialize */
nrows = 20;
ncols  = 50;
for (row = 0; row <= nrows; row++)
  for (col = 0; col <= ncols; col++)
    plot[row][col] = ' ';

/* Load Data */
scanf("%d", &number);
for (index = 0; index < number; index++)
  scanf("%f %f", &y[index], &x[index]);

/* Set scale factors */
ymin  = y[0];
ymax = ymin;
xmin  = x[0];
xmax = xmin;
for (index = 1; index < number; index++)
  {

    if (y[index] < ymin)
      ymin = y[index];
    if (y[index] > ymax)
      ymax = y[index];
    if (x[index] < xmin)
      xmin = x[index];
    if (x[index] > xmax)
      xmax = x[index];
```

```
    }
  yrange = ymax - ymin;
  xrange = xmax - xmin;

  /* Plot values */
  for (index = 0; index < number; index++)
    {
      row = 0.5 + nrows * (ymax - y[index]) / yrange;
      col  = 0.5 + ncols * (x[index] - xmin) / xrange;
      plot[row][col] = '*';
    }
  /* Output */
  for (row = 0; row <= nrows; row++)
    {
      for (col = 0; col <= ncols; col++)
        printf("%c", plot[row][col]);
      printf("\n");
    }
}
```

For the input data

```
5
2.0  1.0
3.0  2.0
8.0  3.0
15.0  4.0
30.0  5.0
```

the following output results:

```
                                                   *




                                            *

                         *


          *
*
```

FORM THE SQUARE OF THE INDEPENDENT VARIABLE

The following program transforms the regression problem values by squaring the values of the independent variable:

```
main()      /* REG6 -- Square transformation */
  {
      float
        y,                  /* Value for dependent variable */
        x,                  /* Value for independent variable */
        t;                  /* Transformed independent variable */
      int
        number,             /* Number of observations*/
        index;              /* Index for observation */

      /* Transform independent variable */
      scanf("%d", &number);
      print("%d\n", number);
      for (index = 0; index < number; index++)
        {
            scanf("%f %f", &y, &x);
            t = x * x;
            printf("%f    %f\n", y, t);
        }
  }
```

The program converts the sample test file

```
5
2.0  1.0
3.0  2.0
8.0  3.0
15.0  4.0
30.0  5.0
```

to the following transformed data:

```
5
2.000000     1.000000
3.000000     4.000000
8.000000     9.000000
15.000000     16.000000
30.000000     25.000000
```

The transformed data is almost linearly associated. The scatter diagram follows:

```
                                                            *









                                            *




              *



     *
*
```

EXPONENTIAL TRANSFORMATION OF INDEPENDENT VARIABLE

The exponential distribution is another transformation which may result in a linear fit. The following program applies the exponential transformation to the independent variable:

```
#include     <math.h>

main()     /* REG7 -- Exponential transformation */
  {
     double
       y,                /* Value for dependent variable */
       x,                /* Value for independent variable */
       t;                /* Transformed independent variable */
     int
       number,           /* Number of observations*/
       index;            /* Index for observation */
```

```
/* Transform independent variable */
scanf("%d", &number);
printf("%d\n", number);
for (index = 0; index < number; index++)
  {
    scanf("%lf %lf", &y, &x);
    t = exp(x);
    printf("%lf     %lf\n", y, t);
  }
}
```

Using this program with the previous data results in the following transformed problem:

```
0
5
2.000000     2.718282
3.000000     7.389056
8.000000     20.085537
15.000000     54.598150
30.000000     148.413159
```

The resulting scatter diagram follows:

```
                                                                                    *









                                         *



          *


     *
  *
```

This transformation results in an association that is almost linear.

NONLINEAR REGRESSON PROGRAM

The following program performs nonlinear curve fitting by transforming the data and fitting a linear line to the transformed data:

```
#include    <STDIO.H>
#include    <math.h>

double
  dep[1000],     /* Dependent variable */
  ind[1000],     /* Independent variable */
  trans[1000];   /* Transformed independent variable */
int
  number;        /* Number of observations */

main()     /* REG8 -- Fit nonlinear functions */
  {
      char
        response;      /* User response */
      double
        slope,         /* Slope of transformed equation */
        intercept;     /* Y-intercept */
      initial();
      getdata();
      response = 'Y';
      while ((response = 'Y') :: (response = 'y'))
        {
          transform();
          solve (&intercept, &slope);
          residuals (intercept, slope);
          printf("\nTry another transformation (Y/N) ? ");
          scanf("%c", &response);
        }
  }

initial()     /* Initial message */
  {
      printf("\nProgram REG8\n");
      printf("\nFit nonlinear regression curve\n");
```

```
      printf("estimating dependent variable as\n");
      printf("as a function of the transformed\n");
      printf("independent variable.\n");
  }


getdata()      /* Load data from data file */
  {
      char
        fname[20],      /* Input file name */
        response;       /* User response */
      FILE
        file1;       /* Input file number */
      int
        i;           /* Index to observations */


      printf("Name of input file ? ");
      scanf("%s", &fname);
      file1 = fopen(fname, "r");
      if (file1 == 0)
        {
          printf("\nUnable to open file\n");
          exit();
        }
      else
        {
          fscanf(file1, "%d", &number);
          for (i = 0; i < number; i++)
            fscanf(filel, "%lf %lf", &dep[i], &ind[i]);
          fclose(file1);
        }
      printf("\nDisplay data values (Y/N) ? ");
      scanf("%c", &response);
      if ((response == 'Y') :: (response == 'y'))
        {
          printf("\n      Dependent Y      Independent X\n");
          for (i = 0; i < number; i++)
            printf("15.8lf      %15.8lf\n", dep[i], ind[i]);
        }
  }

transform()      /* Transform independent variable */
  {
```

```
int
    code,      /* Code number of transformation */
    i;         /* Index for observation*/
   printf("\nCode        Transformation for ind var\n");
   printf("    1       Reciprocal\n");
   printf("    2       Square\n");
   printf("    3       Cube\n");
   printf("    4       Square root\n");
   printf("    5       Logarithm\n");
   printf("    6       Exponential\n");
   printf("    7       No transformation\n");
   printf("\nCode number ? ");
   scanf("%d", &code);
   if ((code < 1) :: (code > 7))
     {
        printf("\nMust be valid code number\n");
        exit();
     }
   for (i = 0; i < number; i++)
     switch (code)
       {
          case 1:
            trans[i] = 1.0 / ind[i];
            break;
          case 2:
            trans[i] = ind[i] * ind[i];
            break;
          case 3:
            trans[i] = ind[i] * ind[i] * ind[i];
            break;
          case 4:
            trans[i] = sqrt(ind[i]);
            break;
          case 5:
            trans[i] = log(ind[i]);
            break;
          case 6:
            trans[i] = exp(ind[i]);
            break;
          default:
            trans[i] = ind[i];
       }
}
```

```
solve (intercept, slope)        /* Solve regression line */
  double
            *intercept,        /* Y-intercept */
            *slope;
        {
            int
              i;              /* Index for observation */
            double
              y,              /* Value of dependent variable */
              x,              /* Value of independent variable */
              sumy,           /* Sum for dep variable */
              sumx,           /* Sum for ind variable */
              sumxx,          /* Sum of squares for dep */
              sumyy,          /* Sum of squares for ind */
              sumxy,          /* Sum of cross products */
              vary,           /* Variation for y */
              varx,           /* Variation for x */
              varxy,          /* covariation */
              b,              /* Slope */
              a,              /* Y-intercept */
              ste,            /* Standard error of estimate */
              r,              /* Correlation coefficient */
              r2;             /* Coefficient of determination */

            /* Clear accumulators */
            sumy  = 0.0;
            sumx  = 0.0;
            sumyy = 0.0;
            sumxx = 0.0;
            sumxy = 0.0;

            /* Form sums and sums of squares */
            for (i = 0; i < number; i++)
              {
                y = dep[i];
                x = trans[i];
                sumy  += y;
                sumx  += x;
                symyy += y * y;
                sumxx += x * x;
                sumxy += x * y;
              }
```

```
        /* Compute summary measures */
        vary   = sumyy - sumy * sumy  / number;
        varx   = sumxx - sumx * sumx  / number;
        varxy  = sumxy - sumx * sumy  / number;
        b      = varxy / varx;
        a      = sumy / number - b * sumx / number;
        r      = varxy / sqrt(varx * vary);
        r2     = r * r;
        ste    = sqrt((1.0 - r2) * vary);
        *intercept = a;
        *slope     = b;

        /* Output */
        printf("\nRegression parameters\n");
        printf("\nY-intercept %15.8lf\n", a);
        printf("Slope       %15.8lf\n", b);
        printf("\nStd error         %15.8lf\n", ste);
        printf("Correlation       %15.8l f\n", r);
        printf("Squared           %15.8lf\n", r2);
    }

residuals(intercept, slope)       /* Compute residuals */
  double
        intercept,             /* Y-intercept */
        slope;                 /* Slope of transformed
                                  equation */
  {
        int
          i;                   /* Index for observations */
        double
          predicted,           /* Predicted value for
                                  dependent variables */
          error;               /* Residual error */
        char
          response;            /* User response */

        printf("\nDisplay residuals (Y/N) ? ");
        scanf("%s", &response);
        if ((response == 'Y') :: (response == 'y'))
          {
             printf("\n       Observed             Predicted");
             printf("        Residual\n");
             for (i = o; i <  number; i++)
```

```
            {
               predicted = intercept + slope * trans [i];
               error     = dep[i] - predicted;
               printf("%15.8lf %15.8lf %15.8lf\n",
                  dep[i], predicted, error);
            }
         }
  }

final ()      /* Final message */
  {
      printf("\nEnd of program REG8\n");
  }
```

The following data has a strong nonlinear association:

Dep var	Ind var
2	1
3	2
8	3
15	4
30	5

Try several transformations and compare their measures of fit. The file FILE8.DAT

```
5
2.0 1.0
3.0 2.0
8.0 3.0
15.0 4.0
30.0 5.0
```

contains the problem data.

The program accepts user requests from the standard input device and provides prompt messages. The problem data is read using disk file functions. The standard output device receives the output. The program asks for the name of the input data file as a text string. It will interactively apply one of several transformations to the independent variable before fitting the regression line.

The following test run tries a linear fit (code 7), the square transformation (code 2), and the exponential transformation (code 6):

```
Program REG8

Fit nonlinear regression curve
estimating dependent variable as
as a function of the transformed
independent variable.

Name of input file   ? FILE8.DAT

Display data values (Y/N) ? Y

      Dependent Y      Independent X
       2.00000000         1.00000000
       3.00000000         2.00000000
       8.00000000         3.00000000
      15.00000000         4.00000000
      30.00000000         5.00000000

Code    Transformation for ind var
   1    Reciprocal
   2    Square
   3    Cube
   4    Square root
   5    Logarithm
   6    Exponential
   7    No transformation

Code number ? 7

Regression parameters

Y-intercept    -8.80000000
Slope           6.80000000

Std error       8.17312670
Correlation      .93475758
Squared          .87377173
```

Display residuals (Y/N) ? Y

Observed	Predicted	Residual
2.00000000	−2.00000000	4.00000000
3.00000000	4.80000000	−1.80000000
8.00000000	11.60000000	−3.60000000
15.00000000	18.40000000	−3.40000000
30.00000000	25.20000000	4.80000000

Try another transformation (Y/N) ? Y

Code	Transformation for ind var
1	Reciprocal
2	Square
3	Cube
4	Square root
5	Longarithm
6	Exponential
7	No transformation

Code number ? 2

Regression parameters

Y-intercept	−1.28235294
Slope	1.17112299
Std error	4.03089672
Correlation	.98452872
Squared	.96929681

Display residuals (Y/N) ? Y

Observed	Predicted	Residual
2.00000000	−.11122995	2.11122995
3.00000000	3.40213904	−.40213904
8.00000000	9.25775401	−1.25775401
15.00000000	17.45561497	−2.45561497
30.00000000	27.99572193	2.00427807

Try another transformation (Y/N) ? Y

```
Code     Transformation for ind var
   1     Reciprocal
   2     Square
   3     Cube
   4     Square root
   5     Logarithm
   6     Exponential
   7     No transformation

Code number ? 6
Regression parameters

Y-intercept      2.79816779
Slope             .18871514

Std error        3.06376921
Correlation       .99109157
Squared           .98226251

Display residuals (Y/N) ?Y

          Observed         Predicted         Residual
         2.00000000        3.31114874      -1.31114874
         3.00000000        4.19259457      -1.19259457
         8.00000000        6.58861277       1.41138723
        15.00000000       13.10166551       1.89833449
        30.00000000       30.80597841       -.80597841

Try another transformation (Y/N) ? N

End of program REG8
```

Exercises

1. Use the scatter diagram program with the following data:

Y	*X*
46	−3
29	−2
17	−1
12	0

19	1
30	2
45	3

2. Use the nonlinear regression program to analyze the data of exercise 1, predicting Y as a function of X.

3. Use the scatter diagram program to display the association between the following variables:

Breakdowns	*Age*
21	0
73	1
112	2
140	3
159	4
172	5
178	6

4. Use the nonlinear regression program to estimate breakdowns as a function of age.

11

Information Representation

This chapter explores the internal representation of information. The computer uses numeric codes to represent letters, digits, punctuation, and special control symbols. Each system includes methods for coding negative integers. (Floating point representations differ greatly among the computer families.)

This chapter illustrates methods for inspecting the internal codes for different types of information. These methods permit the scanning of internal memory in a meaningful way. They are also useful for inspecting the contents of external files.

11.1 ASCII Codes

Most modern computers use 8-bit bytes to represent symbols for communicating with the external world through keyboard input and display or printed output. The formula

$$2^8 = 256$$

gives the number of possible distinct symbols available with an 8-bit coding scheme.

The ASCII (American Standard Code for Information Interchange) codes are employed by most computers. The notable exceptions are the IBM mainframe descendents of the System 360/370 families which use EBCDIC (Extended Binary Coded Decimal Interchange Code).

STANDARD ASCII

The standard ASCII symbols contain seven information bits, allowing only 128 distinct symbols. The eighth bit is a parity bit used to validate the transmission of data over telephone lines which are prone to noise.

Most modern computers define 128 more codes to fill out the 256-symbol potential. These symbols are not standard. Programs using the ASCII codes 128 through 2 the printer, video display, and communication. The control symbols are nonprintable. Attempting to print or display the control characters will have unpredictable results.

DISPLAY PRINTABLE ASCII SYMBOLS 32-127

The following program displays the printable ASCII symbols corresponding to the codes 32 through 127:

```
main()      /* Generate lower 128 ASCII symbols */
  {
      char
        symbol;         /* Generated character */

      for (symbol = 32; symbol < 64; symbol++)
        printf("%c", symbol);
      printf("\n");

      for (symbol = 64; symbol < 97; symbol++)
        printf("%c", symbol);
      printf("\n");

      for (symbol = 97; symbol < 127; symbol ++)
        printf("%c", symbol);
      printf("\n");
  }
```

The output follows:

!"#$%&'()*+,-./0123456789:;<=>?
∂ABCDEFGHIJKLMNOPQRSTUVWXYZ[\]^_'
abcdefghijklmnopqrstuvwxyz{:}~

CHARACTER AND INTEGER VARIABLES

C provides a close correspondence between character and integer variables. A character is an 8-bit byte; an integer contains 16 or 32 bits. It is possible to assign integer values to a character value if the integer values are within the range 0-255. It is also possible to assign the contents of a character variable to an integer which assumes the numeric value of the ASCII code.

CONVERT CHARACTER TO INTEGER CODE

The following program illustrates the interchangeability of character and integer constants:

```
main()      /* Convert symbol to decimal ASCII code */
  {
       printf("%3d    %c\n", 'E', 'E');
       printf("%3d    %c\n", 'e', 'e');
       printf("%3d    %c\n", '$', '$');
       printf("%3d    %c\n", '5', '5');
       printf("%3d    %c\n", 65, 65);
       printf("%3d    %c\n", 52, 52);
  }
```

The output follows:

```
 69  E
101  e
 36  $
 53  5
 65  A
 52  4
```

SYMBOLS AND CORRESPONDING CODES

Each ASCII symbol has a corresponding code number within the decimal range 0-255. We normally use decimal numbers; the computer uses binary information which is more easily coded in hexadecimal (base 16). The printf conversion symbol %d prints the number in decimal form. The conversion symbol %x prints the number in hexadecimal.

The following program gives the decimal and hexadecimal codes for the symbols A, B, . . . F:

```
main()     /* List symbols and ASCII codes */
  {
      int
        first,          /* Starting code */
        last,           /* Last code */
        symbol;         /* Loop control variable */

      scanf("%d %d", &first, &last);
      printf("Dec     Hex     Symbol\n");
      for (symbol = first; symbol <= last; symbol++)
        printf("%3d     %2x     %c\n",
          symbol, symbol, symbol);
  }
```

Input to the program consists of the beginning and ending code numbers for a range of codes to be printed. The input

65 70

results in printing the codes and corresponding symbols for the decimal codes 65, 66, . . . , 70.

The output follows:

```
Dec    Hex    Symbol
 65     41    A
 66     42    B
 67     43    C
 68     44    D
 69     45    E
 70     46    F
```

EXERCISES

1. If your system defines a second set of symbols using the codes 128 through 255, write a program to print or display them.

2. Write a program to display the decimal code, hexadecimal code, and symbol for each printable symbol of your computer.

11.2 STRINGS

A string is a sequence of characters terminated with the '\0' (null symbol). C includes a set of string functions for handling character strings. Of primary interest are the scanf and printf functions for reading and writing strings.

CHARACTER STRING INPUT AND OUTPUT

The following program uses the scanf and printf functions to read character strings from the standard input device and write them to the standard output device:

```
main()      /* String input/output */
  {
      char
        line[80];      /* Character string */
      int
        number,        /* Number of lines */
        counter;       /* Loop control variable */

      number = 4;
      for (counter = 1; counter <= number; counter++)
        {
           scanf("%s", line);
           printf("%s\n", line);
        }
  }
```

The program reads and writes four character strings. The following test file contains four names:

```
Fred
Mary
Helen
John
```

The output is the same as the input.

DECIMAL AND HEXADECIMAL CODES

Each character of the string can be represented using decimal or hexadecimal codes. The following program reads a character string from the standard input device and sends a table of decimal and hexadecimal codes to the standard output device:

```
main()      /* Inspect string */
  {
       char
         line[80];     /* Character string */
       int
         index;        /* Index to string */

       scanf("%s", line);
       printf("Dec      Hex      Symbol\n");
       index = 0;
       while (line[index] != '\0')
         {
            printf("%3d      %2x      %c\n",
              line[index], line[index], line[index]);
            index++;
         {
  {
```

The following is an example test string:

```
E7$3+a?.
```

Output for the sample string follows:

```
Dec   Hex   Symbol
 69    45   E
 55    37   7
 36    24   $
 51    33   3
 43    2B    +
 97    61   a
 63    3F   ?
 46    2E   .
```

STORING VARIABLE LENGTH STRINGS

Some applications—including text processors—require variable length strings. Storing variable length strings in two-dimensional arrays results in wasted space. If each row contains one string, there must be enough columns to store the longest string. The excess columns for the short strings are not available for reallocation.

A common approach is to store the strings head-to-tail in a one-dimensional array. The null symbol '\0' designates the end of each string and consumes one character position. The string

Hello

contains five characters but consumes six character positions including the null symbol.

A vector of pointers gives access to the strings. The pointers are updated as the strings are added to the array. The pointers provide indirect access to the strings.

The following program reads a set of strings into an array and builds the vector of pointers:

```
main()      /* Variable length strings */
  {
      char
        vector[200],     /* Character array for strings */
        *ptr[20],        /* Vector of pointers to strings */
        *cptr;           /* Current pointer */
      int
        number,          /* Number of strings */
        i;               /* Index to pointer vector */

      /* Load strings */
      scanf("%d", &number);
      cptr = vector;
      for (i = 0; i < number; i++)
        {
          scanf("%s", cptr);
          ptr[i] = cptr;
          while (*cptr++ != '\0');
        }
```

```
    /* print strings */
    for (i = 0; i < number; i++)
      printf("%s\n", ptr[1]);
}
```

The program asks for a counter giving the number of strings. The strings follow the counter. A set of test data is:

```
5
Alexandria
Berlin
Halifax
London
Paris
```

The output follows:

```
Alexandria
Berlin
Halifax
London
Paris
```

EXERCISES

1. Write a program that writes one string containing the capital letters A, B, . . . , Z to the standard output device.

2. Write a program that reads several strings from the standard input device, placing them into a character array. Convert all except the last null symbol to spaces to form one combined string. Send the string to the standard output device.

11.3 Binary Integers

Binary numbers use only the digits 0 and 1. The following gives the first few positive binary numbers:

0 1 10 11 100 101 110 111 1000.

These binary integers correspond to the decimal numbers

0 1 2 3 4 5 6 7 8.

HEXADECIMAL AND OCTAL

Binary numbers employ base 2. Hexadecimal numbers use base 16. Octal numbers use base 8. The following table compares the corresponding decimal binary, octal, and hexadecimal integers for the decimal numbers 0-17:

Decimal	*Binary*	*Octal*	*Hexadecimal*
0	0	0	0
1	1	1	1
2	10	2	2
3	11	3	3
4	100	4	4
5	101	5	5
6	110	6	6
7	111	7	7
8	1000	10	8
9	1001	11	9
10	1010	12	A
11	1011	13	B
12	1100	14	C
13	1101	15	D
14	1110	16	E
15	1111	17	F
16	10000	20	10
17	10001	21	11

OCTAL CODED BINARY

The computer uses internal binary codes to represent information. Octal and hexadecimal numbers are easier to read than large binary numbers. The process of converting between binary and octal or between binary and hexadecimal is fast and straightforward.

Some computers use octal representation of binary information. Group the binary number in sets of three bits to convert from binary to octal. Use the table above to assist in the conversion.

Convert the binary number

1001101

to octal. The number

1 001 101

shows the grouping of bits into sets of three. This grouping starts from the right. The octal number

115

results from converting each group of three bits into its corresponding octal digit.

Converting an octal number to its corresponding binary number is also straightforward. The octal number

2705

becomes

010 111 000 101

and shows the grouping into sets of three bits. This becomes

010111000101

as normally written.

Sometimes we keep the lefthand zeros; at other times we suppress them. Circumstances dictate whether to use zero suppression.

HEXADECIMAL CODED BINARY

Converting between hexadecimal and binary requires grouping the bits (binary digits) in sets of four. The binary number

1001111100

becomes

10 0111 1100

when grouped into sets of four bits. The corresponding hexadecimal number is

27C.

Consider converting the hexadecimal number

E50

to decimal. The binary number

1110 0101 0000

shows the grouping into sets of four bits. The symbol E corresponds to the binary number 1110, etc. The binary number is

111001010000.

HEXADECIMAL MOST POPULAR

Most modern computers use 8-bit bytes for communication through printers, video displays, and keyboards. The 8-bit byte divides evenly into two hexadecimal (4-bit) digits. This accounts for the popularity of hexadecimal numbers.

SIGNED BINARY NUMBERS

The common methods of representing signed binary numbers are absolute magnitude, ones complement, and twos complement. The following table compares the three strategies for signed 8-bit numbers:

Decimal	*Signed magnitude*	*Ones complement*	*Twos complement*
−2	10000010	11111101	11111110
−1	10000001	11111110	11111111
−0	10000000	11111111	undefined
0	00000000	00000000	00000000
1	00000001	00000001	00000001
2	00000010	00000010	00000010

All three methods use the lefthand bit as a sign bit. The signed magitude method uses the same righthand representation for both positive and negative numbers. The righthand seven bits are the same for both +2 and −2.

The ones complement of a number is the bitwise complement obtained by converting each 0 to a 1 and each 1 to a 0. The binary number

00000010

represents the decimal quantity +2. The ones complement

11111101

represents the decimal quantity −2.

Signed magnitude and ones complement schemes define a negative zero. This doesn't bother the computer; it's the people using the computer who get upset. The twos complement method avoids the problem of negative zeros by defining it out of existence.

The twos complement of a number involves adding the value 1 to the ones complement. Overflows are ignored so that adding 1 to the value

11111111

representing the ones complement of

00000000

gives the value

00000000

again. Most modern computers use twos complement notation for negative numbers.

SIGNED 16-BIT INTEGERS

The following program gives both the decimal and hexadecimal representation of sequences of signed binary numbers:

```
main()      /* Signed integers */
  {
      int
        value;      /* Current value */

      printf("Decimal      Hexadecimal\n");

      for (value = -32768; value <= -32766; value++)
        printf("%7d      %5x\n", value, value);
      printf("\n");
```

```
        for (value = -3; value <= 3; value ++)
          printf("%7d      %5x\n", value, value);
        printf("\n");

        for value = 32762; value <= 32766; value++)
          printf("%7d      %5x\n", value, value);
  }
```

The format control symbol %d gives the decimal form of the number while %x gives the hexadecimal form. Computers using twos complement notation for negative integers will have the following output:

Decimal	Hexadecimal
−32768	8000
−32767	8001
−32766	8002
−3	FFFD
−2	FFFE
−1	FFFF
0	0
1	1
2	2
3	3
32762	7FFA
32763	7FFB
32764	7FFC
32765	7FFD
32766	7FFE

LONG INTEGERS

The following program illustrates the use of long 32-bit integers:

```
main()      /* Signed integers */
  {
        long int
          first,        /* Starting value */
          last,         /* Last value */
          value;        /* Current value */
```

```
    printf("        Decimal\n");

    first = -2147000003;
    last = -2147000000;
    for (value = first; value <= last; value ++)
      printf("%11ld\n", value);
    printf("\n");

    for (value = -3; value <= 3; value++)
      printf("%11ld\n", value);
    printf("\n");

    first = 2147000000;
    last = 2147000003;
    for (value = first; value <= last; value++)
      printf("%11ld\n", value);
}
```

The output follows:

```
    Decimal
-2147000003
-2147000002
-2147000001
-2147000000

         -3
         -2
         -1
          0
          1
          2
          3

 2147000000
 2147000001
 2147000002
 2147000003
```

The distinction between long and short integers varies among computer families. Among mini and microcomputers, short integers are 16-bit quantities and long integers are 32-bit numbers.

UNSIGNED 16-BIT INTEGERS

Unsigned integers are commonly used for logical operations on quantities that are not to be interpreted as numbers. The contents can be interpreted as numeric. The following program illustrates the use of unsigned 16-bit integers:

```
main()      /* Unsigned integers */
  {
       unsigned int
         values[20];
       int
         number,
         index;

       number = 6;
       values[0] = 0x7fff;
       values[1] = 0xc2f;
       values[2] = 0x43;
       values[3] = 0xd;
       values[4] = 43;
       values[5] = 32767;

       printf("decimal   hexadecimal\n");
       for (index = 0; index < 6; index++)
         printf("%7d      %04x\n",
         values[indexs], values[index]);
  }
```

The output follows:

```
decimal    hexadecimal
 32767         7FFF
  3119         0C2F
    67         0043
    13         000D
    43         002B
 32767         7FFF
```

UNSIGNED 32-BIT INTEGERS

The following program illustrates the use and display of 32-bit integers:

```
main()      /* Unsigned integers */
  {
        unsigned long int
          values[20];
        int
          number,
          index;

        number = 6;
        values[0] = 0x7fffffff;
        values[1] = 0xc2fL;
        values[2] = 0x43L;
        values[3] = 0xdL;
        values[4] = 32767L;
        values[5] = 2147000000;

        printf("     decimal      hexadecimal\n");
        for (index = 0; index < 6; index++)
          printf("%11ld         %08lx\n",
            values[index],      values[index]);
  }
```

The output follows:

```
   decimal     hexadecimal
2147483647      7FFFFFFF
      3119      00000C2F
        67      00000043
        13      0000000D
     32767      00007FFF
2147000000      7FF89ECO
```

EXERCISES

1. Use the programs of this section to investigate the methods used by your system to represent negative integers.

2. Write a program to give the decimal, octal and hexadecimal representations of the decimal numbers $-5, -4, \ldots, 5$.

3. Determine the most negative integer and the most positive integer that your system can represent.

11.4 Floating Point

Computers differ widely in their representation of floating point (scientific notation) numbers. Most use some form of binary (base 2) floating point or hexadecimal (base 16) floating point. Most let the leftmost bit represent the sign of the number. The programs of this section explore internal floating point numbers, but do not address the complex issue of interpreting them.

Several issues complicate the location and interpretation of the hexadecimal coded binary representation of floating point values. Many implementations of C do not provide direct hexadecimal output for variables defined as floating point. For such systems it is necessary to use the union facility to redefine the memory area as containing both a floating point number and one or more integer numbers.

Many computers use boundary alignment conventions. This may make it difficult to locate the boundaries of the floating point number. It may be necessary to scan the bytes immediately to the left and right of the number because of system-imposed boundary alignment.

Many microcomputers and some minicomputers simulate floating point operations in software. The choices of floating point implementations are many and varied. Most microcomputers and mainframe computers place the exponent in the first 8-12 bits and the mantissa in the remaining bits.

Some microcomputers complicate the issue by interchanging the bytes in each 16-bit quantity. Some may reverse the order in which the bytes or 16-bit portions are stored in memory.

FLOATING POINT REPRESENTATION OF INTEGERS

The following program gives the decimal and hexadecimal representation of several integers stored in floating point notation:

```
main()     /* Floating point integers */
  {
     float
```

```
        vector[20];         /* Vector of values */
    union
        {
            float
                value;
            long int
                ival[2];
        } check;
    int
        number,
        index;

    number = 6;
    vector[0] = -64.0;
    vector[1] = -1.0;
    vector[2] = 0.0;
    vector[3] = 1.0;
    vector[4] = 64.0;
    vector[5] = 125732;

    printf("        Decimal     Hexadecimal\n");
    for (index = 0; index < number; index++)
        {
            check-value = vector[index];
            printf("%15.6f        %04x%04x\n",
                check. value, check.ival[0], check.ival[1]);
        }
}
```

The output follows:

```
    Decimal           Hexadecimal
  -64.000000            0000C280
   -1.000000            0000BF80
    0.000000            00000000
    1.000000            00003F80
   64.000000            00004280
125732.000000           920047F5
```

The floating point number requires four bytes totalling 32 bits. The byte C2 gives the sign and 7-bit exponent. The three bytes 800000 give the mantissa for the value −64.

Notice the interchanging of the 16-bit halfwords from the expected form C2800000.

FLOATING POINT FRACTIONS

The following program gives the decimal and hexadecimal representation of several floating point fractions:

```
main()      /* Floating point fractions */
  {
     float
        vector[20];        /* Vector of values */
     union
        {
           float
              value;
           long int
              ival[2];
        } check;
     int
        number,
        index;

     number = 6;
     vector[0] = -7.125;
     vector[1] = -0.25;
     vector[2] = 0.25;
     vector[3] = 7.125;
     vector[4] = 0.1875;
     vector[5] = 0.1;

     printf("       Decimal     Hexadecimal\n");
     for (index = 0; index < number; index++)
        {
           check. value = vector[index];
           printf("%15.6f       %04x%04x\n",
              check.value, check.ival[0], check,ival[1]);
        }
  }
```

The output follows:

Decimal	Hexadecimal
−7.125000	0000C0E4
−.250000	0000BE80
.250000	00003E80
7.125000	000040E4
.187500	00003E40
.100000	CCCD3DCC

DOUBLE PRECISION FLOATING POINT

The following program illustrates double precision floating point representations:

```
main()      /* Double precision fractions */
  {
     double
       vector[20];        /* Vector of values */
     union
       {
          double
            value;
          long int
            ival[4];
       } check;
     int
       number,
       index;

     number = 6;
     vector[0] = -7.125;
     vector[1] = -0.25;
     vector[2] = 0.25;
     vector[3] = 7.125;
     vector[4] = 0.1875;
     vector[5] = 0.1;

     printf("       Decimal      Hexadecimal\n");
     for (index = 0; index < number; index++)
       {
          check.value = vector[index];
          printf("%15.6lf       %04x%04x%04x%04x\n",
            check.value, check,ival[0], check.ival[1],
            check,ival[2], check.ival[3]);
       }
  }
```

The output follows:

Decimal	Hexadecimal
−7.125000	00000000B000C01C
−.250000	000000000000BFD0
.250000	0000000000003FD0
7.125000	000000008000401C
.187500	0000000000003FC8
.100000	9999999999993FB9

Exercises

1. Write a program to illustrate the hexadecimal representation of the floating point values −12.875, −2.1, −1.0, 0.0, 1.0, 2.1, and 12.875.

2. Explore the floating point representation of your system.

11.5 Hex Dumps of Files

Hexadecimal coded binary information requires grouping the bits in sets of four using the hexadecimal representation of the group. The following table shows this relationship:

Binary	*Hexadecimal*
0000	0
0001	1
0010	2
0011	3
0100	4
0101	5
0110	6
0111	7
1000	8
1001	9
1010	A
1011	B
1100	C
1101	D
1110	E
1111	F

HEX DUMPS

A hex dump of a file gives the hexadecimal codes of the internal binary contents. This is the only way of knowing exactly what the file contains. Files containing only printable symbols may never need hex dumps. Hex dumps of files containing internal binary and floating point numbers are used to determine how the file is organized and where variable boundaries lie.

PROGRAM GIVING HEX DUMP OF FILE

The following program gives the hexadecimal codes for the contents of a file:

```
#define     EOF    26
#define     getchar()     ci()

main()      /* Hexadecimal dump of file */
  {
    int
      c;     /* Current character */

    while ((c = getchar ()) != EOF)
      printf("%2x\n", c);
  }
```

This program reads one character at a time and uses the "%2x" format to give the hexadecimal representation. The code corresponding to decimal 26 is the end of file signal for this computer. The standard function ci() is used in place of the more popular getchar() function to fetch one character from the standard input device.

The test file

```
Aeiou
59103
#.%=!
```

contains three lines of five characters each. A carriage return and a line feed follows each line.

The following is a hexadecimal dump of the test file:

```
41
65
69
6F
75
 D
 A
33
39
31
30
33
 D
 A
23
2E
25
3D
21
 D
 A
```

The hex symbol D represents a carriage return and the symbol A is a line feed. The other symbols are in sequence.

DECIMAL AND HEXADECIMAL CODES

Each byte of the file has both a hexadecimal code and a corresponding decimal code. An 8-bit byte has hex codes within the range 00 through FF and corresponding decimal codes 0 through 255. The following program gives the decimal and hexadecimal codes and displays the symbol if it is printable:

```
#define    EOF    26
#define     getchar()                                   ci()

main()      /* Hexadecimal dump of file */
  {
        int
           c;      /* Current character */

        while ((c = getchar ()) != EOF)
           if (c >= 32)
```

```
        printf("%c     %3d      %2x\n", c, c, c);
      else
        printf("      %3d      %02x\n", c, c);
  }
```

The following output results from the previous test file:

```
A    65   41
e   101   65
i   105   69
o   111   6F
u   117   75
     13   0D
     10   0A
5    53   35
9    57   39
1    49   31
0    48   30
3    51   33
     13   0D
     10   0A
#    35   23
.    46   2E
%    37   25
=    61   3D
!    33   21
     13   0D
     10   0A
```

COMPACT DUMP WITH DECIMAL CODES

Displaying one byte per line is inefficient; it is better to display several bytes per line. The following program displays the printable symbols and decimal codes for up to ten bytes per line:

```
#define    EOF    26
#define    getchar()    ci()

main()    /* Decimal codes for file */
  {
      int
        loop,        /* Loop control variable */
```

```
        number,       /* Number of characters per line */
        index,        /* Index to character vector */
        c[10];        /* Current character */

    number = 10;
    loop = 1;
    while (loop == 1)
      {
        for (index = 0; index < number; index++)
          {
            if (loop == 1)
              c[index] = getchar ();
            else
              c[index] = -1;
            if (c[index] == EOF)
              loop = 0;
          }
        for (index = 0; index < number; index++)
          {
            if (c[index] == -1)
              printf(" ");
            else if (c[index] < 32)
              printf(".");
            else
              printf("%c", c[index]);
          }
        printf("      ");
        for (index = 0; index < number; index++)
          {
            if (c[index] == -1)
              printf("      ");
            else
              printf(" %3d", c[index]);
          }
        printf("\n");
      }
}
```

The following output results for the previous test file:

```
Aeiou..591     65  101  105  111  117  13  10  53  57  49
03..#.%=!.     48   51   13   10   35  46  37  61  33  13
```

COMPACT DUMP WITH HEXADECIMAL CODES

The following program displays the printable symbols and hexadecimal codes for up to ten bytes per line:

```
#define    EOF    26
#define    getchar()    ci()

main()     /*Decimal codes for file*/
  {
      int
        loop,          /* Loop control variable */
        number,        /* Number of characters per line */
        index,         /* Index to character vector */
        c[10];         /* Current character */

      number = 10;
      loop = 1;
      while (loop == 1)
        {
           for (index = 0; index < number; index++)
             {
                if (loop == 1)
                  c[index] = getchar ();
                else
                  c[index] = -1;
                if (c[index] == EOF)
                  loop = 0;
             }
           for (index = 0; index < number; index++)
             {
                if (c[index] == -1)
                  printf(" ");
                else if (c[index] < 32)
                  printf(".");
                else
                  printf("%c", c[index]);
             }
           printf("     ");
           for (index = 0; index < number; index++)
             {
                if (c[index] == -1)
                  printf("     ");
```

```
                else
                   printf(" %O2x", c[index]);
             }
          printf("\n");
       }
}
```

The sample output follows:

```
Aeiou..591    41  65  69  6F  75  0D  0A  35  39  31
03..#.%!.     30  33  0D  0A  23  2E  25  3D  21  0D
```

The program outputs a period if the symbol is not a printable character. The period serves as a place holder for ease of locating specific bytes in the file.

Exercises

1. Use the hexadecimal file dump program with compact output to inspect a C source program file.

2. Use the hexadecimal file dump program to inspect the contents of a C object program file.

11.6 Hex Memory Dump

Hexadecimal coded dumps of internal memory are just as useful as hex dumps of files but may be more difficult to obtain. Many computers employ addressing techniques with base registers or segment registers; this increases the difficulty of obtaining hex dumps of internal memory.

The programs of this section must be modified for each family of computers. Commands may be necessary for loading the base registers or data segment registers. The programs request the beginning address of a section of memory. A value of zero results in dumping the next section of memory; a value of one stops the program.

HEXADECIMAL MEMORY DUMP

The following program displays the hexadecimal coded contents of memory 480 bytes at a time:

```
main()     /* Internal memory dump */
  {
       char
          *ptr;          /* Pointer to memory */
       int
          location,  /* Location to begin dump */
          lines,       /* Number of lines */
          columns, /* Number of columns */
          loop1,       /* Outer loop control */
          loop2,       /* Inner loop control */

       lines     = 20;
       columns = 24;

       scanf("%x", &location);
       while (location != 1)
          {
              ptr = location;
              for (loop1 = 0; loop 1 < lines; loop1++)
                 {
                     printf("\n%6x   ", location + 24 * loop1);
                     for (loop2 = 0; loop 2 < columns; loop2++)
                        printf("%02x", *ptr++);
                 }
              printf("\n\n");
              scanf("%x", &location);
              if (location == 0)
                 location = ptr;
          }
  }
```

3
The test file

```
0
6A8
1000
0
1
```

dumps the first 480 bytes of memory, the 480 bytes starting with location 6A8, the 480 bytes starting with hex location 1000, the next 480 bytes, and terminates the program.

The output from the test run follows:

```
   0   0101B1052578000A2536782020200025303278000A0A0025
  18   78006E6F7420656E6F756768206D656D6F72790AB4060006
  30   F0FF01000000000000000000000000000000000000000000
  48   000000000000000000000000434F4E3A0050524E3A004C53
  60   543A002A436F6E74726F6C20432A00000000000000000000
  78   00000000F03F00000000000024409A9999999999B93F0000
  90   000080842E418DEDB5A0F7C6B03E0000000000000000002A
  A8   446976696465206279205A65726F2A002A4F766572666C6F
  C0   772A002A4572726F7220696E20466C6F6174696E6720506F
  D8   696E742A002A537175617265207260F6F74206F662061206E
  F0   65676174697665206E756D6265722A000D00000000000000
 108   000000000000000000000000000000000000000000000000
 120   000000000000000000000000000000000000000000000000
 138   000000000000000000000000000000000000000000000000
 150   000000000000000000000000000000000000000000000000
 168   000000000000000000000000000000000000000000000000
 180   000000000000000000000000000000000000000000000000
 198   000000000000000000000000000000000000000000000000
 1B0   000000000000000000000000000000000000000000000000
 1C8   000000000000000000000000000000000000000000000000


 6A8   000000000000000047FF00F3A4B117E8CBFD8B1EA60153E8
 6C0   FE00B116E8BEFD5B0AC0754753C7068E000100BA4C02B41A
 6D8   E8B2FD5B33F68A074388844C024681FE800075125053B980
 6F0   00B428E894FD0AC05B58752C33F63C1A75DC8BCE0BC97409
 708   B428E87DFD0AC07571EB6FE89ED120202A2A2A2044697265
 720   63746F727900EB13B110E858FD00001006202A2A2A204469
 738   736B00E876D12066756C6C00E8C7FCB113E839FB803E4502
 750   007434C606F801FFBE8100BF90001E07C6050047B90F00FC
 768   F3A4C606890042C7068A00414BB117E80BFDC606450200E9
 780   7CF9B110E8FEFCC606450200C3B150BA4153880E89008916
 798   8A0053E8A9D9B03E800000750AB119E8E6FCFEC0A280005B
 7B0   C3BF8000E80C001E07B90600FCF3A5C3BF80005783C70C1E
 7C8   07B9190033C0FCF3AA5FC3E8DED0446972206D61736B00E8
 7E0   4AF9E848D9A080000AC07507B119E89FFCFEC0A2FA01BA4C
 7F8   02B41AE88FFC33D2B11152E87FFC5A0AC0754FB6FFBB4C02
 810   0AD27516A0FA010440E872D02EA06A01FEC8B2FFFEC22C0F
 828   73FAE887D03A2000B10B438A07247FE854D080F9047505B0
 840   20E84AD0FEC975EAFECA7407B020E83DD0EB03E831D0B112
 858   EBA80AD2750F0AF6750EE84FD04E6F2066696C6500E817D0
 870   803EFB0102723BE80DD08A16FA01B436E80AFC3DFFFF742A


1000   DEC38BF38BFA1E07FCF3A48BDE8BD7C38BF38BFA1E07FDF3
1018   A4FC8BDE8BD7C333C0A2E502BFCC02B91C001E07FCF3AA40
1030   BFE802B90200F3AA40BFF002B90200F3ABB8FFFFBFEA02B9
1048   0600F3AAB89503BFF402B90600F3ABB87503BF0003B90200
1060   F3ABB000BF0403B96500F3AAC606040303C60608031EC606
1078   29031EC6064A030AC60657030FC60669031AC7066A030D0A
1090   C3E820112E8A166B01FECAB600E894C9A17003A3A900E955
10A8   F0E82DFEBBFFFFA1A900A37003C706A900D34E538B1EA801
10C0   C747FF0D0AC606D80200C606E90201C7061404B050E829C8
10D8   5A428B1EA60103DAE89905A00403FEC87416BB0000E87415
10F0   A0040302C08AE8B020E892C7FECD75F9E8260EE84601E864
```

```
1108    00733274D680FE7F720DC606F801FFC60692010080E67FBB
1120    E3395352BBFB02BAFF02B90800E9E0FEE89700C606040303
1138    E8F914EB08A2F801C6069201008B1EF60281FB1204739480
1150    3EEA0200740550E84C145888074353E8F2135B891EF602E8
1168    2012E976FFE8C4143C7F74043C20733BBB0403C607014388
1180    0753BB0403BE734FB5FFE879005B0AC0751253BB0403BE3B
1198    50B51FE868005B0AC0F9740FFEC8740CBBC65003D903D92E
11B0    8B17F9C3E813009CE87914FE0604034388079D75BCE80200
11C8    EBB7E82614E8851475E15333DBE88C14BB04038A0750438A

11E0    07E8070058FEC875F45BC350E8900E583C207203E997C650
11F8    50B05EE890C6580440E88AC658C3B1FF51535B592E8A0446
1210    0AC0742CFEC151538A0F432AC1730402C8EB239F502E8A04
1228    2A0722C575134643FEC975F1589E5B59B500B0FF7402B001
1240    C35802C18AC8B50003F1EBBEE8A413E8031475ECBBD8028A
1258    070AC0757AC607FFBB000891ED902C606DB0200E8F513E8
1270    410DE8000E2E803E6A01387209BB002AE8E113E87EFBBB00
1288    06E841134C696E652000BB0010E83513436F6C2000BB0018
12A0    803EEA0200741 1E82313496E7365727420202020000E90E00
12B8    E812134F7665727772697465200080 3EEB0200740AE80013
12D0    496E64656E7400A0D4020206D602FEC03A06DB027415A2DB
12E8    02BB0014E87513E8830D8AD8B700B003E85A008B1EF4023B
1300    1ED9027503E9D907E8D6078B3EA6018B0EF402BA01002BCF
1318    7420E8D612E835137530FC1E07B00AF2AE750F420AD275F5
1330    E8C012E81F1374EAEB18BB000B52E82313E8310D5BB005E8
1348    0B008B1EF402891ED902E98C0750B500E811005802C5740B
1360    8AE8B020E827C5FECD75F9C383FB00B0307433BA1027E815
1378    00BAE803E80F00BA6400E80900BA0A00E80300BA010032C0
1390    2BDA7204FEC0EBF803DA04303C307506FEC5FECD74C5FECD
13A8    E9E3C4E806C53A20008BDA8BF2438A37C6070043C606ED02
```

The computer used for the test run has a data segment register; all addresses are relative to its contents. The data segment register provides a window on a region of 65,536 bytes. The segment register must be modified to inspect other regions.

HEX DUMP AND PRINTABLE SYMBOLS

The text strings within a program help locate regions of interest. The following program displays the printable symbols along with the hex codes:

```
main()      /* Internal memory dump */
  {
      char
        *ptr;        /* Pointer to memory */
```

```
int
  location, /* Location to begin dump */
  lines,    /* Number of lines */
  columns,  /* Number of columns */
  loop1,    /* Outer loop control */
  loop2;    /* Inner loop control */

lines   = 20;
columns = 16;

scanf("%x", &location);
while (location != 1)
  {
    ptr = location;
    for (loop1 = 0; loop 1 < lines; loop1 + +)
      {
        printf("\n%6x  ", location + columns *
          loop1);
        for (loop2 = 0; loop 2 < columns; loop2+ +)
          printf("%02x", *ptr+ +);
        printf("     ");
        ptr = - columns;
        for (loop2 = 0; loop2 < columns; loop 2+ +)
          {
            if ((31 < *ptr) && (127 > *ptr))
              printf("%c", *ptr);
            else
              printf(".");
            ptr+ +;
            }
        }
    printf("\n\n");
    scanf("%x", & location);
    if (location = = 0)
      location = ptr;
  }
}
```

This program displays the contents of 320 bytes per video display. Each line displays 16 bytes. The following file contains a set of addresses:

0
6A8
1000
0
1

The following is the resulting memory dump:

```
  0    0A01B1052578000A25367820202000025   ....%x..%6x    .%
 10    30327800202020002563002E000A0A00    02x.    .%c......
 20    2578006E6F7420656E6F756768206D65    %x.not enough me
 30    6D6F72790ABC060006F0FF0100000000    mory............
 40    00000000000000000000000000000000    ................
 50    0000000000000000000000000434F4E     .............CON
 60    3A0050524E3A004C53543A002A436F6E    :.PRN:.LST:.*Con
 70    74726F6C20432A000000000000000000    trol C*.........
 80    0000000000F03F0000000000000024409A  ......?......$@.
 90    999999999B93F0000000080842E418D     ......?.......A.
 A0    EDB5A0F7C6B03E0000000000000000000   ......>.........
 B0    2A446976696465206279205A65726F2A    *Divide by Zero*
 C0    002A4F766572666C6F772A002A457272    .*Overflow*.*Err
 D0    6F7220696E20466C6F6174696E672050    or in Floating P
 E0    6F696E742A002A537175617265207266F   oint*.*Square ro
 F0    6F74206F662061206E6567617469766 5   ot of a negative
100    206E756D6265722A000D000000000000     number*........
110    00000000000000000000000000000000    ................
120    00000000000000000000000000000000    ................
130    00000000000000000000000000000000    ................


6A8    00000000000000000000000000000000    ................
6B8    0047FF7299EB9C5A58505250E8EBFF5B    .G.r...ZXPRP...[
6C8    0AC07501C35A58505250E8B9FF5B3501    ..u..ZXPRP...[5.
6D8    00C35A58503C4172063C5A77020420FF    ..ZXP<Ar.<Zw..  .
6E8    E25A5F5E5983EC06EB095A5F5E83EC04    .Z_^Y.....Z_^...
6F8    B9E8FD8BC78A1C881D46470ADB7402E2    .........FG..t..
708    F4FFE25B5F5E5983EC06EB095B5F5E83    ...[_^Y.....[_^.
718    EC04B9DCFF8BC78A150AD2740347EBF7    ...........t.G..
728    8A14881546470AD27405E2F4C6050000    ....FG..t.......
738    10065E5633C0803C0074044046EBF7FF    ..^V3..<.t.@F...
748    E25A5F5E5983EC06EB095A5F5E83EC04    .Z_^Y.....Z_^...
758    B9E8FD8A043805720F771246470AC074    .....8.r.w.FG..t
768    02E2F0B80000FFE2B8FFFFFFE2B80100    ................
778    FFE25A5B535255533C033EDBE00008A0F   ..Z[SRU3.3......
788    4380F92074F880F90974F380F92D7506    C.. t....t...-u.
798    BE01008A0F4380F930722480F939771F    .....C..0r$..9w.
7A8    50B80A00F7E58BE85880E930B500BF0A    P.......X..0....
7B8    00F7E703C183D20003EA8A0F43EBD78B    .............C...
7C8    D583FE007407F7D2F7D883DAFF5DC35A    ....t........].Z
7D8    5F595883EC068CDB8EC3FCF3AAFFE25A    _YX............Z
```

```
1000   015F6670757368001500015F6673746F   ._fpush...._fsto
1010   7265640016000015F6673746F72656500  red...._fstoree.
1020   1700015F6673746F72656C001800015F   ..._fstorel...._
1030   6678636800190001 5F66636C65617200  fxch...._fclear.
1040   1A00015F66636D706B656570001B0001   ..._fcmpkeep....
1050   5F66636D70001E00015F666E6567001F   _fcmp...._fneg..
1060   00015F666E6F7400200001 5F667A6572  .._fnot. .._fzer
1070   6F002400015F666973002100015F6664   o.$.._fis.!.._fd
1080   6563002500015F66696E63002600015F   ec.%.._finc.&.._
1090   66737562002700015F6661646400 2800  fsub.'.._fadd.(.
10A0   015F6664697600290001 5F666D756C00  ._fdiv.).._fmul.
10B0   2A00017371727 45F002B000310000000  *..sqrt_.+......
10C0   03120007000313000E00031100210003   ..............!..
10D0   14002900031500320003160049000317   ..)....2....I...
10E0   004D000318005100031900 7D00031A00  .M....Q....}....
10F0   8100031B008A00031D00A400031C00A5   ................
1100   00031E00A600031F00C000032000C500   ................
1110   032300CA00032200D100032400D40003   .#...."....$....
1120   2100EC00032500F300032600FC000327   !....%....&....'
1130   0005010328000A010329000F01032A00   ....(....)....*.

1140   1401032B001901032C00350104048800   ...+....,.5.....
1150   0000000000F03F880000000000002440   ......?.......$@
1160   889A999999999 9B93F88000000008084  ........?.......
1170   2E41888DEDB5A0F7C6B03E8100840000   .A........>.....
1180   0000820000820000912A446976696465   .........*Divide
1190   2062792 05A65726F2A008B2A4F766572   by Zero*..*Over
11A0   666C6F772A009A2A4572726F7220696E   flow*..*Error in
11B0   20466C6F6174696E6720506F696E742A   Floating Point*
11C0   00A32A53717561726520726F6F74206F   ..*Square root o
11D0   662061206E656761746976652 06E756D  f a negative num
11E0   6265722A000583E8000007 1100849BDD  ber*............
11F0   04C383E80000071100849BD904C383A3   ................
1200   0000060700848916020006070083E800   ................
1210   000711008456BE00000607008 59BDB04  .....V..........
1220   5EC384803E0000060600810082740181   ^...>.........t..
1230   C384C606000006060085019BDBE3C392   ................
1240   83EC06558BEC568B760887760087EE83   ...U..V.v..v....
1250   C60283E8000007160082 5EC3849BDD1C  ..........^.....
1260   C3849BD91CC386569BD93E0000060800   .......V..>.....
1270   84810E000006080087000C9BD92E0000   ................
```

Exercises

1. Write a program to dump the contents of your system's internal memory.

2. If your system uses base registers or data segment registers, explore changing the register contents so that you may inspect any region of internal memory.

12

Performance

Pointers are more efficient than subscripts. Unformatted I/O is more efficient than formatted I/O. Function calls add to program execution time. Programs in this chapter illustrate how to measure the relative efficiency of these methods.

12.1 Subscripts or Pointers

Pointers are more efficient than subscripts. The programs of this section generate two matrices of stated size and perform a matrix multiplication. The first two programs contrast subscripts and pointers for integer matrix multiplication. Two programs compare subscripts and pointers for floating point multiplication. The final two programs contrast subscripts and pointers for double precision matrix multiplication.

INTEGER MULTIPLICATION WITH SUBSCRIPTS

The following program generates two integer matrices and computes their matrix product:

```
main()     /* Integer multiplication with subscripts */
  {
     double
        frand();        /* Generate random number */
     int
        a[50][50],      /* First matrix */
        b[50][50],      /* Second matrix */
```

```
        c[50][50],      /* Result matrix */
        ni,             /* Rows for first matrix */
        nj,             /* Number of columns for second */
        nk,             /* Cols of first and rows of second */
        i,              /* Index */
        j,              /* Index */
        k,              /* Index */
        sum;            /* Sum of the products */

    /* Dimensions */
    scanf("%d %d %d", &ni, &nk, &nj);

    /* Generate first matrix */
    for (i = 0; i < ni; i++)
      for (k = 0; k < nk; k++)
        a[i][k] = 20.0 * frand() - 10.0;

    /* Generate second matrix */
    for (k = 0; k < nk; k++)
      for (j = 0; j < nj; j++)
        b[k][j] = 20.0 * frand () - 10.0;

    /* Matrix multiplication */
    printf ("Start\n");
    for (i = 0; i < ni; i++)
      for (j = 0; j < nj; j++)
        {
          sum = 0;
          for (k = 0; k < nk; k++)
            sum += a[i][k] * b[k][j];
          c[i][j] = sum;
        }
    printf ("Stop\n");
}
```

Input to the program consists of three dimensions giving the number of rows and columns for the first matrix and the number of columns for the second matrix. The number of rows for the second must equal the number of columns for the first. The test file

```
50 50 50
```

results in mulitplying two 50-row by 50-column matrices.

The program output follows:

```
Start
Stop
```

The program displays the first line when ready to begin the matrix multiplication and the scond line when finished. Use a stopwatch to estimate the time required to perform the multiplication.

The matrix dimensions may need to be increased to obtain measurable times with mainframe computers. Some microcomputers may not be able to multiply two 50-byte matrices in a reasonable period of time.

INTEGER MULTIPLICATION WITH POINTERS

The following program multiplies two integer matrices using pointers to address the elements:

```
main()     /* Integer multiplication with pointers */
  {
      double
        frand();        /* Generate random number */
      int
        a[50][50],      /* First matrix */
        b[50][50],      /* Second matrix */
        c[50][50],      /* Result matrix */
        *aptr,          /* Pointer to first matrix */
        *bptr,          /* Pointer to second matrix */
        ni,             /* Rows for first matrix */
        nj,             /* Number of columns for second */
        nk,             /* Cols of first and rows of second */
        i,              /* Index */
        j,              /* Index */
        k,              /* Index */
        sum;            /* Sum of the products */

      /* Dimensions */
      scanf("%d %d %d", &ni, &nk, &nj);

      /* Generate first matrix */
      for (i = 0; i < ni; i++)
```

```
        for (k = 0; k < nk; k++)
            a[i][k] = 20.0 * frand() - 10.0;

    /* Generate second matrix */
    for (k = 0; k < nk; k++)
        for (j = 0; j < nj; j++)
            b[k][j] = 20.0 * frand () - 10/0;

    /* Matrix multiplication */
    printf ("Start\n");
    for (i = 0; i < ni; i++)
        for (j = 0; j < nj; j++)
            {
                aptr = &a[i][0];
                bptr = &b[0][j];
                sum = 0;
                for (k = 0; k < nk; k++)
                    {
                        sum += (*aptr++) * (*bptr);
                        bptr += 50;
                    }
                c[i][j] = sum;
            }
    printf ("Stop\n");
}
```

The inpupt and output is the same for all programs of this section. Most computers perform fast integer arithmetic. From 90 to 98 percent of the compute time is spent inside the innermost loop of the triply nested matrix multiplication loop.

Using pointers within the innermost loop may save 45-50 percent of the time needed to perform the integer matrix multiplication. The amount of savings depends on the computer and the efficiency of the object code generated by the compiler.

Subscript calculations for matrices require a multiplication and an addition to give the relative location of the element with respect to the base. Still another addition is required to give the actual memory location.

A pointer variable gives the actual address of the element. The pointer is incremented directly so that the new value for the pointer variable references the next element of the matrix. One multiplication and two additions for each matrix reference are eliminated by using pointer variables.

A pointer variable will gain access to a matrix element in one-third of the time needed with subscripts. After including the loop overhead, integer matrix multiplication will be twice as fast with pointers as with subscripts.

FLOATING POINT WITH SUBSCRIPTS

The following program generates two floating point matrices and computes their product:

```
main()      /* Real multiplication with subscripts */
  {
      double
        frand();          /* Generate random number */
      float
        a[50][50],        /* First matrix */
        b[50][50],        /* Second matrix */
        c[50][50],        /* Result matrix */
        sum;              /* Sum of the products */
      int
        ni,               /* Rows for first matrix */
        nj,               /* Number of columns for second */
        nk,               /* Cols of first and rows of second */
        i,                /* Index */
        j,                /* Index */
        k;                /* Index */

      /* Dimensions */
      scanf("%d %d %d", &ni, &nk, &nj);

      /* Generate first matrix */
      for (i = 0; i < ni; i++)
        for (k = 0; k < nk; k++)
          a[i][k] = 20.0 * frand() - 10.0;

      /* Generate second matrix */
      for (k = 0; k < nk; k++)
```

```
        for (j = 0; j < nj; j+ +)
          b[k][j] = 20.0 * frand () - 10.0;

    /* Matrix multiplication */
    printf ("Start\n");
    for (i = 0; i < ni; i+ +)
        for (j = 0; < nj; j+ +)
          {
            sum = 0;
            for (k = 0; k < nk; k+ +)
              sum + = a[i][k] * b[k][j];
            c[i][j] = sum;
          }
    printf ("Stop\n");
}
```

Most microcomputers and many minicomputers do not have floating point hardware. Use this program with large matrices only for systems capable of fast floating point arithmetic.

FLOATING POINT WITH POINTERS

The following program generates two floating point matrices and computes their product using pointer variables for the innermost loop:

```
main()     /* Real multiplication with pointers */
  {
    double
      frand();        /* Generate random number */
    float
      a[50][50],      /* First matrix */
      b[50][50],      /* Second matrix */
      c[50][50],      /* Result matrix */
      *aptr,          /* Pointer to first matrix */
      *bptr,          /* Pointer to second matrix */
      sum;
    int
      ni,             /* Rows for first matrix */
      nj,             /* Number of columns for second */
```

```
        nk,            /* Cols of first and rows of second */
        i,             /* Index */
        j,             /* Index */
        k;             /* Index */

    /* Dimensions */
    scanf("%d %d %d", &ni, &nk, &nj);

    /* Generate first matrix */
    for (i = 0; i < ni; i++)
        for (k = 0; k < nk; k++)
            a[i][k] = 20.0 * frand() - 10.0;

    /* Generate second matrix */
    for (k = 0; k < nk; k++)
        for (j = 0; j < nj; j++)
            b[k][j] = 20.0 * frand () - 10/0;

    /* Matrix multiplication */
    printf ("Start\n");
    for (i = 0; i < ni; i++)
        for (j = 0; j < nj; j++)
            {
        aptr = &a[i][0];
        bptr = (&b[0][j];
        sum = 0;
        for (k = 0; k < nk; k++)
            {
                sum += (*aptr++) * (*bptr);
                bptr += 50;
            }
        c[i][j] = sum;
        }
    printf ("Stop\n");
}
```

Most computers show a 20 to 30 percent improvement when using pointers rather than subscripts to access matrix elements. There may be no measurable improvement for computers that do not have floating point hardware. The improvement is less on a percentage basis because floating point arithmetic is often three to ten times slower than integer arithmetic.

DOUBLE PRECISION WITH SUBSCRIPTS

The following program uses subscripts and double precision matrices:

```
main()     /* Double precision with subscripts */
  {
       double
         frand(),         /* Generate random number */
         a[50][50],       /* First matrix */
         b[50][50],       /* Second matrix */
         c[50][50],       /* Result matrix */
         sum;             /* Sum of the products */
       int
         ni,              /* Rows for first matrix */
         nj,              /* Number of columns for second */
         nk,              /* Cols of first and rows of second */
         i,               /* Index */
         j,               /* Index */
         k;               /* Index */

       /* Dimensions */
       scanf("%d %d %d", &ni, &nk, &nj);

       /* Generate first matrix */
       for (i = 0; i < ni; i++)
         for (k = 0; k < nk; k++)
           a[i][k] = 20.0 * frand() - 10.0;

       /* Generate second matrix */
       for (k = 0; k < nk; k++)
         for (j = 0; j < nj; j++)
           b[k][j] = 20.0 * frand () - 10.0;

       /* Matrix multiplication */
       printf ("Start\n");
       for (i = 0; i < ni; i++)
         for (j = 0; j < nj; j++)
           {
             sum = 0;
             for (k = 0; k < nk; k++)
```

```
                sum += a[i][k] * b[k][j];
            c[i][j] = sum;
        }
    printf ("Stop\n");
}
```

DOUBLE PRECISION WITH POINTERS

The following program uses pointers for the innermost loop and double precision matrices:

```
main()      /* Double precision with pointers */
  {
      double
        frand();        /* Generate random number */
        a[50][50],      /* First matrix */
        b[50][50],      /* Second matrix */
        c[50][50],      /* Result matrix */
        *aptr,          /* Pointer to first matrix */
        *bptr,          /* Pointer to second matrix */
        sum;
      int
        ni,             /* Rows for first matrix */
        nj,             /* Number of columns for second */
        nk,             /* Cols of first and rows of second */
        i,              /* Index */
        j,              /* Index */
        k;              /* Index */

      /* Dimensions */
      scanf("%d %d %d", &ni, &nk, &nj);

      /* Generate first matrix */
      for (i = 0; i < ni; i++)
        for (k = 0; k < nk; k++)
          a[i][k] = 20.0 * frand() - 10.0;

      /* Generate second matrix */
      for (k = 0; k < nk; k++)
        for (j = 0; j < nj; j++)
          b[k][j] = 20.0 * frand () - 10.0;
```

```
        /* Matrix multiplication */
        printf ("Start\n");
        for (i = 0; i < ni; i++)
          for (j = 0; < nj; j++)
            {
              aptr = &a[i][0];
              bprt = &b[0][j];
              sum = 0;
              for (k = 0; k < nk; k++)
                {
                sum += (*aptr++) * (*bptr);
                  bptr += 50;
                }
              c[i][j] = sum;
            }
        printf ("Stop\n");
}
```

Some computers perform double precision calculations just as quickly as single precision. For such computers the pointer variables will offer the same improvement for both single and double precision. If double precision arithmetic is more time-consuming, the improvement may be only 10 to 20 percent.

The improvement resulting from using pointers rather than subscripts for matrix references ranges from negligible for systems not having floating point hardware, to 20 percent for most computers, to 50 percent for some mainframe computers with fast floating point arithmetic. The theoretical limit is an improvement of 70 percent for a system with very fast looping instructions.

Exercises

1. Compare the efficiency of subscripts and pointers for integer matrices for your system.

2. Compare the efficiency of subscripts and pointers for floating point matrices for your system.

3. Compare the efficiency of subscripts and pointers for double precision matrices for your system.

12.2 Formatted or Unformated I/O

The internal form for integers and floating point numbers differs from the external printable symbols. Converting external symbols to internal form every time a file is read is very time-consuming. C provides direct I/O without format conversion. The resulting files are exact byte-for-byte copies of the internal values.

GENERATE FILE OF FORMATTED VALUES

The following program generates a file of formatted double precision numbers using the random number generator:

```
#include    <math.h>
#include    <STDIO.H>
#define     EOF          -1

main()     /* Generate file of formatted numbers */
  {
      FILE
        file1;               /* File descriptor */
      double
        frand();
      int
        number,              /* Number of values */
        index;               /* Index */
      double
        vector [10000];      /* Vector of values */

      scanf("%d", &number);
      for (index = 0; index < number; index++)
        vector[index] = 100.0 * frand();

      file1 = fopen("B:FORM.DAT", "w");
      fprintf(file1, "%5d\n", number);
      for (index = 0; index < number; index++)
        fprintf(file1, "%15.8lf\n", vector[index]);
      fclose(file1);

  }
```

The input parameter is the number of values to generate. Use the program to generate several thousand values and write them to a disk file.

READ FILE OF FORMATTED VALUES

The following companion program reads the formatted file generated by the previous program:

```
#include    <math.h>
#include    <STDIO.H>
#define     EOF          -1

main()      /* Read file of formatted numbers */
  {
       FILE
         file1;                 /* File descriptor */
       double
         frand();
       int
         number,                /* Number of values */
         index;                 /* Index */
       double
         vector [10000];        /* Vector of values */

       file1 = fopen("B:FORM.DAT", "r");
       fscanf(file1, "%5d\n", &number);
       for (index = 0; index < number; index++)
         fprintf(file1, "%lf\n", &vector[index]);
       fclose(file1);

  }
```

A substantial portion of the time for reading the file is spent converting the external formatted numbers to internal double precision representation. The input speed could be increased up to 20 times by avoiding the format conversion.

GENERATE FILE OF UNFORMATTED VALUES

The following program generates a file of unformatted double precision values:

```
#include    <math.h>
#include    <STDIO.H>
#define     EOF          -1

main()    /* Generate file of unformatted numbers */
  {
     FILE
       file1;                /* File descriptor */
     double
       frand();
     int
       number,               /* Number of values */
       index;                /* Index */
     double
       vector [10000];       /* Vector of values */

     scanf("%d", &number);
     for (index = 0; index < number; index++)
       vector[index] = 100.0 * frand();

     file1 = creat("B:UNFORM.DAT");
     write(file1, &number, 2);
     write(file1, &vector[0], number * 8);
     close(file1);

  }
```

The input parameter is the number of values to generate and place in the file. This program uses direct output to dump the double precision values in internal form as a sequence of bytes. Each double precision value requires eight bytes. The functions creat(), write(), and close() dump memory regions to a disk file.

The function creat() creates a new file. Another function—open()—opens a file that already exists. The functions read() and write() move information between a buffer area and external memory.

READ FILE OF UNFORMATTED VALUES

The following program reads the file of unformatted values created by the previous program:

```
#include      <math.h>
#include      <STDIO.H>
#define       EOF            -1

main()      /* Read file of unformatted numbers */
  {
      FILE
        file1;               /* File descriptor */
      double
        frand();
      int
        number,              /* Number of values */
        index;               /* Index */
      double
        vector [10000];      /* Vector of values */

      file1 = open("B:UNFORM.DAT", 0);
      read(file1, &number, 2);
      read(file1, &vector[0], number * 8);

      close(file1);
  }
```

The reading time for several thousand double precision values in unformatted form is a small fraction of that for a similar set of formatted values. Large files should be in unformatted form for processing efficiency.

Exercises

1. Write a program to generate 5,000 integers and store them in a file in formatted form.

2. Write a program to read the 5,000 formatted integers created by the program of exercise 1.

3. Write a program to generate 5,000 integers and store them in a file in unformatted form.

4. Write a program to read the 5,000 unformatted integers created by the program of exercise 3.

5. Write a program to generate 5,000 floating point numbers and store them in a file in formatted form.

6. Write a program to read the 5,000 formatted floating values generated by the program of exercise 5.

7. Write a program to generate 5,000 double precision values and store them in a file in unformatted form.

8. Write a program to read the 5,000 unformatted double precision values generated by the program of exercise 7.

12.3 Local or Global Variables

Higher-level languages, including C, incur execution time overhead for each function call. Much of the overhead comes from passing arguments to the function and returning results to the calling program. More overhead may result from saving general-purpose registers.

The programs of this section measure the overhead for several types of functions. Each program calculates the area and circumference of a rectangle many times. The calculations take place inside a double loop. The program asks for two parameters: the first gives the number of times through the outer loop, and the second gives the number of inner loops.

The calculations are done in double precision which is much slower than integer calculations for most computers. Function calling overhead is sizeable; it is large relative to fast integer calculations, but not as noticeable for slower double precision arithmetic.

TWO FUNCTION CALLS

The following program calls one function to calculate the area and a second function to calculate the circumference:

```
main()      /* Function calls with actual parameters */
  {
      double
        fnc1(),     /* Function computing area */
        fnc2(),     /* Function computing circumference */
        length,     /* Length of box */
```

```
        width,      /* Width of box */
        area,       /* Area of box */
        circ;       /* Circumference of box */
    int
        outer,      /* Number of outer loops */
        inner,      /* Number of inner loops */
        i,          /* Index */
        j;          /* Index */

    scanf("%d %d", &outer, &inner);
    length = 40.0;
    width  = 30.0;

    printf("Start\n");
    for (i = 0; i < outer; i++)
        for (j = 0; j < inner; j++)
            {
                area = fnc1(length, width);
                circ = fnc2(length, width);
            }
    printf("Stop\n");
}

double fnc1(length, width)
  double
    length,
    width;
  {
    double
      area;

    area = length * width;
    return (area);
  }

double fnc2(length, width)
  double
    length,
    width;
  {
    double
      circ;
```

```
    circc = 2.0 * (length + width);
    return (circ);
}
```

This program follows the recommended form for functions. Each function has only one output value. The calling program passes actual parameters rather than addresses. The main program and functions exhibit the desirable qualities of low coupling and high cohesion.

ONE FUNCTION WITH TWO OUTPUTS

The following program combines the two calculations into one function. The output is in terms of variable addresses. The main program sends the addresses of the variables area and circ.

```
main()      /* Function calls with actual parameters */
  {
     double
        length,      /* Length of box */
        width,       /* Width of box */
        area,        /* Area of box */
        circ;        /* Circumference of box */
     int
        outer,       /* Number of outer loops */
        inner,       /* Number of inner loops */
        i,           /* Index */
        j;           /* Index */

     scanf("%d %d", &outer, &inner);
     length = 40.0;
     width  = 30.0;

     printf("Start\n");
        for (i = 0; i < outer; i++)
        for (j = 0; j < inner; j++)
           {
              fnc(length, width, &area, &circ);
           }
     printf("Stop\n");
  }
```

```
fnc(length, width, area, circ)
  double
      length,
      width,
      *area,
      *circ;
  {

      *area = length * width;
      *circ = 2.0 * (length + width);
  }
```

This program may be 30 percent faster than the previous one using two function calls per loop. The execution time per function call is substantial. This overhead is between 20 microseconds (millionths of a second) and 300 microseconds, depending upon your computer system.

FUNCTION CALL WITH GLOBAL VARIABLES

The following program calls a function to perform the calculations, but uses global variables rather than subroutine arguments.

```
double
  length,     /* Length of box */
  width,      /* Width of box */
  area,       /* Area of box */
  circ;       /* Circumference of box */

main()      /* Functions with global variables */
  {
      int
        outer,      /* Number of outer loops */
        inner,      /* Number of inner loops */
        i,          /* Index */
        j;          /* Index */

      scanf("%d %d", &outer, &inner);
      length = 40.0;
      width  = 30.0;
```

```
        printf("Start\n");
        for (i = 0; i < outer; i++)
           for (j = 0; j < inner; j++)
              {
                 compute();
              }
        printf("Stop\n");
   }

compute()
   {

        area = length * width;
        circ  = 2.0 * (length + width);
   }
```

This program runs two to three times faster than the first program on many computers. If it is so much faster, why not make all variables global? Readability is important. Programs with hundreds of global variables are very difficult to understand. The speed issue is important only for those functions called repeatedly thousands of times per run.

PROGRAM WITHOUT FUNCTION CALLS

The following program performs the calculations within the loop rather than calling a subroutine:

```
main()      /* Program without function call */
   {
        double
           length,      /* Length of box */
           width,       /* Width of box */
           area,        /* Area of box */
           circ;        /* Circumference of box */
        int
           outer,       /* Number of outer loops */
           inner,       /* Number of inner loops */
           i,           /* Index */
           j;           /* Index */
```

```
        scanf("%d %d", &outer, &inner);
        length = 40.0;
        width  = 30.0;

        printf("Start\n");
        for (i = 0; i < outer; i++)
           for (j = 0; j < inner; j++)
              {
                 area = length * width;
                 circ = 2.0 * (length + width);
              }
        printf("Stop\n");
}
```

The improvement in speed is minor for most computers. Speed improvements have come primarily from reducing the parameter passing overhead.

Exercises

1. Run the programs of this section on your system to measure its function calling overhead for double precision variables.

2. Modify the programs to measure the overhead with single precision variables.

3. Modify the programs to measure the function calling overhead with integer variables for length, width, area and circumference.

12.4 Increment or Add

C provides special operator symbols for incrementing or decrementing variables and for adding one variable to another. This can be very effective when used with subscripted variables. This section explores the increment and sum operators and compares them with the general-purpose operations available with other higher-level languages.

LOOP WITH STANDARD INCREMENT STATEMENT

The following program has a simple inner loop with the statement j = j + 1;

incrementing the variable j:

```
main()      /* Add 1 to value */
  {
      int
        outer,      /* Number of outer loops */
        inner,      /* Number of inner loops */
        i,          /* Index for outer loop */
        j;          /* Index for inner loop */

      scanf("%d %d", &outer, &inner);
      printf("Start\n");

      for (i = 0; i < outer; i++)
        {
          j = 0;
          while (inner > j)
            j = j + 1;
          }

      printf("stop\n");
  }
```

This program asks for two parameters. The first gives the number of iterations of the outer loop. The second gives the number for the inner loop. The parameters

500 1000

result in 500,000 iterations of the inner loop. This provides a measurable time for microcomputers; mainframe computers require larger parameters, giving more iterations.

SPECIAL C INCREMENT INSTRUCTION

The following program uses the C increment instruction and places it inside the while loop test:

```
main()      /* Increment */
  {
      int
        outer,      /* Number of outer loops */
        inner,      /* Number of inner loops */
        i,          /* Index for outer loop */
        j;          /* Index for inner loop */

      scanf("%d %d", &outer, &inner);
      printf("Start\n");

      for (i = 0; i < outer; i++)
        {
          j = 0;
          while (inner > j++);
        }

      printf("stop\n");
  }
```

The 10 to 15 percent improvement is not dramatic.

STANDARD ARITHMETIC PROGRESSION

The following program computes the sum of the values calculated within the inner loop:

```
main()      /* Sum values */
  {
      int
        value,      /* Current value */
        sum,        /* Sum of values */
        outer,      /* Number of outer loops */
        inner,      /* Number of inner loops */
        i,          /* Index for outer loop */
        j,          /* Index for inner loop */

      scanf("%d %d", &outer, &inner);
      printf("Start\n");

      for (i = 0; i < outer; i++)
```

```
        {
          sum = 0;
          value = 0;
          while (value < inner)
            {
              sum = sum + values;
              value = value + 1;
            }
        }

      printf("stop\n");
  }
```

This program adds the instruction

```
sum = sum + value;
```

to the earlier program. Use a stopwatch to measure the calculation speed; substitute other commands to measure their speeds.

SPECIAL C OPERATORS

The following program uses the special C operators:

```
main()     /* Sum values */
  {
      int
        value,     /* Current value */
        sum,       /* Sum of values */
        outer,     /* Number of outer loops */
        inner,     /* Number of inner loops */
        i,         /* Index for outer loop */
        j;         /* Index for inner loop */

      scanf("%d %d", &outer, &inner);
      printf("Start\n");
      for (i = 0; i < outer; i++)
        {
          sum = 0;
          value = 0;
          while (value < inner)
```

```
            {
              sum += values;
              value++;
            }
        }

      printf("stop\n");
  }
```

The 10 to 15 percent improvement is noticeable but not dramatic.

COMBINING OPERATIONS

The following program performs the incrementing as part of the summation operation:

```
main()      /* Sum values */
  {
     int
       value,      /* Current value */
       sum,        /* Sum of values */
       outer,      /* Number of outer loops */
       inner,      /* Number of inner loops */
       i,          /* Index for outer loop */
       j;          /* Index for inner loop */

     scanf("%d %d", &outer, &inner);
     printf("Start\n");

     for (i = 0; i < outer; i++)
       {
         sum = 0;
         value = 0;
         while (value < inner)
           sum += value++;
       }

     printf("stop\n");
  }
```

Most systems will exhibit little improvement in speed. Some programmers find the command

```
sum += value++;
```

more appealing than the set of two commands

```
sum += values;
value++;
```

There is almost no measurable difference in speed.

READABILITY AND EFFICIENCY

Efficiency and readability are often conflicting goals. Most programmers find subscripts easier to understand than pointers, but pointers are often more efficient. A program that uses parameters as communication between a calling program and its subsidiary functions is easier to understand and more reliable; however, the parameter passing adds to the execution time overhead.

Unformatted I/O is often dramatically faster than formatted I/O, but the data is buried in the file in a form that is difficult to interpret, even with a hexadecimal coded dump of portions of the file. The increment and summation operators may improve performances by 10 or 15 percent, but the resulting programs may not be as easy to read.

The C programmer chooses language constructs for the task at hand. Efficiency is the primary goal for some programs. Other programs require improved readability.

Exercises

1. Compare the performance of the programs of this section on your system.

2. Determine the effective speed of integer multiplication on your system.

3. Determine the effective speed of double precision multiplication on your system.

Appendices

Appendix A
Reserved Words

Most languages have a set of reserved words which cannot be used as user-supplied names. The following list of reserved words is typical.

auto	do	for	return	switch
break	double	goto	sizeof	typedef
case	else	if	short	union
char	entry	int	static	unsigned
continue	extern	long	struct	while
default	float	register		

Appendix B
Format Codes

The following summarizes the format % codes for the printf() function:

Code	*Number type*
%d	Decimal integer
%o	Octal (base 8) integer
%x	Hexadecimal (base 16) integer
%u	Unsigned decimal
%f	Decimal format for float or double
%e	Scientific notation format for float or double
%g	Decimal or scientific notation, whichever is shorter
%c	Single character
%s	Character string

The following format codes are used by the scanf() function:

Code	*Type*
%d	Decimal integer
%f	Floating point number
%c	Character
%s	Character string
%o	Octal integer
%x	Hexadecimal integer
*	Skip field (%*d, %*f, etc.)

Appendix C
Special Symbols

The C language provides a set of escape sequences with its backslash character \ followed by a character. The common escape characters follow:

Symbol	*Description*
\n	Newline (carriage return and line feed)
\r	Carriage return only
\f	Form feed (eject page)
\'	Single quote
\t	Horizontal tab
\b	Backspace
\\	Backslash
\0	Null character

Appendix D

Operators

ARITHMETIC OPERATORS

+	Add
−	Substract
*	Multiply
/	Divide
%	Modulo (remainder)

RELATIONAL OPERATORS

<	Less than
<=	Less than or equal
>	Greater than
>=	Greater than or equal
==	Equal
!=	Not equal

INCREMENT AND DECREMENT OPERATORS

++a	Preincrement
a++	Postincrement
−−a	Predecrement
a−−	Postdecrement

LOGICAL OPERATORS

&&	AND
!!	OR
!	NOT

BITWISE LOGICAL OPERATORS

&	Bitwise AND
:	Bitwise inclusive OR
^	Bitwise exclusive OR
<<	Left shift
>>	Right shift
~	Onex complement

ASSIGNMENT OPERATORS

+=	Add
−=	Subtract
*=	Multiply
/=	Divide
&=	And
!=	Inclusive OR
^=	Exclusive OR

Appendix E
Standard Functions

STANDARD MATH FUNCTIONS

Name	*Description*
abs(x)	absolute value, integer = abs(integer)
fabs(x)	absolute value, double = fabs(double)
acos(x)	Arccosine, result in radians
asin(x)	Arcsine, result in radians
atan(x)	Arctangent, result in radians
cos(x)	Cosine, argument in radians
sin(x)	Sine, argument in radians
tan(x)	Tangent, argument in radians
exp(x)	Exponential
exp10(x)	Exponential base 10
pow(x,a)	Raise x to the power a
log(x)	Natural logarithm
log10(x)	Base 10 logarithm
sqrt(x)	Square root
srand(x)	Set new seed for random number generator
rand()	Return random integer
frand()	Return random real value in interval 0-1

FORMATTED INPUT AND OUTPUT

Name	*Description*
printf()	Formatted print to standard output device
fprintf()	Formatted print to file
sprint()	Formatted output to string
scanf()	Formatted input from standard input device

fscanf()	Formatted input from file
sscan()	Formatted input from string

DISK I/O ROUTINES

Name	*Description*
creat(f)	Create file and assign file name
open(f)	Open existing file
close(f)	Close file
fopen()	Alternate routine for file open
fclose()	Alternate routine for file close
fgetc(f)	Get next character
fputc(f)	Put next character
fgets(f)	Get string from file
fputs(f)	Put string

CHARACTER ROUTINES

Name	*Description*
isalnum()	Is argument alphanumeric?
isalpha()	Is argument alphabetic?
iscntrl()	Is argument control symbol?
isdigit()	Is argument numeric digit?
islower()	Is argument lowercase?
isupper()	Is argument uppercase?
isspace()	Is argument blank, tab, LF, or CR?
tolower()	Convert to lowercase
toupper()	Convert to uppercase

STRING ROUTINES

Name	*Description*
atoi(s)	Convert string to integer
atof(s)	Convert string to double precision
atol(s)	Convert string to long integer
index(s,c)	Return pointer to first occurrence of c in s
rindex(s,c)	Return pointer to last occurrence
strcat(a,b)	Concatenate b to end of a
strcmp(a,b)	Compare two strings
strlen(s)	Length of string

Index

A

actual value parameters, 167, 171
add, 394
address of variable, 162, 191
address calculation sort, 308
alternation, 109
AND, 89
area under a curve, 265
argument, 144, 155
arithmetic expression, 39
arithmetic mean, 289
array initialization, 125
arrays, 121, 139, 201, 210
ASCII, 85, 105, 341, 343
assembly language, 4
automatic variables, 124
average, 289

B

Babbage, 78
binary numbers, 52, 348
bind, 10
bit, 8
bit fields, 224
bit operations, 51
bitwise logical operators, 57
blank lines, 31, 69
block structured languages, 168
Boolean expressions, 89, 114
Boolean variables, 75
braces, 12, 30
branch, 186
break, 179
break command, 77, 179, 181, 186
bubble sort, 302
built-in math functions, 82
byte, 8

C

C compiler, 9
C language, 3
C operators, 397
C preprocessor, 230
cc, 9
calculus, 239
case convention, 30
case sensitive, 31
char, 35
character array, 122, 130, 140
character codes, 132, 342
character routines, 145
character strings, 345

coefficient of determination, 311
cohesion, 143
comma operator, 226
comments, 67, 70
compilers, 5
complement, 55
compound interest, 242
compound logical expressions, 89
conditional execution, 75, 101, 108
continue, 184, 186
control characters, 85
control variable, 76, 84
correlation, 311

D

data analysis, 289
data entry, 86
data file, 126
data format, 37
data types, 35, 37
decimal character codes, 132, 225, 346, 364
declarations, 29
decrement, 7, 43, 201
definite integral, 265
derivative, 256
differential calculus, 239
dimensions, 121
disk files, 230
disk I/O, 145
do while, 96
double, 35
double precision, 82, 148, 262, 382
double precision function, 160

E

EBCDIC, 342
editor, 9
efficiency, 4, 6, 8, 44, 175, 203, 378, 389, 394
EOF, 106, 231
error messages, 39
execution, 10
exponent, 357
exponential, 240, 329
extended operators, 7, 44

F

factorials, 38, 93
file copy, 60
files, 66
finite series, 247
float, 35
floating point, 79, 147, 357, 380
flow of control, 101, 177
for loops, 19, 76, 123
format codes, 36
formatted input, 62, 145, 235, 385
formatted output, 145, 385
frequency count, 105, 295
fudge factor, 92
function calls, 389
function definitions, 155
function library, 30
function results, 157
functions, 142

future value, 249
fuzz, 92

G

Gaussian elimination, 276
getchar, 105
global variables, 168, 389
goodness of fit, 316
goto, 186

H

hex dumps, 361, 367, 370
hexadecimal, 52, 56, 349
hexadecimal character codes, 132, 225, 346
hexadecimal coded binary, 350, 363
hierarchical program, 152
histogram, 298

I

identity matrix, 273, 282
increment, 43, 202, 394
incrementing, 6
indentation, 14, 68
indirect addressing, 193
infinite loops, 97
infinite sequence, 246
infinite series, 247, 250
information representation, 341
int, 35
integer division, 41
integer function, 159
integral calculus, 265
integration, 265
interactive data entry, 64, 86, 321
interpreters, 5

J

K

key words, 34

L

limit of a sequence, 244
line editor, 9
linear regression, 310
link, 10
local variables, 169, 389
location, 208
logical expressions, 89
logical operators, 47
long, 35
long integers, 94, 353
looping, 75, 173
loop testing, 21
loose coupling, 143
lower case convention, 30

M

machine language, 4
main, 12
main function, 29
mantissa, 357
math functions, 82
matrix inversion, 276
matrix multiplication, 274
matrix transposition, 270
matrix operations, 270

maximum value, 103
memory dump, 367
modulo operation, 41, 180
multidimensional arrays, 134

N

negation, 40
negative numbers, 55
nested if . . else, 112, 118
nested recursion, 172
nonlinear curve fitting, 325
nonlinear regression, 331
numeric arrays, 121
numerical calculus, 254
numerical differentiation, 255
numerical integration, 265

O

object program, 10
octal, 52, 349
octal character codes, 225
octal coded binary, 349
ones complement, 351
OR, 89
ordered list, 302

P

paragraphing, 69
parentheses, 40
pointers, 191, 196, 203, 375, 377
portability, 4
postincrement, 43, 45, 203
power series, 252
prime numbers, 179
printf, 12, 233
printing, 11
preincrement, 43, 45, 203
program editor, 9
program flow, 177, 213
program organization, 29
program quality, 26
program style, 33
programming process, 25
prompt messages, 64
push down stack, 175

Q

quality, 26
quick sort, 305

R

readability, 27, 32
real numbers, 79, 147, 357, 380
recursion, 172
redirection, 61
reference parameters, 167, 198
register variables, 228
registers, 8
regression analysis, 310
relational operators, 89
relations, 46
repeat until, 23
residual errors, 318
results, 157
rounding errors, 82, 246

S

sample mean, 291
sample standard deviation, 291

scanf, 63, 233
scatter diagram, 325
scope, 168
screen editor, 9
semicolon, 12, 30
sequence, 239
series, 239, 247
shift operators, 58
short, 35
signed integers, 352
signed numbers, 351
signed magnitude, 351
Simpson's method, 268
simultaneous linear equations, 282
single precision, 147, 260
slope, 255, 311
solving equations, 284
sort by insertion, 302
sort by selection and exchange, 303
sorting, 302
source program, 10
special characters, 36
special operators, 397
stack, 175
standard deviation, 290, 292
standard error, 311
standard functions, 143
standard input, 60, 231
standard math functions, 82, 144
standard output, 60, 231
statement, 12
static variables, 124
statistics, 289
STDIO.H, 232
string arrays, 129, 345, 347
string copy function, 132
string output, 131
string routines, 146
structured pointer, 219
structured variable, 215
structures, 213
subscript, 121, 123, 201, 375
sum of squares, 312
swap, 199
switch, 177, 181, 186
symbolic name, 191
syntax errors, 39
system of functions, 164

T

tables, 134
tabulating frequencies, 295
trailer value, 94, 99, 127
transformations, 328
transpose matrix, 270
trapezoid method, 266
two-dimensional arrays, 134
twos complement, 351
type declarations, 34
TYPEDEF, 227

U

unconditional branch, 186
unformatted I/O, 386
unions, 221
unsigned integers, 355

V

value parameters, 197
variable addresses, 195
variable declarations, 29
variable names, 34

variable transformations, 328
variables, 34, 343
variance, 290
variation, 312
vector, 122

W

while, 21, 88, 107

X

Y

y-intercept, 311

Z